To John & Cathy
Many happy &
productive years
To you both.
Love. Vicki.

"Some things you just do for the buzz"
The LUSTY MEN
R. Walsh
said by R. Mitchum

D1266206

**SOON TO BE
A MAJOR
MOTION
PICTURE**

SOON TO BE A MAJOR MOTION PICTURE

THE ANATOMY OF AN ALL-STAR, BIG-BUDGET, MULTIMILLION-DOLLAR DISASTER

by Theodore Gershuny

HOLT, RINEHART AND WINSTON
New York

Copyright © 1980 by Theodore Gershuny

All rights reserved, including the right to reproduce this book or portions thereof in any form.

Published by Holt, Rinehart and Winston, 383 Madison Avenue, New York, New York 10017.

Published simultaneously in Canada by Holt, Rinehart and Winston of Canada, Limited.

Library of Congress Cataloging in Publication Data

Gershuny, Theodore.
Soon to be a major motion picture.

Includes index.
1. Rosebud. [Motion picture] I. Title.
PN1997.R57583G4   791.43'7   79-3433
ISBN 0-03-053591-3

First Edition

Designer: Robert Bull
Printed in the United States of America

10 9 8 7 6 5 4 3 2 1

To my mother and father

Acknowledgments

Many people have generously helped with this book. Besides those mentioned in the introduction, there are five individuals whose contributions must be recorded.

My agents, Roberta Kent and Warren Bayless, offered suggestions and advice which were unfailingly useful. And their faith, even when I was in doubt, was a sustaining force.

The editor of the manuscript, Marian Wood, enriched it with invaluable energy, professionalism, and critical lucidity.

Finally, Paul Bartel and Claire Francy have my enduring gratitude and affection for their many gifts.

T. G.

Contents

Photos appear on pages 185–208.

Introduction

From the start, I wanted to write about a special kind of film. Not TV and not a studio project on a backlot. The world of studio filming had already been treated, perhaps most brilliantly in Lillian Ross's *Picture*. But by the mid-1970s another kind of parallel work was taking place far outside the studios.

The movie I covered would not be English or American or European, but multinational. It would be an independent venture with a producer-director whose reputation and personality would dominate the film. Shooting would stretch across varied locations and attract that gypsy cadre of artist-technicians who specialize in extended travels.

Partly this would be a study of work—a book I wished I had had when I started in film—about the planning, casting, crewing, and producing a major movie. It would be the story of how money is spent and misspent. Inevitably, one feared it might also become the anatomy of a disaster, a view of how serious, talented people can make an awful picture and still survive. Most films, after all, are flawed, and survival is always an issue.

Beyond the work, a whole social experience beckoned. Filmmakers know that most pictures are quickly forgotten. Even more, they know that when a production ends, the life around it evaporates. So I wanted to celebrate that life, the way it was at a certain moment in film history.

Beneath these reasonable intentions something more emotional was also churning. I began this book as a mystery about real people, an exploration of that secret territory, that hidden war zone, where a director fights it out with physical reality to make his movie. Having written and directed three low-budget films, I knew something of that struggle. Now I hoped to follow the chain of choices—rational, whimsical, gut-level—by which a director shaped a film. In the deepest sense, I wanted to reveal where movies—at least one of them—came from.

I would describe a world I knew but, as I promised myself, stand apart from it. Not get involved.

Of course I had no idea what would happen.

I didn't foresee a star walking off the film, an ex-politician descending with half the European press in pursuit, a consuming love affair, bomb threats, or a brilliant comic actor sounding like Lenny Bruce on the Grand Tour. Or being haunted by *Lawrence of Arabia,* then playing scenes with "Lawrence" himself.

I could not know that a multimillion-dollar effort would be a study in futility.

As for the producer-director, I did not foresee that halfway through the film I would loathe the man; or that later, despite the tyranny and ensuing depression, I would root for him—yes, and be glad that he somehow had the last, liberating laugh.

The only thing I really expected was that it would be fun. Movie-making is always fun in a left-handed way. Otherwise, why would anyone put up with all the grief?

The film I chose didn't merely fail. It was executed in public by a critical firing squad.

"... Only someone with his arm being twisted could take credit for it ... consistently idiotic...."
—Canby, *The New York Times.*

"... a bloodless bore." —Crist, *New York* magazine.

"... unspeakable ... the enormous ethical questions raised are tempestuously ignored ... the movie's disorder and vainglory are particularly painful in these weeks of further crisis for Israel. . . . " —Penelope Gilliat, *New Yorker.*

". . . appalling disaster." —*Cue.*

Radio and television were equally warming: The director was "third rate" said WCBS-TV, and the movie had "the urgency of an overdue notice from the public library," according to WNEW–TV.

Not exactly a paean of praise. Yet, a year earlier, one might have hoped it would turn out differently. Whatever the problems, there had been time and money to fix them. Otto Preminger had complete creative control.

The first brief stories appeared in *Variety* in late 1973. United Artists would finance and distribute Preminger's film *Rosebud,* based on the French novel by Paul Bonnecarrère and Joan Hemingway. The screenplay would be written by Otto's son, Erik Lee Preminger, and filming would start in the spring of 1974.

That was enough. I had never met Preminger but had admired many of his films, especially *Laura.* For no better reason than the existence of that detective story, I thought he might tolerate my own investigation. So I sent him a letter. And read the book.

Rosebud had been published in France in 1973 and subsequently in twenty editions around the globe. Whatever its literary merits, it clearly evoked a nightmare of the Western world:

Palestinian terrorists kidnap five young women of influential families from a yacht in the Mediterranean, hide them, and force them to make statements on film, which are then telecast worldwide.

The kidnapping becomes an international, page-one drama.

The films make carefully escalating demands. For each one that is met, a girl will be released. For each refusal, a girl will die.

The first order seems relatively harmless. A film must be shown of the five hostages standing nude on the yacht, announcing their capture. The Western governments realize the thrust of the plot but fear the public outcry if a hostage is killed. So the film is shown. And one young woman is freed.

The Arabs then ask for a confession by an arms supplier. This is followed by a contest for suggestions to help the Palestinian refugees. When the entries are unsatisfactory, the Arabs change tactics, angrily demanding a boycott on all Israeli exports. The three remaining hostages will be released over the course of a year, if the boycott is successful.

That final demand is never aired. By the time it is delivered, secret agents of France and Israel have discovered the Corsican farm where the young women are imprisoned. The agents free the captives, subduing and capturing their Arab guards with a secret "sleeping gas."

Once the women are safe, Jewish commandos parachute down to the desert headquarters of the guerrillas in Lebanon. The terrorist leader is taken, his ring is smashed, and a lie is broadcast announcing that the girls have been released for a mere payment of ransom. Thus the guerrillas are demeaned and public opinion turns back against them.

The novel ends with a glimpse of its true subjects, a crowd of news-hungry Parisians, devouring the early morning papers. "L'Affaire Rosebud" is over, leaving them at once sated and disappointed, until the next drama that threatens their consumer society.

There was potential for triumph or disaster.

Though the book read like a political comic strip, though it crudely mixed documentary realism and Ian Fleming melodrama, and though the story ran downhill as the Arab demands got wilder, Preminger would still be trying to wrest from the material a gripping Mideast thriller. Just the possibility of such a victory was fascinating. He would be aided by the novel's cynicism, which seemed so in tune with the post-Watergate American temper. And his production would surely offer abundant opportunity to trace the life of a multinational location film. Most important, the central theme of the work—the manipulation of world opinion—seemed perfect for the director of *Exodus, Advise and Consent,* and *Anatomy of a Murder.*

He called me the day my letter reached him. Shortly afterward, in his office, I told him, "I want to see how you make a film on this scale. I want to show people what it's like to *be* Otto Preminger."

He laughed. The idea appealed to him, as I'd hoped it would.

"Fine," he told me. "Come along. You can see everything. With a different director, it would be hard. A man like Zinnemann, he's very quiet. Very private. But with me it's easy. I have no secrets. The door is always open!"

That's all there was to it.

Few in this book would have chosen to be here at first. Some were hired, only to find me waiting, taking notes. I was present almost always, and it became impossible for them to be constantly on guard. Eventually their reserve gave way to a grudging understanding between us. "Tell the truth. Use your judgment. Remember, you're talking about my career."

At times I have combined dialogue on the same theme which was spoken on different occasions. The text is rendered grammatically when the speaker might have done the same, given the chance. Some bitterness has been tempered, lest it provoke more bitterness now. And a few names that have been changed are marked with an asterisk in the list of "real life" characters that follows.

But the deeds and words contained here were done and spoken in my presence or reliably reported to me. They are as close as I can get to the life of the film.

By the time the work was ending, my subjects and I had become almost dependent on one another. I had absorbed myself in their lives; they in turn would come to me saying, "Why weren't you there today? You missed something—" Finally it became hard to leave them, to give up their stories, to say, Enough. Now I can only express my deep gratitude to all those who gave me their help. Without such people, there would be no book, no story to tell, and, very probably, no movies.

I am indebted to the following individuals, on or around the film, who tolerated my observations with good nature:

Brigitte Ariel	Colin Jamison
Yoram Ben Ami	Richard Jenkins
Yves Beneyton	John Lake
Debbie Berger	Peter Lawford
Françoise Brion	Florence Favre Le Bret
Gary Bunce	Anatole Litvak
David Cadwallader	Bernard Mazauric
Georges Cravenne	Robert Mitchum
Norman Cross	Thom Noble
Claude Dauphin	Julian Pettifer
Colin Davidson	Max Seeburg
Peter Downey	Terry Sharratt
Ray Evans	Robert Simmons
Patrick Floershein	John Slaughter
Marc Frederix	Ron Taberer
Tony Gittleson	Charles Tarbot
Alan Grayley	Tony Teiger
Jim Guild	Hans Verner
Robin Hilyard	Russ Woolnough
Simon Holland	

Special thanks are due to those who patiently and helpfully filled in my view of the production with their own recollections and responses:

Barbara Allen
Amidou
Sir Richard Attenborough
Georges Beller
Judd Bernard
Paul Bonnecarrère
Penelope Bonnecarrère
Mark Burns
Margot Capelier
Kim Cattrall
Denys Coop
Anne Alvarez Correa
Adrienne Corri
Anna Cottle
Graham Cottle
Dick Dassonville
James Devis
René Donzelot
Olivier Eyquem
Wolfgang Glattes
Cliff Gorman
Robin Gregory
Keith Hamshere
Rudolph Hertzog

Willy Holt
Dewi Humphries
Isabelle Huppert
Ken Kaufman
John Lindsay
Klaus Lowitsch
Angela Martelli
Eva Monley
Mickey Murchan
Peter O'Toole
Ron Pearce
Laurent Petitgirard
Erik Preminger
Paul Rabiger
Cliff Richardson
John Richardson
Michael Seymour
Josef Shiloah
Peter Thornton
Raf Vallone
Lalla Ward
David White
Nigel Wooll
Fred Zinnemann

And to one man I owe the existence of this book. I watched him as closely as possible for almost a year. Whatever emotions I saw in him, I never saw fear.

I wish to thank Otto Preminger.

Who hid nothing.

Main Characters in the Novel

Rosebud teems with guerrillas on one side, victims on the other, and agents in between, all seeking favor from the great, dumb god, public opinion. They are briefly noted here, as they appear in print.

The agents:

LAURENT MARTIN: Dashing Frenchman, half James Bond, half Kissinger; master of diplomacy, weapons, women; cast as American, then as Englishman.

YEFET HAMLEKH: Israeli; shrewd, middle-aged, with a touch of Le Carré's spiritual fatigue; cast younger.

HANS SCHLOSS: German; less prominent; like Hamlekh, middle-aged but cast younger.

These professionals virtually breathe cynicism. To them, all political conviction only masks the same selfish drives. Their chief concern, their fear, is the power of public opinion. Witless and huge, it waits to be molded. They know that whoever sways it, regardless in what direction, gains power from doing so. Any change is enough. And all their cynical fears are fully confirmed by the acts of other characters in *Rosebud*.

The terrorists:

KARL SCHEIDEMANN: Mastermind of the plot; anti-Semitic Jewish radical using Arabs to destroy the "false state" of Israel; changed in the film to SCHRANTZ, a German anarchist, then to SLOAT, an English Arabist.

ULRICKA RAAD: Scheidemann's mistress; beautiful, drug-crazed, Amazonian nymphomaniac; cut from screenplay.

HACAM: Palestinian; looks like a thug, talks like a martyr; willing to die for his cause; played by an Israeli.

KIRKBANE: Younger Palestinian; more sensitive; hates to see his victims in agony; invents painless killing spike; played by a French-Moroccan.

ADRIEN TARDETS: North African refugee; Arabs finance his Corsican farm, hide hostages there, use him as a front.

MRS. TARDETS: Catatonic since the accidental death of her children; sleeps through the novel and the film.

Victims, families, friends:

CHARLES-ANDRÉ FARGEAU: Ruthless, corrupt French industrialist; smuggled guns to Jordan that were used to massacre Palestinian refugees during Black September; hides his Jewishness; owns *Rosebud*, the yacht from which the girls are abducted; cares only for his granddaughter, Sabine.

SABINE FARGEAU: French hostage; a pawn to pressure her grandfather; played first by American, then by Frenchwoman.

PATRICE THIBAUD: Sabine's lover; young, radical professor; exploits Sabine's capture to promote his politics; much more romantic in the film.

HÉLÈNE NIKOLAOS: The brightest, poorest hostage; Greek; has brief affair with Martin; in the film he rejects her, but then, in his aloof way, he rejects everyone.

GEORGE and FREDERIQUE NIKOLAOS: Poor Greek exiles; their daughter, Hélène, is Sabine Fargeau's best friend; for this they are given a luxury apartment; for this their daughter is kidnapped.

Minor characters, hardly more than names attached to a bank account, a piece of real estate, or a violent destiny:

MARIAN CARTER: English hostage, renamed MARGARET in film.

LORD and LADY CARTER: Marian's parents; own shipyards.

JOYCE DONOVAN: American hostage.

SENATOR DONOVAN: Joyce's father; owns steel mills.

GERTRUD FRYER: German hostage.

GUNTER FRYER: Gertrud's father; owns banks.

FRANÇOIS LOCCI: Owns Corsican farm near Tardets; helps agents.

FRANK WOODS: *Rosebud* crewman; first victim; Arabs bribe him to let them on board, then kill him.

There is, finally, one presence in the novel as strong as any character, the *Rosebud* itself, Fargeau's yacht and the scene of the abduction.

Its crewmen have helped Fargeau smuggle guns—and are therefore "executed" when the Arabs take the ship. The boat is then sent by auto pilot to crash against the Israeli coastline as a grim warning. In the movie, the craft is saved from going aground at the last second.

Fargeau has named his boat because of a youthful fascination with *Citizen Kane.* The word "Rosebud," uttered on Kane's deathbed amid baroque splendor, reminds Fargeau of all the wealth and power he himself has sought.

But he, or the novelists, misunderstand. To Charles Foster Kane, "Rosebud" is a name on a sled, snatched away from him as a boy and recalled a lifetime later. The word evokes a lost youth, a world away from wealth and power.

... And in Real Life

Maggie Abbott—London talent agent
Barbara Allen—English production secretary
Amidou—French-Moroccan actor playing Kirkbane
Brigitte Ariel—French actress playing Sabine Fargeau
Richard Attenborough—English producer-director-actor playing Sloat
Raoul Baum*—French second assistant director
Georges Beller—French actor playing Thibaud
Yoram Ben Ami—Israeli location manager
Yves Beneyton—French actor originally playing Thibaud
Debbie Berger—American actress playing Gertrud Fryer
Betty Berman*—American actress originally playing Sabine Fargeau
Richard Blodgett—London talent agent

Paul Bonnecarrère—French author of *Rosebud*
The Brave Goose—English yacht playing the *Rosebud*
Françoise Brion—French actress playing Mrs. Nikolaos
Jules Buck—American producer-partner of Peter O'Toole
Mark Burns—English actor playing the yacht broker
Margot Capelier—French casting director
Kim Cattrall—American actress playing Joyce Donovan
Denys Coop—English director of photography
Anne Correa—Paris talent agent
Adrienne Corri—English actress playing Lady Carter
Anna Cottle—Independent production executive and wife of
    Graham
Graham Cottle—English associate producer
Georges Cravenne—French publicist
Crystal*—Duenna, bodyguard, and nuisance
Dick Dassonville—Paris talent agent
Claude Dauphin—French actor playing Fargeau
James Devis—English camera operator
Captain Farrago*—Corsican liaison and layabout
Pierre Flambeau*—Frenchman originally doing special effects
Patrick Floershein—American actor playing Frank Woods
Wolfgang Glattes—German assistant director
Cliff Gorman—American actor playing Hamlekh
Robin Gregory—English sound recorder
Helmut Griem—German actor
Keith Hamshere—English still photographer
Rudolph Hertzog—German location manager
Herr Hochbaum*—Wealthy German yacht owner
Simon Holland—English art director
Willy Holt—Original French art director
Dewi Humphries—Welsh camera crewman
Isabelle Huppert—French actress playing Hélène Nikolaos
Richard Jenkins—English second assistant director
Marjorie Kellogg—American novelist and screenwriter
Klaus*—Dutch gigolo with a twist

Peter Lawford–English actor playing Lord Carter
David Lewin–English trade paper editor and bon vivant
John Lindsay–Former New York mayor playing Senator
    Donovan
Anatole Litvak–Major director living in France
Klaus Lowitsch–German actor playing Schloss
Angela Martelli–English continuity woman
Bernard Mazauric–French location manager
Robert Mitchum–American star originally playing Martin
Eva Monley–Original English production manager
Mickey Murchan–Irish rigger
Annalise Nascalli-Rocca–Original Italian costume designer
Thom Noble–English film editor
Peter O'Toole–Irish star playing Martin
Ron Pearce–English chief electrician
Laurent Petitgirard–French composer
Julian Pettifer–English newscaster playing himself
Erik Preminger–American screenwriter
Otto Preminger–American producer-director
Paul Rabiger–French makeup man
Cliff Richardson–English special-effects artist
John Richardson–English special-effects artist and son of Cliff
Max Seeburg–English shipping agent
Michael Seymour–English production designer
Terry Sharratt–English microphone-boom operator
Josef Shiloah–Israeli actor playing Hacam
Peter Thornton–English film editor
Topol–Israeli star
Raf Vallone–Italian star playing George Nikolaos
Hans Verner–German actor playing Gunter Fryer
Lalla Ward–English actress playing Marian Carter
David ("Chalky") White–English production accountant

• ONE •
PRE-PRODUCTION

"So we went to work. And he would say, no, there is something not quite right here. I mean it does not have your flair. . . . It just somehow lacks genius that the other scenes have . . . And I said, Otto, for god's sake, if we have every scene equally excellent, do you realize how monotonous this picture is going to be? . . . And he said, oh. He paced back one more time and said, tell you what—you make them all excellent and then I'll direct them unevenly."

—DALTON TRUMBO on writing
the screenplay of Exodus*

"My father wants everyone to be a character."
—ERIK PREMINGER

---

*Excerpted from Hollywood on Trial, a James C. Gutman/David Helpern, Jr., Production.

THE GRAND VOYAGE

Innocence

At sixty-seven, Otto Preminger was one of a tiny group of filmmakers, including Hitchcock, Wilder, Huston, Zinnemann, and a very few others, who had made international reputations in the 1940s in Hollywood and whose names, in the '70s, still stood for movie entertainment around the world.

A Jew born in Vienna, Preminger had been an actor, an assistant to Max Reinhardt, and, later, a director of plays and films in Europe. He emigrated to the United States in 1935.

The success of *Laura* (1944) established him as a major stylist. Starting with *The Moon Is Blue* (1953), he had also produced all but two of his features. *Rosebud* would be his thirty-sixth film as director and the sixteenth to carry the signature of his complete control, "An Otto Preminger Film."

To win and retain his control, he had fought some battles. He challenged Zanuck successfully to preserve the ending of *Laura,* sued (and lost) to keep *Anatomy of a Murder* from being cut for TV, and was the first to hire a blacklisted writer to work under his own name (Dalton Trumbo on *Exodus*).

Now he faced another battle. He had not made a major critical or commercial hit for over a decade. As Erik Preminger would say later, "There's a lot riding on this film."

I visited the director just before a Christmas weekend.

It was to be my only formal interview with him during all of *Rosebud.*

Rain flooded Fifth Avenue that morning, and a dirty sky

3

blanketed the city. His suite was on the seventeenth floor of the Columbia Pictures building. Going up, the elevator doors opened on glimpses of color ads for "Hits of Tomorrow." But on seventeen, one faced a bare, black wall. Beside a black door, tiny silver letters announced OTTO PREMINGER.

A receptionist sent me down a long hall to his private office. There, across a half-acre of carpet, he sat upstage center at a white marble desk. The large room was aggressively modern, furnished in chrome, leather, and Plexiglas. The paintings were by Sutherland, Rivera, Dubuffet, and Kandinsky. The only personal touches were photos of his wife, Hope, his brother, Ingo, his twins, Victoria and Mark, his son Erik, and two Presidents, Franklin Roosevelt and John Kennedy. The room was all in black and white, except for the art, and for Preminger's forehead, glowing pink beneath a ceiling spotlight. Hearing me, he looked up.

"Come in," he called. "Come . . ."

The rumbling basso and the Viennese accent were familiar from film and TV appearances. But he was bigger than I had expected, with a powerful, meaty handshake. The bullet head was wide and polished baby-smooth. Though his face was creased, his blue eyes shone bright and curious. His shoulders and chest, under a navy blazer, were barrel-shaped. Time had merely added a bulging stomach.

"He is a *fauve*!" Raf Vallone said months later. "A fighter. That's why we understand each other. We're both fighters."

Yes, one felt an old fighter's reflexes measuring a stranger automatically. Waves of sooty water whipped against his windows. The walls were shadowy, but the pink glow over his desk made the room almost cozy. He waved me to a chair. It was like a movie scene—Everett Sloan in *Citizen Kane*, reminiscing as the rains beat down and he had "nothing but time."

"You know, there have been other books about me?" He handed over a photo-memoir of *Anatomy of a Murder*, even as he dismissed it.

"I've learned to forget the past. Don't misunderstand me. I

4

have a good memory. If we met two years from now, I'd certainly remember your face and why we met. But about my films . . ." In the pause, water drummed on the windows. "I remember a few scenes . . . here and there."

I closed the book on my lap.

"About that film I remember an agent who came to see me . . . a gentlewoman who wore white gloves. She insisted I see an unknown actor, not even her client. It became the first part for George C. Scott."

Preminger's work existed for him as memories of other people. Underlying his comments was a tenacious fascination with character—an omnivorous, gossipy curiosity about other lives. As we sat together, he took all calls, and after each one came a brief recital of the caller's personality. One man "never said an intelligent thing in his life. Except once, at a funeral, he said, 'By now I know more dead people than live ones.' "

Preminger enjoyed telling how he had acquired *Rosebud.* The book had been offered by both a French agent and an American one. The Frenchman had been instructed only to sell it outright.

"What could I do?" Preminger asked innocently. "I called the American and *he* sold me an option."

The story had another twist. After buying his option, Preminger called Arthur Krim at United Artists. It was a Friday afternoon. "I said I needed an answer by Monday. They asked me to send over three copies. By Monday at eleven we had a deal."

Later Preminger found out that the novel had already been recommended to the UA home office by a staff member working in Paris. But no one had read it.

"So today we're partners! UA and I!" Preminger laughed. "That's what this business is. By the way—" he lowered his voice confidentially, "—are you Jewish?"

"Yes."

"Well, they felt that Scheidemann would not be acceptable. I agreed. So now—" he boomed in triumph, "—he is *Schrantz*! A German. He may have been a Nazi. We're working it out."

The anti-Semitic Jew was the kind of contradictory character that usually intrigued Preminger. "I promised UA—they didn't want to put Jew against Jew—but it was not a bad idea."

Suddenly he glanced at me suspiciously and mentioned another book about him. "It's just a collection of scandal. Not *one fact* is true!" All he liked in it was Billy Wilder's foreword.

"Wilder said I am really Martin Borman. Despite plastic surgery, my friends see the resemblance at once."

He laughed and offhandedly remarked that in his movie the girls and Fargeau would be developed more. And Martin, the French agent, would be American. "We felt it was necessary. So much of the audience is American. It won't hurt anything." He shrugged off the whole subject. "Believe me, I don't think anyone can foresee the commercial success of a film."

Saul Bass, the designer, called from California about a sketch he had sent. Preminger carefully jotted down information while peering through a pair of glasses with fat, black rims perched halfway down his nose.

The call completed, he turned back to me. "My life is centered on the film. That's how I am. Even the screenplay—I never take credit, but I direct all my screenplays. Just as I direct the actors. In this I'm omitting the first four chapters."

Those early chapters detailed the real-life hijacking of a Lufthansa jet, which was released only after the German government gave up three Arab prisoners who had taken part in the Munich Olympics killings. *Rosebud* appropriated this history to introduce its main characters. In the novel, agent Laurent Martin arranged the hijacking to help Bonn get the Arabs out of the country and avoid a dangerous trial scheduled just before an election. And the plane was taken by Hacam and Kirkbane, the same PLO guerrillas who would later capture the *Rosebud*. They never knew their guns held blanks or that they were pawns in a public-relations spectacle.

"I don't show the incident," said Preminger. "There isn't time. But it's covered in dialogue. It's a director's decision."

I left with his invitation to "Come anytime. You don't need an appointment." Walking into the rain, I found that my main impression was awe: at a life full of people, at so much ego and energy, and at all those feelings so nakedly displayed.

"One thing about Otto," Peter O'Toole's partner said months later. "You know exactly where you stand. He says what he thinks. Exactly."

Erik Lee Kirkland was eighteen when he found where *he* stood: as Otto Preminger's natural son. A few years later, after his mother, Gypsy Rose Lee, died, Erik was publicly acknowledged by Otto and adopted.

The crucial facts of their three lives were that Gypsy Rose Lee, for her own reasons, had let Erik think he was the child of a former husband. And for eighteen years Otto had deeply missed his son.

Erik first heard from Otto while serving in the army.

"I didn't know much about him. *Exodus* was playing at the post theater so I thought I'd better see it."

Physically, the two men shared the same eyes and profile. But where Otto was round and bald, Erik was thin and long-haired. Where Otto boomed, Erik was quiet. Where Otto was tailored, Erik wore jeans. The effect was all-American—a Preminger without Europe.

At twenty-nine, Erik spoke reasonably, deliberately, often pausing to relight his pipe. If he didn't understand you, he squinted through the pipe smoke as if trying to penetrate your opacity. When people didn't understand his father, Erik erupted in high, nervous laughter.

He had reason to be nervous. *Rosebud* was his first paid screenplay assignment. Earlier, he had studied computers in the army, then worked on productions for his father and for Elaine May. For two years he had been writing a script he hoped to direct.

"I just kept going over and over it, grinding it out. Then my father said, 'If you weren't so wrapped up I'd like you to write *Rosebud.*' I thought it over and, well"—he relit his pipe, "—I agreed."

Later, some on the film would envy Erik his once-in-a-lifetime opportunity. It was true he was under enormous pressure, but by the calculations of the film business he had nothing to lose. The risk was all with Otto.

Erik worked in a small room down the hall from his father, wearing metal earmuffs to shut out noise.

"Is he tough on you?" I asked.

"It's no harder for me than for any other writer. He filters every scene through his personality until he likes it."

"Don't you ever want to stop when it's right?"

"Who knows what's right? Saul Bass had a wonderful line. On an Otto Preminger film *only Otto* knows!"

As we chatted, Erik offered some further clues. "My father," he said, "caters to reality."

Thus, since Martin would be played by an American he had to *be* one. "My father's terribly concerned with the truth."

Again, relighting his pipe: "My father likes scenes with strong antagonists. I'll tell you what is good about this movie. It's direct. Character subtleties aren't as important as confrontation. On this film he won't have to futz—[puff]—with levels of cool."

Erik suddenly looked concerned.

"I don't care what you write about me, but if you do anything to hurt my relationship with my father—"

"Why should I?"

"—I'll sue you for every cent."

"There's not much to sue."

"Profits from the book?"

I shrugged, and he turned to other fictions.

"My father wants everyone to be a character." Thus the hostages were a problem. "Anyone with action can be a character. But those girls don't *do* anything." The solution was to let them give a dinner party on the yacht; it amounted to a new scene. And instead of Martin seducing Hélène (the "poor" hostage), it might happen the other way around. "It's better, considering their age difference. She's young. The more mistakes she makes, the more appealing she is."

The first draft would be done February 1. "You can read it then—if it's all right with my father."

At home later I tossed aside my notes and poured a large vodka. For company, I could entertain doubts.

The film had no script, no budget, no cast, and no schedule. A speculative air hung about the project, as if Preminger were still weighing ideas. *Rosebud* was a conception based on his reputation, which was now troubled. A William Morris agent had reminded me sourly that after *Such Good Friends* it had taken Otto two years to get a picture on. Well, whatever the gossip, Preminger *was* trusted with money. The proof lay in a sixty-page contract with United Artists, providing for financing, distribution, profit sharing—every detail down to when the picture would be delivered, eight months after the start of principal photography or four months after the finish, whichever came first.

Another question was the collaboration of father and son. Having directed my wife in three movies (before we separated), I knew the mixed blessing of working with a loved one. It was warm, it was comfortable, and it was painfully easy to be uncritical—or too critical.

One hoped it would be different here, that Otto and Erik might complement each other. Erik, with his long hair and meditation and bemused style, was totally present tense, while Otto sounded echoes of history and other social orders. Nothing could happen to him for the first time.

Erik believed in logic and analysis, pursued down a river of data, while Otto worked from his instincts; his "reasons" sprang from feelings. As Erik had said, Otto would go on changing the script until it *felt* right. "My father doesn't analyze films." A French critic added, "When Otto is working, he's too busy. When it's over, he doesn't like to look back." And Preminger had the last word: "When I'm dead people will decide if I had a style. By then it won't matter."

They had much to offer each other. Otto had claimed one of the great subjects of the decade. Erik had the will to "grind it out." And in those innocent days, anything seemed possible.

Then the doorbell rang.

Margo stood in the doorway in a raincoat and long scarf. She was twenty, fresh-faced, and outrageously coincidental in a way barely permissible even in a real character. When I had met her the night before in a neighborhood bar, she'd said she was a dancer. Now, at one-thirty in the morning, she brought the cold in with her, clinging to her flushed cheeks.

"I thought you'd be in bed. Can I come in?" She had fought with her boyfriend and wanted to talk to someone. Did I mind?

"No, sit down. I'll make you some coffee."

She sat stiffly on the edge of a velvet armchair, her shoulders trembling, hands folded in her lap.

"You all right?"

"Fine. I will be. How's your book?"

I mumbled something and went into the kitchen to start the coffee. When I got back, her legs were drawn up and her arms linked around them. She stared up at me as if waiting for a verdict on herself. Her clothes were folded on the coffee table as if they were just back from the laundry, as if she didn't want to give offense.

"I was sure you'd be in bed . . . I don't need coffee." More than anything, she sought to please. "If you don't want to make it," she whispered, "we could just lie down."

I told her gently it was better if she left.

"Don't you like me?"

No, she was fine. Just beautiful. Such reassurances were the only thing that came to mind, the truth being impossible to explain. For I was amazed to be thinking then of the movie, particularly something Erik had said. "We think maybe *she* tries to seduce Martin, considering their age difference." I wondered, truly, what misgivings Martin might feel, what doubts and hesitations? Such feelings had little place in a film like *Rosebud.* Nothing really had a place in it but action.

I walked Margo home and kissed her good night, still thinking of Otto and Erik and the work they had taken for themselves.

Preminger's permanent staff in New York included his accountant, a tailored woman in her fifties, surrounded by ledgers in a small office where one window looked out on a bleak snowfall. At the end of the day she set down her glasses, showing tired eyes. "I'm not prejudiced," she announced, "but to me Otto Preminger is a genius. He can talk about anything. If he has a movie panned he'll come in the next morning and you wouldn't know anything was wrong. And he has great regard for human beings. It *disturbs* him when others don't."

She combed and sprayed her hair, then tied on a plastic rainhat. A blue vein flickered at her temple as she declared that a production accountant would keep books for the film. "*I* wouldn't! It's a whole year's work jammed into twelve weeks."

But no matter who handled accounts, she knew one thing. Preminger would sign all checks.

As he always did.

Down the hall another aide dealt with media, agents, and actors. *His* style was politically cautious, revealing as little as a press release.

About casting: "Otto's open on everything. Though, ah, we wouldn't want to issue an invitation. For the leads, . . . ah, talk to Erik. We're calling agents who represent certain names."

As to other actors: "I look at their backgrounds. I watch them. I hope to see some, uh, spark."

Later the room crackled. A call had gone out for the seventeen-year-old daughter of a U.S. Senator. They especially wanted poise and breeding.

Wait now. Freeze frame. I knew I was flying to Europe February 11. The ticket was in my pocket. Good-byes had begun. But the movie remained hypothetical, almost a drinking fantasy, until that first girl entered and it came to life.

I should have said good-bye then to reflection. Except for listening to explanations given with saintly patience by the English production staff, there would be no time to think. And there would be too many people. Far too many.

Now. Enter the first.

She was a pale, southern ingenue who quite simply believed in *Rosebud.* Overdressed and breathless, she tugged at her scarf while getting lost in the story of her soap opera.

"Reminds me of Julie Harris," said the aide later.

Indeed, most of the women were types, like the Malibu sun queen in slacks that advertised every curve, and Miss Clean with a batch of toothpaste commercials.

But the last girl was special—dark, intense, squirming with energy in her tight jeans—all hot ambition and heaving breasts. She would *use* this time!

"I made a movie with Won Ron!"

"Sounds Puerto Rican."

"*No!* This guy's the number-one Hong Kong actor. He had his office right in with Bruce Lee. And I did *The Last House on the Left*—with all those kids abducted. You forgot the movie? I'd like to! I saw it at a drive-in—and people got *sick*! Then I was mutilated in *Massage Parlor*—I had my throat slit and was hung upside down. I was in a picture about a man who castrated horses. And a drug movie. I was the roommate in *Massage Parlor.* I didn't do tricks . . . well, just a couple—this cop knocked . . . and woo woo woo. Listen, you're not gonna tell me about your film?"

He told her she didn't look the part.

"So I'm not right?" She suddenly raised an imaginary machine gun and sprayed the man with bullets—"Pah pah pah pah"—then slung her bag over her shoulder, swept to the door, flashed a smile and a peace sign.

"I thought you were going to throw your bag at me."

"No! I'm really not hostile! Good luck with your movie!"

Real Life

Back in Preminger's office another kind of casting went on. We were no longer in the realm of earnest looks, nervous fingers, and "sparks."

Cliff Gorman had come to talk about playing Hamlekh, the Israeli secret agent. He had won a Tony award as Lenny Bruce in the Broadway production of *Lenny*, starred in the film *Cops and Robbers* and in both the film and stage productions of *The Boys in the Band*.

Cliff sat across from Preminger while Erik and I were drawn up on the sidelines like kibitzers at a gin game.

Both players were actors. Gorman looked about forty, with medium height, heavy brows, and a dark, hawkish, city face. He had the tautness of a man who worked out regularly—a middleweight with good moves, relaxed now in one of Preminger's leather chairs, holding a lighted cigar between strong fingers, listening with a faint smile. Dressed in a cord jacket and wide, aviator-style glasses, he seemed amused and casual to the last inch, sending a clear message through the chatter: "I'm only curious. . . . I don't need this. . . . What have you got?"

Preminger began by praising him in *Lenny*. "The play lived in your performance." Then he got to business. "It's a book called *Rosebud*."

"There's no script?"

"Not yet. But it doesn't matter. I don't give script approval, you know." No reaction. Preminger held up a blue paperback of bound, advance proofs. "The character who is the French agent will be American. . . . "

Cliff puffed his cigar and listened. As in every gambling scene in every B movie, a cloud of smoke rose around him.

"Your character is called Hamlekh. It's the second character."

"Who's the third?" His manner had a New York push, a sarcastic edge. I could see him as a cop.

"Hacam is third. He's an Arab." Preminger started on the story, then broke off as if bored. "Look, you read the book. You will see everything. And you won't be able to put it down."

He handed it across the desk. "Your character could speak—well, he could speak like you."

"Like *me*?"

"Yes, I don't want to emphasize a particular accent, but if the dialogue is not too colloquial, that in itself will be foreign. Aren't you Jewish?"

Cliff laughed, sounding tough. "That's irrelevant."

"Have you been to Israel?"

"No."

"Ah, once you go there you will be crazy about it, believe me. . . . Don't forget the book. You can bring it back later."

Cliff smiled. "Is it two cents a day if overdue?"

"Read it. It will become better in the screenplay."

They shook hands and Preminger said, "Shalom."

"Sha-*lom*?" Cliff shrugged and left.

Afterward came the obligatory thoughtful silence.

"I didn't think his accent was *bad*," said Erik. "Was he trying to do an Israeli?"

"You louse!" Otto walked to his son and put his arm around him. "Gorman's a great actor . . . but a real Israeli might fit better. Hmm . . ."

Clearly he had made no decisions yet. And there would be a lot of looking.

"Erik!" he demanded suddenly, "how are we doing?"

"I don't know how casting's coming, but the writing's going terrifically."

"Then don't sit! Go to work!"

14

One evening, Erik pulled off his metal earmuffs and prepared to hurry off to supper with his father and some UA executives. "People think these parties help, but projects don't get on because of parties. You know what happens at parties? I met a girl from a studio who told me they turned down *Rosebud* because it was too contrived."

That same day Patricia Hearst was kidnapped.

The most outrageous inventions of the novel were suddenly on the front pages, and I remembered Erik saying, "My father has an uncanny sense of what will become topical."

The similarities were astonishing.

Both kidnappings were hushed up briefly for tactical reasons, both terrorist groups sent letters to the press, and both families (Hearst and Fargeau) ordered the "law" not to pursue the hostages lest their daughters be endangered.

On February 13, the SLA asked "food for the poor," beginning a series of demands as complex as those in *Rosebud.*

Hostages in both cases traveled blindfolded, spoke on recordings to their powerful families, and were innocent victims in a larger plan. Said Patricia Hearst on tape, "I just hope you'll do what they say, Daddy. . . . This is not . . . just a simple kidnapping."

Both cases involved death threats. "Field Marshal Cinque" declared that he would execute Patty "to save . . . starving people," and the *Rosebud* terrorists promised to deliver a hostage's body for every unmet demand.

We were hooked.

Rosebud was contemporary, vital—now.

All they had to do was finish the script.

Eva Monley, the production manager in London, was amazed. "Did you see the Hearst thing? It's incredible!"

"Hearst? Well, I will tell you . . ." Preminger spoke to me with a straight face, even repeating his words weeks later to a

London journalist. "If someone came to me with a script about Hearst, I definitely would not do it. It's too sensational in a way. Gershy, why are you smiling? What's wrong? You are usually so serious."

During his last hours in the city, Preminger enjoyed a flurry of activity, checking memos, crumpling correspondence in balls at his feet.

"This Eva Monley! She makes me so nervous I can't read. Look, her accountant got sick. But there is *another* accountant."

Again he conferred with an aide about possible stars. "Tell them we will start in mid-April to mid-May. . . . Hmm. Newman . . . Brando—don't ask him again. We left it that we might send him a script. . . . Now, Mitchum—how old is he?"

"Fifty-five, Otto."

"Ah, too old."

He bounded up from his chair. "Ah, I'm so overweight. But now I'm going to the barber!"

Erik was dubious. "You're getting a haircut?"

"You should be *proud*." Laughing, he wagged his finger. "I at least *get* a haircut."

The last good-bye was made that night, to my wife at Kennedy Airport. We had separated three months before, just as she gained success in her first Broadway play. After five years together, we were left with the knowledge that we had once loved each other.

"Did I ever say it?" she asked.

"Three times. You were drunk."

"And you believed me?"

"I was drunk too."

"Now don't get sad. I want you frisky and happy. That's why you're going. We weren't happy together. Remember that. You're much better when you're alone."

"Right. I'm happy *now.*"

"Right!"

Drinking coffee in that hideously cheerful canteen, I thought again how beautiful she was: tall and rangy, all legs and cheekbones. A cloud of soft brown hair fell to her back and her gray-green cat's eyes were cool and slitted with challenge. But I knew how that imperturbable mask could dissolve into sudden, bewildered uncertainty. And that, as they say, is what got me.

I understood her orphan's fear of being touched, or of truly needing anyone, or of reaching out to ask for help. I had only to watch her and remember these things, to plunge into sadness. And I couldn't tell her how beautiful she was. She hated to hear it from me.

So we sat and drank coffee and reminded each other we were free to do as we liked. The flight was finally called and I got up with my hands full of carry-on luggage, feeling burdened with all the things I wanted to tell her.

"Remember I love you."

"You are not to *say that*!"

"Sorry. It slipped out."

"You're going to Europe. You're having a good time! Now remember!"

"Over and over. I'll repeat it."

"That's right. And write a good book. And make money. And enjoy yourself."

We were laughing as I kissed her cheek and turned to board the plane. She could always make me laugh, at least until we were apart.

"The trouble with you, Gershy, is that you are like so many men. You always want what you can't have. I should write a book about *you*!"

Somewhere over the Atlantic, Preminger padded stocking-footed into the tourist section and tapped me awake. His tie was loose and he looked as if he'd been enjoying life in first class.

"Gershy, are you having a good flight?"

"Yes, fine thanks. What about you?"

"I always have a good flight!" It was one hour till dawn.

On board, Otto and Erik were carrying the first-draft screenplay minus a final scene with Schrantz. That character was largely unborn, but there were a hundred and forty pages in shiny red covers, which I hoped to read soon.

And in London, Eva Monley waited to bring the film her portion of real life.

Starting as a location worker on *African Queen* (1951), she had moved up to location manager (holding that job on five Preminger films), and gradually had become one of two top female production managers in Europe. Most recently, she had graduated to associate producer on *The Black Windmill* (1973) for Don Siegel.

Eva knew personnel all through the industry and had sifted through a dozen candidates for some jobs, seeking, as she put it, the "bestest" for Preminger.

Her notes, filed almost daily from London, were encyclopedic. They questioned which actors and equipment to use, which vehicles to take where, which suppliers to rent from— on and on. Doubts blossomed into whole arias.

The truth was that Eva was worried. With the production due to start in eight weeks, she wanted answers. "What I need is to walk through it with Papa, see how he imagines it. That's the only way we'll get to final decisions."

And Eva walked very slowly, at random, because there was no other way. The true nature of her job can only be understood by moving close, until the pattern of rational decision making dissolves into masses of maddening detail.

Consider the schedule. On New Year's Day, 1974, Eva speculated that the unit would travel Nice-Corsica-Paris-

Berlin-Israel. Israel would also stand in for Lebanon. As Preminger said, his Lebanese welcome, after *Exodus*, was "not enthusiastic." Eva also guessed that the film would be shot in twelve weeks, including travel time. Nine months later her schedule proved almost exactly right.

But nothing in films moves in straight lines. Nothing. On January 5, she urgently asked to come to New York to discuss, in part, the schedule.

The trip was not made.

January 8. Many support vehicles were considered, including the big, customized vans that hold cameras, lights, and a generator. Eva estimated that just moving such a vehicle to the locations and back to London would take nine workdays.

January 9. Trouble. Flights into Corsica could not carry big film vans. Nor could the Corsican ferries. Eva considered hiring a larger ferry; but the energy crisis, just hitting then, made such charters doubtful.

February 11. Eva got the first-draft screenplay, rushed to her from New York. She met immediately with Max Seeburg, a shipping agent who would forward the equipment and move the rushes to and from a London lab. Together they created a schedule and estimated shipping costs, including a charter flight, Paris to Berlin, to save time.

Meanwhile, a travel agent, an elegant young man sporting a watch given him by the Beatles, started quoting passenger fares. (By Preminger's order, everyone would fly tourist.)

All these plans were acts of faith. Three people in London were arranging trips across Europe based on a script that was still changing in New York, depending on the availability of unknown actors and the home berth of an unchartered yacht.

For nothing. The shooting didn't start in Corsica *or* Nice. And there was no flight, chartered or regular, from Paris to Berlin because Hamburg came between. The rushes weren't processed in England. And films don't move in straight lines.

Scheduling took perhaps one percent of Eva's time. It was

nothing compared to reconnaissance trips, which the English called "recces." (Pronounced *wreck-ease*, with the accent on wreck.)

At the end of January, Eva flew to Nice and Paris, ravenous for facts in the face of an implacable deadline. Thirty to fifty technicians, a dozen or more actors, various press hustlers, families, lovers, and hangers-on would descend on some as yet undecided location at some unspecified date in May to make a movie. It was her job to get them contracts, transport, rooms, a caterer to feed them, a doctor to cure them, and all the equipment they needed for "action."

In Paris, she was reminded that the production had to apply for permission to shoot in France from the French Cinema Board (C.N.C.), had to seek authorization to import and export supplies, and had to ask reimbursement of the French TVA it paid (a 20 percent value-added tax). With endless bookkeeping, they might recover the money six months after shooting.

(Preminger snorted at the whole idea. "They are such *little* men.")

Earlier, in London, Eva had given the English unions the right to review crew deals, but *Rosebud* would shoot in Europe and not be subject to union rules. The English crew would make "all-in" one-price deals for weeks running seventy-two hours or longer.

At Studio Victorine in Nice, Eva compared the cost of a French crew. Amazingly, it proved more economical to bring a London grip to Nice, house and feed him, wash his laundry, and give him Sunday lunch than to use a local worker. The Frenchman got the equivalent of £126.50 for forty hours of daylight work, Monday to Friday. With thirty-two "overtime" hours, all at double-time, he would earn £329. The Englishman worked seventy-two hours "all-in" for £159, including social security. Even with another £100 a week for expenses and hotels, he remained cheaper.

The recce continued as Eva went yacht-hunting. The central image of the book was a luxury boat, its passengers abducted, its crew murdered, its auto pilot set on a crash course against the Israeli shoreline. That image sent Eva searching for a symbol of careless wealth, a dream on water. Even the names shimmered: *Nefertiti, Silver Trident, Briseis, Cynara, Southern Breeze.* They ran from ninety to two hundred feet, with crews to twenty-five and rental fees to $3,000 a day.

Eva knew that Preminger must one day "cast" his boat like an actor. She only hoped it would be on the Riviera, to avoid a costly trip from some distant Greek or Italian port. But nothing in films moves in a straight line. Nothing.

Eva's fact-finding also created arabesques of niggling over such issues as where to buy film (depending on the relative TVA and VAT in France and England).

And all the data and questions were waiting for Preminger. As we landed, I wondered how he and Eva would work together. Certainly he would not be hurried.

"I tell her it's too soon to worry. If *I* am not worried, why should she be? Look, I'm not shooting a schedule, I'm shooting a picture."

Dorchester Suite

London produced a sudden rush of liberation.

The surroundings hardly mattered. Heathrow was a dim, noisy barn where porters played hit-and-run with handcarts. Driving into the city, the ancient Austin cab smelled of stale tobacco and dusty leather. Cramped in the back, needing showers and shaves, Otto and Erik faced a murderous day. Yet they were buoyant.

For the movie, Erik suggested a French actress he had met at the Teheran Film Festival. When Otto had been unable to accept an invitation there, he had sent his son instead.

"Sometimes I spoil my son, but then my son is worth spoiling." On cue, we rolled up to the Dorchester.

Filmmakers often stay in the best hotels as partial compensation for the troubles ahead. The Dorchester was old London and money of all ages: a low, gray stone building facing its own traffic oval across from Hyde Park, with porters in clawhammer coats and green-striped vests scurrying up the front steps. A cold sun burnished the façade in dry gold.

Preminger had his usual suite. "This is like coming home. They put the liquor bottles back in the cabinet and they have exactly the same amount as when I left!"

The large living room held two fat sofas, a scattering of armchairs, a Frigidaire full of fresh fruit and Perrier, and a shy, pretty English girl who came each morning to "take the flowers out for air."

"It's dangerous for these girls." Preminger scowled at me. "Arab sex maniacs could grab them."

Erik sounded amazed. *"Arab?"*

"Doesn't he look Arab? He could be one of the terrorists."

Downstairs, Eva Monley waited to come up. Meeting her in the lobby, I thought, Yes, she's like her memos. Short, square-jawed, with graying, close-cropped hair, she spoke staccato English riddled with contractions and nicknames, anything to say more in less time. Dressed in no-nonsense pants and a velour shirt, with a scarf around her neck, she looked fiercely impatient to get *out* and get *going.*

Listening, I felt her nerves: "I want to keep the people I've lined up. Luckily, I've had time to plan and scheme—talking to the labs, I've gotten their quotes below *Black Windmill.*"

She talked so fast I could barely make notes. "I've had time to show that a British crew is cheaper than a French one. OP wanted to make this picture with an all-French crew, but that's wrong. They aren't on your side. They laugh at you behind your back!"

She wasn't worried about *Rosebud.* "I'd rather take on a big challenge and have a go. And these days I can work on projects I like and not have to subdue my instincts. I turned down the new Kubrick film. Frankly, I loathe the way he treats women. Maybe he has a problem. I hated every frame of *Clockwork Orange*! Oh, I'm acid to say it, but that's the privilege of a woman PM."

Talking about her old bosses, Siegel, Huston, Carl Foreman, Anatole Litvak, and others, bolstered her. Once, Siegel had exploded at her. "I stood there and let it wash over me. You have to. Then when he finished, I told him, 'You run a poor second to Otto Preminger!' Later we became terrific friends."

Her real worry was Preminger. "When he yells, he has the ability to destroy people's dignity in public. It's a bad gift. You know, he brooks *no discussion*!"

She was chafing to go up and face him.

"OP gave me my first break as a location manager. Now I really know something. I only hope he realizes."

The Dorchester suite felt like the setting for a French farce, played by an English company, with an American director firing orders in a Viennese accent. Doors flew open. Suites nearby were being remodeled, to the sound of drills and hammers. Phones rang from outside and downstairs, and Preminger's response was always the same: "Send him up. Send them up! Send them *all* up!"

There were newsmen, radio interviewers, friends, technicians, talent agents, and yacht brokers offering bouquets of *Rosebuds*. There were dark actors for Arabs and blondes for hostages. There were calls to Paris, Nice, and New York and the first tremors of a collapsible phone system. There was Eva with her green notebook, leaning forward on a sofa across from Preminger as appointments overlapped, so that half a dozen people sat through each others' interviews, all swept along, all part of Preminger's audience.

With no cast, no crew, and a start date eight weeks away, the question was: Where to begin?

Eva urgently needed to commit members of the crew and

offered Preminger a list of names. But to him it was enough that *she* knew the people. And that many were English. "Artistically it's nicer. And anyone connected with sound must be English."

("It's changing my way," Eva said later. "With a little persuasion, I'll get this picture set up the way I want it!")

When Eva gave out scripts, he told her, "Make it clear every word will be rewritten. This is not a script, it's an *idea*!"

Some jobs were a problem. Several top art directors were busy, but Eva "liked the sound of this Willy Holt," who had done *The Day of the Jackal.*

"He speaks fine English, and he's young. Fifty."

"*That* is young. When you get older, everyone stays the same age. To me, you're still a little girl."

"I worry you won't listen to me."

"I will if you *speak loud enough*! Your English is so . . . so . . . *English*!"

The last name was Angela Martelli's. She had done continuity on *Exodus,* Hitchcock's *Frenzy,* and many, many more.

By now, blue twilight filled the suite, and Preminger ordered drinks. "You know," he mused, "Angela was wonderful on *Exodus.* And about Hitchcock . . ." He paused, thoughtfully. "I will tell you something. He is the director I most admire. He is never afraid to try something new. As much as he is praised, he is *underpraised*!" Then he smiled, looking gentler than I'd ever seen. "He said once to me that *Laura* was better than all his pictures. I should quote that . . . and pretend he cared." His smile deepened into a soft chuckle. A few minutes later, the first visitors arrived, Eva's notebook closed, and they were laughing with old friends.

The laughter couldn't last.

Besides her other work, Eva had to make a "below-the-line" budget. It meant doing separate budgets for each country in local currency, and then a consolidated budget in dollars.

"Eva, why so sad?"

"I'm concentrating. You want a budget for five currencies . . . over four countries . . . in three days. It's impossible."

"You should figure high."

"It'll be a ballpark figure."

"Much depends on it."

The tone of all this was deceptively low-key, like the careless jingle of small change. Yet Preminger—according to the custom in such production contracts—was personally liable for any budget overruns.

Why would he take such a risk?

"He knows he's a good producer," said Eva.

Erik added, "And he gets to make the picture."

Preparing the budget involved relentless questioning as Eva reduced the work to salaries, fees, bodies, days, feet, miles, kilos, reels, dollars, francs, marks, and pounds.

Arriving the second morning, she looked haggard. "I was up till two-thirty phoning and figuring and up again this morning at six. By seven-thirty I couldn't get a line to France."

Preminger opened his door to us while shaving with a cordless razor. Wearing a turtleneck and a big Gucci belt, he was nursing a cold. Room service brought coffee. Next door, Erik was typing. Down the hall they were still hammering.

And the interrogation began.

Some questions had clear answers. More or less.

How long would the picture be?

"Evaaa—" the bass rumbled with paternal rebuke. "As long as it has to!"

They settled on two hours—eleven thousand feet.

Editor Peter Thornton would travel with the company, cutting as they shot. "It's easier for me," said Preminger. "I shoot in long takes because I was trained in the theater. And I'm impatient. I don't like to sit in an editing room for a year."

Realism was vital. "No sets. And no day-for-night. It *never* works. I will shoot real night, and for a sunset on the boat, there will be a *real sunset!*"

He demanded anamorphic lenses, though they cost £7,000 more. The lenses created a panoramic image two-and-a-third times wider than high.

"The look is worth it! A tremendous look!"

Some questions would be answered . . . soon.

Could director of photography Denys Coop use a smaller crane than the big Chapman "Hercules"? And what about a lab?

"They must pay the cost of sending rushes," said Preminger.

"I mentioned it."

"Why are you so sad?"

"I'm not sad."

"You've become soft, Eva. You *tell* them. They *must* pay!"

"I tried, but it's immensely costly—"

"Bring them here. Coop and I will *talk* to them!"

Many questions simply hung in the air, waiting.

Should *Rosebud* be an English national film to get Eady Plan subsidy money?

Or French national, to get the French subsidy?

Or a French-English co-production to get both?

What about the sales taxes—VAT, TVA, and German *Mehrwertsteuer*? An American company would recover them later. Should *Rosebud* be American, recover the taxes, and lose the subsidies? Or be foreign, pay the taxes, and gain the subsidies?

Which crew members would go everywhere?

Who would be picked up locally?

Who was going on recces?

Where were the Arab actors?

Where was Topol?

Where was Michael Caine?

Where were we?

It was the third day, and I had begun carrying aspirin. Clearly, Eva and Otto were slightly at odds.

She wanted the assistant director to start soon, to help with scheduling.

"Eva, you're so scared . . ."

"I'm protecting you and me."

"Not me."

"Then me."

He spoke without emotion. "It won't help."

The room seemed to contract. Going over a set of tickets, Eva checked off cities.

"You added a Paris."

"I'm concentrating a hundred and twenty-five percent and it's so hot in here!"

Hammering punctuated the exchanges. Preminger called the manager. "They *drill* and it goes through your bones . . ."

"Seven years ago," said Eva, "you wouldn't have paid for a suite with this noise. Now I can say *you've* changed."

Moments later, magically, the hammering stopped. Preminger smiled with genuine surprise. Something had been accomplished.

During these inquisitions, there were moments when Preminger revealed some feeling for the film. It happened once when he was explaining his new final scene. This had changed radically from the book, where Hélène went on TV and discredited the Arabs by saying they had "released" the hostages for ransom.

"It's a terrible trick to lie," said Preminger. "It makes the Arabs sympathetic at the wrong time." Now Schrantz would discredit himself after being captured by the Israelis. He would rant contemptuously to Martin and Hamlekh about the Arab guerrillas he had manipulated—while unknowingly being videotaped through a two-way mirror. "Then he would suddenly see himself on TV, speaking to Martin. It would be technically interesting to do this without a cut. Martin would turn on the TV and the scene in the room would continue exactly on it. It *proves* the reality to Schrantz!" Preminger spoke with fervor, reaching Eva.

"The message of his picture," she exclaimed, "is TV! The power of TV!" For a moment all the planning and calculating seemed informed by an idea.

With budgeting came bargaining. An American agent wanted $100,000 for a French actor. So Preminger called the actor's French agent.

"I'll pay only the price he gets for pictures in France. . . . Out of the question! I *know* what he got for his last one. A hundred and fifty thousand *francs!*"

He hung up with nothing settled, tapping his gold Mark Cross pencil on the coffee table. "There are always other actors."

It was a verdict. He would not go beyond his price. Take it or leave it.

Chalky White, his accountant, saw it at once. He was a jolly, stocky chainsmoker, harrumphing and massaging his English vowels until they became the perfect evocation of evening pleasures in a Wardour Street pub and "I'm broke, old boy" emerged as "Eim browke, owld bhoay."

He would start in April.

But Preminger wanted him to do a budget now, for no extra pay.

Chalky offered to work on weekends, while he finished a film for Brut Productions, a part of the cosmetics firm. But there should be a fee.

"*No!* We're not Brut. We don't make money by putting something stinking in a little water."

He had to be tough. *Rosebud* drew every film hustler in London. One lab sent flowers—while their salesman sat with a button open on his purple shirt and offered a discount of 17½ percent.

28

"By what dreaming do you arrive at that? I usually get twenty-five percent."

"We only *give* fifteen percent."

"Be nice. Call a board meeting and make us twenty."

("These laboratories make so much money they can afford the discount. When the flowers wilt, send them back.")

The yacht brokers worked even harder, like the clubman-type with pinstripes and dandruff: "All our boats are rich men's yachts."

"Then they should be generous."

"Oh, but how did they *get* rich? By being stingy!"

("These brokers have no principles.")

Best of all the salespeople were the agents. No dandruff here. No slobs in peek-a-boo shirts.

Maggie Abbott of CMA had shoulder-length brown hair framing a strong profile and spoke in a softly resonant English voice. One hoped her actresses showed the same understated sexiness.

Preminger especially liked her idea of Louis Jourdan for the industrialist, Fargeau. "Too young, but he *is* great. Handsome and virile. . . . Perhaps he's not taken seriously enough. People know that decisions are made by us ugly old men."

("Gershy, you were leering at her like an Arab sex maniac.")

Most polished was Richard Blodgett of IFA, who elevated selling almost to a performing art. The son of Cornelia Otis Skinner, he had studied at Harvard and now lived in London. Tall and bearded, wearing a blue blazer over a turtleneck, he balanced informality and elegance. His speech was also balanced, half English, half Boston. And his greeting to Otto was friendly but not intimate. A *balanced* greeting.

For the girls, he offered ideas as if they were semiprecious stones. One was "very gifted." A second had just been married. "She's so much more mature now."

Preminger favored Lalla Ward, another client, whom Eva

had shown him in a news clipping. "Her father is a Lord. Can she be funny and snobbish?"

"Oh, I think so." Very reassuring. "What about men?"

"I need two Arabs. One is very charming. He has to kill but doesn't like to hurt people."

"Well, I've *got* him. It's Ian McShane."

"First I want to try to get an Arab. Perhaps even a Jew."

"But Ian's Jewish! And he has limitless charm."

For the hostages' fathers, Blodgett offered more names. "Harry Andrews? Eric Porter? Tony Quayle? Or even Lord Olivier? Is it big enough for the Lord?" No reaction.

Blodgett stroked his lip idly and moved to the main event. "Any feelings about the star part? How about Donald Sutherland?"

"Good," said Preminger without enthusiasm.

Who was first choice then?

"Someone like McQueen. Brando . . ."

"Ah."

"Any actor with charm and personality. You could play it, Dick."

"What would you say to Burt Lancaster?"

"It's possible. How old is he?"

"In his late fifties."

"How late?"

"He celebrated his sixtieth birthday in Rome. . . . Is the picture for UA?"

"Yes, why?"

"Just wondering. Burt had a five-picture deal with them." The idea was planted. UA *liked* Burt.

For the Israeli agent, Blodgett had another notion. Nicol Williamson."

"I saw him in *Uncle Vanya* . . ."

"I know. Nicol's doing *The Wilby Conspiracy* with Caine and Poitier. I got him equal billing."

Had UA objected to the billing?

On cue, Blodgett's hands spread as if smoothing troubled water. He spoke with scholarly detachment.

"Let me give you an argument. . . . By his presence he makes the other two more important. Neither is an absolutely first-rank star. But opinion-makers know Nicol. With him in the trio the whole cast is stronger. Marty Baum [the producer] wanted the same thing."

He might have been back at Harvard in a tutorial session, watching the afternoon sun set through mullioned windows.

Next morning Preminger considered the part of Schrantz. "It's trite to make him a German. Maybe he'll be an Englishman. What do you think of Nicol Williamson?"

Casting unknowns was harder than names, for it required faith in a business that mostly taught cynicism. With the young actresses he liked, Preminger looked at sample reels and listened avidly to readings. But readings and films could be deceptive. Finally, he had to believe—and gamble.

"Do you still strip them?" Eva asked.

"Not personally. But they are still nude, if that's what you mean." So they had to be warned. Gently.

He explained to the actresses that "they don't do anything obscene. The nudity is harmless and necessary."

He didn't add that they would be standing naked through repeated takes in front of a crew on a windswept afterdeck. And no one asked. Nudity just wasn't an issue.

One actress fluttered her lashes. "I don't make a habit of it, but yes."

Another shot her cuffs and snapped, "Depends on how it's done, really."

Only one girl, Judi Bowker, refused. "It's not worth it," she told Preminger. And he liked her for it. But the others had all decided long ago. It *was* worth it.

In London, Preminger saw everyone the agents sent. In New York, his office would have screened Christine, Sonia, Françoise, Iris, Caroline, Marie-Christine, Kristina, Barbara, Jenny, Judy, Cathryn, and the rest. But not here.

Many were too old, too dark, too tall, too affected. I squirmed as one agent told a ravishing Jackie Bisset type to sit up and speak up! Preminger turned to an Arab actor who was also waiting in the room and asked if he was nervous too.

"No."

"Thank God! Are you a good actor?"

"I can't tell."

"You keep it a secret, you fool?"

As if to prove his impatience, he almost cast the first girl he saw as the English hostage. Ann Shetland wasn't her real name, but she *was* slightly horse-faced. Primly cheerful in a pink dress, she sat demurely through her interview.

"You're very good for the part."

Ann smiled hopefully.

"Marvelous!" he exclaimed. "She gives me the impression of being a good actress."

Eva was cooler. "She photographs better than she looks."

"She *looks* like an aristocrat in the movie sense." Despite his cold, he would visit her play. "And if she is even halfway good, I shall hire her without further ado!"

I'll call her first rival Eve Harrington. Because she was cute.

For ten dizzy minutes she gave a preview of the ego bruises that lay ahead. Preminger had seen her in a movie, playing an American girl. Her accent had been shaky then and her face plump. Thus the slender young woman who arrived was a revelation: a tall, liquid figure poured into a flaring pants suit.

"That cameraman should be shot! This girl is *beautiful*!"

"It was baby fat. Once you lose it, it stays off."

"You have the part! You're an American. Why do you live in England?"

"My father is English. Frankly, I'm surprised at being cast as an American."

One second after she left, he realized he'd confused her playing an American with being one. "With that English accent, no one would believe she was a Senator's daughter."

Reactions poured in by phone. Eve's agent called. Preminger said she couldn't play an American. When the agency head called, Preminger promised to consider Eve for the English girl—if Ann Shetland didn't work out. Finally Eve called.

"I thought," said Preminger, "because of your film, you're for the American girl. If I don't sign Miss Shetland I'll come back to you. . . . It's all right, it's my fault. . . ." He would have come back, too, but for Eva Monley.

"You just don't know the trouble on her last picture. She wouldn't lose weight and she wouldn't study. Now suddenly she's ambitious!" Exercising the "privilege of a woman PM to be acid," she closed the door on Eve Harrington. "She's charming but quickly on attack. Not like Miss Shetland, who's prim and frilly and composed."

A year later, Eve Harrington married a top international film actor and her career raced ahead, regardless of *Rosebud*. (And two years after their marriage, the happy couple began a bitter divorce suit.)

Miss Shetland, meanwhile, was becoming part of the family. She and her agent came one evening to read the nude scene and "confer," while friends relaxed and Erik poured drinks.

Eva ordered hers without water.

"She just wants to see the scotch," said David Lewin with a laugh. He was the editor of *Cinema-TV*, a British trade paper, and looked like a jollier version of Henry Kissinger, a frizzy-haired Semitic satyr. "I'll have a large vodka with lots of ice," he announced. "And you may quote me!"

For a few minutes everyone was desperately glad not to be talking business. Whether it was the vodka or the laughter, Miss Shetland was even looking attractive.

"She will have a small tonic before the show," said her agent.

"You should relax and have a drink too," Preminger advised.

He giggled and fluttered his hand. "Oh, I *am* relaxed."

"Wherever we shoot, you are welcome."

David Lewin eyed Miss Shetland. "Certainly *I'll* visit. You're pretty."

"Thank you."

"*Ha!*" That was Otto.

"Dear Otto," exclaimed Lewin. "He loves me because we always laugh. Too bad the day can't start that way. Too bad they don't make films with pretty girls like her instead of old men! Otto, did you say you wanted *five* women? What an interesting study!"

There was lots more laughter, and more tonic, potato chips, and pretzels. "Oh," said Miss Shetland, "it reminds me of a children's party."

"Her agent asked ten thousand pounds. I offered a hundred and fifty a week and he accepted! She is so *right*! And she has a humor! Gershy, this is all for *your* benefit."

That night, tickets waited at the theater for "Mr. Pellinger."

("I'm very well known here.")

Playing a princess in distress, Miss Shetland looked like Disney's Snow White. Afterward, because the dressing room was tiny, Preminger congratulated her in the auditorium, as the audience struggled past them. Hearing she would do the part, she erupted in a swoony, fairy-tale smile.

Preminger's belief in her talent had been verified and it gave him a lift. At midnight, in a freezing drizzle, we waited for a taxi under the iron canopy of Charing Cross Station. The director had come out with a cold after an endless day. Yet he talked enthusiastically about his Viennese theater, about a Greek girl to contrast with Ann Shetland, about Graham Greene, who had done the screenplay of *St. Joan*—"my greatest flop."

As I finally got home and lay down, exhausted, I wondered where he got his energy. And how could Snow White be an English aristocrat?

Casting, he often said, was a matter of luck. The next day Ann's ran out.

Preminger finished an interview in the bedroom, answering yet again the same old questions. ("I don't like to sit in an editing room for a year . . .") Beyond the hotel window, a construction crane rose over Hyde Park, slowly crossing the scrubbed, February sky.

In the living room, Lalla Ward waited. The first word I scrawled about her was "lovely."

She looked eighteen—had never played older. Mixing delicacy and sensuality, her face was a wide oval framed by long, blonde hair that fell to below her breasts. She wore no makeup and didn't need any. With her clear skin, wide, carnal mouth, and blue-green eyes that reflected every feeling, Lalla at least *looked* deeply romantic.

She sat amid the flowers and floral drapes and flowered teacups, dressed in sensible pants, describing her experience. "I drowned as Shelley's wife." She had also done a film "about a girl who's going to be married in three days and realizes she's got the wrong man."

Preminger nodded encouragement.

"I suppose if everyone finds me wildly fascinating the picture will be a success. Otherwise they're in trouble."

He gave her the nude scene to scan quickly.

"All I've got against taking my clothes off is if there's no point."

Erik puffed his pipe vigorously. "The scene is very brief and clinical."

She laughed. "How boring." Lalla read quickly, heedless of the chatter around her. The nude scene was acceptable. She left a picture and departed with a summer smile, producing an awkward silence in the wake of the obvious.

"She's younger than the other girl . . ."

"And sexy . . ."

"And . . ." And beautiful and the daughter of a Lord and bright.

Preminger told Eva to bring Lalla's sample reel to Paris for screening. Then he dictated the option clauses for the girls' contracts, giving him the right to use each one in a picture a year for five years at escalating prices. If he missed a year, the contract was still good for the remaining years. He felt it was a fair reward for a man who was gambling, a reward for belief in the face of skepticism.

What Preminger trusted most was equipment: the latest, the best, the most expensive. At the same time he didn't want to spend needlessly. So the game began.

His director of photography, Denys Coop, had years of experience and an irreducible body of skills that combined to give him the power to say which equipment was "essential" and which technicians would assist him. He had worked up through the ranks, in the English way, greatly influenced by Oswald Morris, who, with John Huston, had pioneered color filtration (*Moulin Rouge, Moby Dick*) and desaturated color (*Reflections in a Golden Eye*). Denys had learned an approach from Morris and been his operator for years. Most important, Denys had been Preminger's cinematographer on *Bunny Lake Is Missing* (1965).

Now Denys was president of the British Society of Cinematographers, and he *looked* presidential. In his solid arms and shoulders, in his bulging gut, one saw the massing effect of heavy work and heavy lunches. One felt solidity in his brush mustache; his glasses with their thick, black rims; his half-bald dome fringed with wisps of black hair. He mixed a dry humor with what I would later see was a stubborn pride. Rubbed the wrong way, it might produce a large measure of hurt.

As they met in the Dorchester, Preminger described his first scene: "following a terrorist in the port of Bastia as he comes off the ship and goes through pass control, all in one shot." He talked hardware, not concepts. And for every scene, Denys knew proper equipment: for the opening, an industrial crane or a Chapman Nike (smaller than the Hercules); for aerial work, the Mobius, a gyro-stabilized, remote-controlled electronic wonder. For cramped interiors, the Panaflex was ideal, though no camera could galvanize long dialogue scenes in a plane. "The interior of a plane," said Denys, "is just not interesting."

For a lab, they would use Coop's favorite in England (if it paid for shipping rushes) and buy film in France (for the best discount).

Everything was possible. They could even shoot actors watching real TV and film. A movie projector would be interlocked with the Panaflex so both shutters opened together. And a TV monitor (showing a videotape) could be connected to the movie camera by a "sync pulse generator," which emitted a regular impulse, synchronizing both the TV scanning and the Panaflex shutter, so that no black "phase bar" marred the TV face.

A waiter hovered, ready to take lunch orders, as Denys explained that they could avoid all the interlocks and pulse generators by just "matting in" images. A master shot would be made with blank TV and film screens. The media images could be added later in a lab. But Preminger preferred to have real actors watching real pictures, even if it was more trouble. And he trusted that all the proper, expensive equipment would give him that reality.

After lunch they set off on a ritual visit to Samuelson's to discuss equipment and stress frugality. Preminger as usual rode in the front seat, studying the view and ruminating.

Down Abbey Road he grew restless. "Where does Mr. Samuelson live, Liverpool?"

At the legendary Samuelson's one could rent anything for a film. Amid chattering telexes in a central control area, customer liaison men were constantly phoning movie units around the world, keeping track of every piece of rental gear and dealing with any problems. The foyer was hung with dozens of souvenir clapsticks, including the one from *Bunny Lake.*

It looked like a state occasion. Sidney Samuelson, one of four founding brothers, guided Preminger, who forged ahead in a leather greatcoat amid a susurrus of recognition.

Otto reminded Sidney that they had no money. As everyone was lofted up on the power-tailgate of a seven-ton Sammobile, Otto stressed to Sidney that the big film van was too awkward for Corsican roads.

"But, Otto, you can't have all this gear in a minibus." Denys even wanted to take two "brutes," powerful old carbon-arc lamps.

Preminger thundered, "Denys, you still want bruuuutes? A young cameraman doesn't *know* brutes!"

"Otto, I'm still young enough to *lift* them."

Leaving, Otto emphasized to Sidney, "I make you my representative. Negotiate against the other brothers. I feel whatever we don't need we shouldn't take."

Yet they took everything. It was insurance. Spending so much already, they could not risk any delay for lack of gear.

Denys planned to take two zoom lenses and three high-speed fixed lenses for night shooting. What he finally took were four zooms (50–90mm, 25–250mm, 50–500mm, 40–200mm) and six prime lenses (30mm, 35mm, 40mm, 50mm, 75mm, and 100mm).

Shooting with anamorphic lenses increased the equipment load. The second camera also had to be anamorphic and turned out to be a big Panavision PVSR studio reflex.

Later, during the second day of shooting, I walked to the dock where the *Rosebud* was moored and saw a Nike crane sitting in the blistering sun, charging its batteries after a costly flight from London.

And later still came the brutes.

"Whatever we don't need we shouldn't take," Preminger had said. But it was a losing battle. *Rosebud* needed everything.

At this time Preminger began to meet some of his future crew members. Approaching a new employer, often for the first time, they behaved with a strained sobriety.

Tony Teiger, the shaggy prop master, hid his Cockney street smarts behind a guarded quiet. ("Isn't it amazing," asked Preminger, "how we all liked him better when he said he was Jewish?")

Robin Gregory, "our best soundman" according to Eva, was serious, polite, and round-faced, with a touch of the fervid high school scientist. "Kubrick insisted on *Barry Lyndon* that every take be perfect. Even a clothes rustle or a noise in the clear and he would redo the scene!"

Peter Thornton, the wistful, gray-haired editor whom Preminger had started in features, still at times yearned to go to sea. "I was trained for it, you know." He suggested the diabolic misery of a sailor locked in an editing cubicle, rerunning endless footage of the cruising yacht.

At times all the seriousness of these visitors was too much for Preminger. But old friends and even older jokes kept the boredom at bay.

He told one bon vivant who appeared in a turtleneck, "I remember when everyone in London wore white or black tie."

39

"But I'm *with it,* Otto," said the man with a laugh. "You say your film is a period piece?"

"No! The only period pieces are you and I!"

Preminger was especially delighted to see Jules Buck, even with his strudel story. Buck and the director had been friends since their days at Fox. Round and dark and energetic, Buck now puffed a cigar and told of a Jewish husband who lay dying while the family gathered.

A delicious smell came from the kitchen. The dying man pleaded with his wife, "Sarah, I know I'm going . . . all I ask is one last piece of strudel."

"No, Sam! That's for *after* the funeral."

Their laughter led to business: Preminger recommended a novel to Buck—and to Buck's partner.

That, of course, was Peter O'Toole.

The good times seemed like a distraction in London. The talk and jokes merely emphasized the silence at the center of *Rosebud.* I had not been offered a script or invited to observe any conferences between Otto and Erik. My glimpses of their collaboration were accidental and trivial.

("Erik, in New York you would have already been at work fifty minutes ago. Just reminding you.")

I hadn't even heard a concept of the film. Actors, crew, and equipment accumulated around a mystery that, for all I knew, might just be a void.

If Preminger was worried, he didn't show it. Meeting Topol for lunch, he was never more confident or compelling about the film. Stars brought out the best in him. At such moments, he gave *Rosebud* its greatest excitement, leaning forward, gesturing with the thumbs and forefingers of both hands like a man spreading a butterfly's wings, creating *his* Hamlekh, selling his project, all the while he was looking and shopping.

"You are the top agent in the Shin Beth," he told Topol. "Israel is not invited to help in recovering the girls—though the boat is found there. *You,* however, have information the others don't have. You know the mastermind behind the plot. And you tell Martin where to find him. Representing Israel, you say that giving in to blackmail won't work."

Sitting in the Dorchester, Topol could have been a Jewish James Bond: tall, handsome, smart, and with a sense of humor. He had once thought of doing a film about terrorists himself, but hesitated. "It felt silly to glorify these people. Today it's too late to worry about that. They're part of our world." That was the first time on *Rosebud* I heard anyone discuss the morality of the film.

"Tell your agent if you're interested," said Preminger. "Hamlekh is the part."

"Too bad you can't make it with a T. No! I have no desire to play Hamlet."

Preminger and Eva finished in London with a rush of decisions:

"Letters of intent" to crew members would specify a start "on or about May 15," wording which gave the production two weeks leeway either side.

They would negotiate with LTC Labs in Paris, since the English labs would not pay for shipping rushes.

The young actors must start rehearsal two weeks early.

Shooting would begin in Nice, then go to Corsica.

Lee Electric would supply all lights, positioning the ones in Israel through their Tel Aviv branch. That eliminated the big film vans.

And Preminger would find a way to get the rest of the gear to Corsica. "Even if I have to swim with it on my back!"

The last night in London he spoke at the "President's Dinner" of the British Society of Cinematographers. He had prepared no speech and wasn't worried. "You cannot plan these things. It destroys the spontaneity." With his jokes about Presidents and Watergate, he was a smash.

And I thought that maybe I worried too much. After all, it was a long time to May 15.

At three in the morning I folded a rented tuxedo into its box, packed my notes, and dozed off until a seven o'clock call. It was February 16. We had been in London five days.

Foreigners

As the Air France jet banked over the Nice airport, our cabin turned blue with light reflected off the water.

Later, on the tarmac, we leaned into the wind, walking from the plane to the terminal, where a bored customs guard with acne waved us through like schoolchildren at a crossing. Soon our taxi headed toward Nice, that central city linking the jewel towns of the coast: further east lay Cap Ferrat, Villefranche, and Monte Carlo; behind us in the west were Antibes, Juan-les-Pins, Cannes, and St. Tropez.

Here Preminger had left behind a staff who knew his habits and a people who spoke his language. For a while he could joke about it, flipping off a local TV set with a laugh: "It's amazing how they all speak French so well."

The Grand Hotels of Nice lined up cheerlessly along the Promenade des Anglais, overlooking a long, gritty beach, deserted now in the off season. Preminger naturally stayed at the Negresco, a mass of plaster fringe and stone curls where the staff wore red livery. My own hotel, the Westminster, was an even larger Museum of Social Decline, featuring vast halls with pitted mirrors and a grand staircase leading down to a shuttered discotheque.

"Nice," declared Peter O'Toole later, "is a graveyard for arthritic Englishmen." Still, my window opened onto the Promenade. By day the life of the city called up in thick, rapid French, without subtitles. And at night the starry lamps along the avenue outlined the Baie des Anges, giving Nice a measure of beauty as the sound of traffic yielded to the lulling tidal wash.

Preminger spent two days at the start of the week seeking his dream boat, escorted along the rainy coast by an indefatigable young English broker.

The director knew an ideal boat already. Its owner, Herr Hochbaum, had commissioned *Utopia IV* with tremendous speed and a radical design at a cost of $6 million. Almost at once it had sunk. But great wealth is persistent, and Hochbaum had sent the builders a legendary telegram: PLEASE REPEAT BOAT.

Berthed in Cannes, *Utopia V* was a blue-white projectile with slitted windows as menacing as dark glasses on a bully. Even at rest, the boat spoke of predatory wealth. And the owner actually arrived by helicopter, landing on the dock. Just as Fargeau would.

No visitors were allowed while Hochbaum was away, but Preminger did talk to the German captain. "Hochbaum will be here in March and I *bet* you he'll invite me to lunch or dinner! The minute you talk German they open up. The English are easygoing and polite. The Germans are also polite but behind it is a little fist."

Preminger himself had no real interest in yachts. He was shown many he dismissed as "too old" or "too crummy for a rich man." The few he asked to see were intriguing mostly because of their owners. Thus he would go to Monte Carlo to visit the Onassis and Burton-Taylor boats. And on the way he could also stop at Cap Ferrat to check the progress on his new villa.

The Cap was a peninsula with one luxury hotel, a tiny harbor, and perhaps a hundred villas separated by palms, cedars, and eucalypti. A house on the water, according to one English broker, could cost a million. Prices had been bidden up steadily by waves of cosmetic queens, advertising geniuses, and cognac barons—millionaires who would pay for having millionaire neighbors.

Their homes were a genteel flowering of turrets and pastel-colored stucco, a fairyland through which Preminger's design cut like a meat cleaver. His house was an arc of blue-gray marble, set on a hill so that every room faced the pool below and the sea beyond. "They told me you can't have all the rooms face the same way. But they do! It's like a stage set." Instead of stairs there were sweeping marble ramps. "Useful if I have a heart attack."

Looking up from the pool, the place curved around a viewer as if in Cinemascope. The empty white rooms formed geometric abstractions punctuated by bronze glass and recessed lights. In that high-bourgeois setting, the villa somehow reminded me of an air terminal, except that it wasn't as big or as warm.

"Wait till you see the view from my house! But don't say you like it—say you *are surprised it isn't finished*!"

Preminger shouted in slow-motion French at his architect—"the greatest disappointment of my life"—then strolled onto a terrace. Across the water, he watched wispy clouds clinging to yellow hilltops and masses of cedars swaying in the breeze.

Preminger breathed deeply.

All around, every prospect pleased.

If Villa Alpha was a celebration of wealth far beyond *nouveau chutzpah*, the last word in such pursuits was still to come.

As we arrived in Monte Carlo, the sun broke out, flaring off a mass of hotels fit for Miami Beach.

The Burton boat, docked here, turned out to be too modest—a retreat for stars rather than a star itself.

In the bathroom Preminger shrugged, "Here washed Elizabeth Taylor."

Which brought him to Onassis's vessel.

With a thick, yellow smokestack, the *Christina* looked like a freighter, over three hundred feet long. Indeed, it had been converted from industrial use.

The idea of running it with a small crew was laughable, even to Preminger.

"Johnnie Meyer told me they had eight *cooks!*" (Meyer handled "public relations" for Onassis.)

Boldly Preminger led the way up the gangplank. One expected to be met by armed guards. Instead, after a few words, we were miraculously offered a tour. That pious, silent stroll, like a pilgrimage through Chartres, was the one time on the film I saw the director speechless.

The vessel approached the boundary of imaginable private indulgence. It was a castle by Ludwig of Bavaria, a floating caprice.

On deck, a gaggle of Greek seamen were polishing the mahogany railing around the pool and the mosaic top that slid over it to form a dance floor. We were led below decks, down a three-story, curved, carpeted staircase, beneath a crystal chandelier. At one level were nine guest rooms—large suites decorated in soft pastels, rose- and aqua-hued. They suggested a luxury hotel, with double beds, dressing space, writing tables, and no sense of shipboard crowding. Farther down were galleys, a dining room, and a huge lounge with scattered groups of sofas and armchairs lost in paneled shadows. It might have been a men's club on Park Avenue. How much brandy had been drunk in this room? How many cigars smoked? Was that a piano in the corner? Our guide pointed proudly to a small landscape by Winston Churchill.

On the lowest level, Onassis's private study was filled with antiques, carved objects, porcelain, leather-bound books, and, above the desk, a typically murky, elongated portrait of a pope by El Greco.

"Magnificent! And it's *not* too big!" Driving back to Nice, Preminger exclaimed, "For this boat I'd pay *five* thousand a day! Photographically it's . . . this is a very cultured man! Not *nouveau*. Onassis is used to his money. That captain was impressed by a Churchill that cost maybe fifteen hundred and ignored an El Greco worth a million and a half. For us it would be *great!* I will find out where Onassis is."

Preminger did not have high hopes of getting the *Christina*. Yet he would try when he got to Paris. "You know," he mused, "I would have *bet* we couldn't go on it . . ."

At the Westminster, Eva took the yacht broker's call as she worked amid scattered notes, cold coffee, and a swelling misunderstanding.

"My error," she said, "was telling OP we could get a boat for a thousand dollars a day. . . . Wait, they can use how many tons of fuel?. . . Now what is bunkering? . . . You have to pay for *water* as well? . . . And harbor fees! *Gor blimey!!*"

Arriving in Paris, Preminger checked into the Plaza Athenée and the city promptly descended. In a few days, he hired art director Willy Holt, an assistant director, a casting director, and a composer.

He discussed actors with the William Morris Agency, set a schedule for recces, gave some interviews, and had a few inspiring meals, especially at the Plaza Relais, where lunch included the sweet distraction of dozens of women from the couture shops nearby, workers as well as customers. The air was vaporous with their gossip and perfumes as their heads bobbed together, coiffed in bangs, billows, and shimmering helmets of blonde, auburn, and strawberry hair. Sparkling with laughter, makeup, and cheap jewelry, they were beauty armored, style celebrating itself.

In London, people had complained that the English movie business was dead. Here they were too busy to complain. Art director Willy Holt took time from *Marseilles Contract* to discuss the look of *Rosebud* over lunch. It didn't hurt that his own look was riveting. Tall, gaunt, ascetic, he had a salt-and-pepper beard, and lank hair that fell below his collar. A faded khaki work suit and a pair of half-lens spectacles in gold rims, hanging from a neck chain, added to his thoughtful air. When he smiled, his deep-set eyes took on gentleness and—yes— compassion.

46

Preminger asked, "Are you also an actor?"

Then he turned from art to logistics. A Corsican expert would soon conduct Willy and Eva over the island. Meanwhile, Willy shouldn't feel "bound" by the script. He had room for choice. Indeed, some earlier decisions seemed no longer to be decided. Willy had *lots* of room. For example, Schrantz's hideout, scheduled for Israel, might be done in Tunisia. And Frankfurt was a doubtful site. Preminger found it dull.

About the yacht, he would call Onassis and Hochbaum. For the Corsican farm where the girls were hidden, "We must adapt what we find. . . . You go with Eva. Use your judgment."

The big change was that a real flight simulator would no longer be used in Corsica to confuse the hostages and make them think they were flying. Now Preminger wanted a simulator that looked "homemade."

He cautioned Willy, who had worked for Fred Zinnemann on *Day of the Jackal,* that, unlike Zinnemann, "I am not so given to detail. . . . It's more important that things go quick."

On leaving, Willy remarked in his thick, muffled accent, "Ahm from Flow-ree-dah. My fazhair was from Flow-ree-dah."

"An American who can't speak English. Like me!"

Willy nodded and departed.

Said Preminger, "I do the same thing. People talk to me, but when I don't understand I just nod."

And so began the work of the French crew.

Willy's first job was finding Corsican locations—the port, a passport office, a customshouse, a shoreline where the hostages would be taken off a motorboat, the Tardets farm where they were kept (including caves for the hostages and the armory), and a network of roads, forests, hills, mills, bars, hotel rooms, airfields, and police stations. The list for Corsica covered a fifth of the total screenplay and included sets *within* sets—corridors, foyers, kitchens, et cetera. Preminger also liked to follow action from room to room, and Willy had to allow for that.

Aesthetics were always tied to logistics. Therefore, the hostages' dungeon had to connect to the rest of the Tardets farm, to speed the shooting. There should be room to park vehicles and move in equipment. The cellar should require a minimum of extra dressing (a steel door, bunks, prop lights) and feel like a Black Hole—while being fifteen minutes from a luxury hotel. Finally, sets should cluster together to reduce travel time: thus, all Corsican locations would depend on where the farm was.

And this same search with the same strictures would go on in Israel, Paris, Berlin, the south of France—plus Frankfurt or Düsseldorf or Hamburg—and maybe Tunisia.

Whipping through traffic to the last day of shooting on *Marseilles Contract*, Willy seemed serene. *Rosebud* was not his first tough job. On *Jackal* they had filmed the attempted assassination of de Gaulle in just four days on a Parisian plaza, during the August holidays. Problems didn't bother Willy after spending, as he casually mentioned, two years in Auschwitz, Bergen Belsen, and Buchenwald.

He had been captured while working for the Resistance.

"I was accused to be Jewish . . . held by head in water of bathtub. The Gestapo give me a star to wear. I stay with it a long time. That's why I have good philosophy. When big problems arrive . . . I know they are not so big. If Preminger is hard, I have seen harder."

On the set, Willy introduced me to Judd Bernard, producer of *Marseilles Contract*.

"Hi. You can hang out," he told me. "Come over to the next set and have lunch with us."

Judd had no part in *Rosebud*, yet he must be included here to reflect a world of international production far removed from Preminger's. Judd's was the cheery purgatory of evaporating projects, expense accounts that are suddenly shut off, executives who no longer take one's calls. Whereas *Rosebud* had been a going film from the day Arthur Krim and Preminger had shaken hands, *Marseilles Contract* had a list of titles depending on whether it was shown to the police, the press, or the U.S. distributor. One of its stars, Anthony Quinn, had actually switched roles; and another, Omar Sharif, finally dropped out. The movie had been "canceled" on Christmas Eve, two days before its start, leaving Judd broke in a luxury hotel.

"All I had was my toothpaste."

That same picture was finishing today—"about sixty hours from now. They're gonna have to hustle for a change."

An assistant cautioned that one actor felt this was an important scene.

"If he farts, he thinks it's important. Let's see what they're doing."

The location was the Gare D'Orsay, an abandoned railway station where Orson Welles had shot much of *The Trial*. Under a sooty wrought-iron canopy, grips hooked a camera car to a black Citroën and focused lights on the back seat while Anthony Quinn paced around looking dolorous.

This was Judd's tenth production, including *Double Trouble* (1966) with Elvis Presley, *Point Blank* with Lee Marvin, *Blue* with Terence Stamp, *Fade-In* with Burt Reynolds, *Negatives* with Glenda Jackson—and some even more obscure.

A forty-six-year-old ex-Chicagoan, Judd was compactly built, with a rueful manner and a restlessness that made him seem even younger. He had written, as well as produced, *Marseilles Contract*. But at the moment he could only wait for it.

"Maybe I should do the whole thing. Look at *Zardoz*. Written, produced, and directed by John Boorman. But it's such . . . people chanting!

"The trouble is, a producer is always going to bat. It's hard to earn a living. A director, well, if he has a hit, one decent film, anybody will take another shot with him. But a *producer*! You know all the films I made but, believe me, you don't know the ones I didn't make. That list is longer!"

Constantly fighting himself, Judd naturally admired Preminger. "He is so professional! He proves you don't have to

49

be a Triple A shortstop to make a film about baseball. Everything he does has flair, style—I mean, it's visual. Any of those guys, Tola Litvak, Preminger—they don't hit every time, but, boy, wowee, you look at *Anastasia* or *Advise and Consent*! You won't *find* better mounted pictures. And audiences appreciate it. . . . Look! They're going!"

The cars crept into traffic as the remaining crew milled about, stamping their feet against the cold.

"Have a coffee," Judd urged. "Have a sandwich."

He told of coming to Europe originally for Paramount.

"Charlie Bluhdorn sent me to make *Negatives.* I brought it in for a hundred and sixty thousand pounds, forty thousand under. During that time, Paramount also gave me *The Man Who Had Power over Women.* But after they saw *Negatives* they canceled *Man.* Now I'm really persona non grata there."

He managed to resell both films to other distributors and stayed in Europe after his divorce to be with his children.

Now he waited for the cars. And studied the pavement.

"Pictures get screwed. Redford walked out of *Blue* two-and-a-half weeks before shooting. So we found Terry Stamp and gave him speech lessons at UCLA. Had him talking with a twang, but then Karl Malden was speaking regularly so it was no good. . . . God, as soon as he opened his mouth with that accent we were dead. We showed a rough cut to the Paramount guys from New York and they *loved* it. They were gonna blow it up to seventy millimeter. I'll never forget—one of their guys cried. . . . This was when they were furious because Polanski had gone twenty-six days over on *Rosemary's Baby.* Then *Variety* reviewed *Blue* and that was the end. They killed it. Picture got *no* good reviews except in Europe. Last I heard, Stamp was living in India with hair down to his ankles."

The Citroën pulled in.

"How long they gonna be?"

"Makeup. Have to fix his cheek."

"Oh!" Judd turned away. "Waiting . . . that's all this business is. Waiting and scrounging. I used to have good relations with Paramount. Charlie Bluhdorn said to me, if *Negatives* was any good, I could have five years of work with Paramount. *I never talked to him after that phone call!"*

Back at the hotel, Preminger met another staff member, the casting director Margot Capelier. Through her he could reach virtually every name with an acting credit in European films over the last decade, plus an underground army struggling toward recognition.

He told William Morris to "send everything to Margot . . . she is doing everything."

"Oh," said an agent, "she is the greatest."

The men kissed her cheeks and the women called her with their problems while she accepted all courtesies like tokens paid at a toll booth. But Margot had her favorites, who were sure to see every director. Friendship with her increased one's share of chances. It was a currency to be hoarded.

Short and stocky, about sixty, she bustled through the Plaza with grim humor, carrying a shoulderbag and a valise bulging with photos. At first she was not worried about Preminger, having already served a legendary French tyrant, Marcel Carné, director of *Children of Paradise.* "I *liked* him. And it is always interesting to meet a big director . . . a new monster. Maybe he hides himself and once a week you see inside.

"For how long shall I work, Monsieur?" she asked Preminger.

"As long as you can stand me." He gave her a script. "This is not final but you can get an idea of the parts."

"Monsieur, are we close to the book with the characters?"

He assured her they were and that the part of Thibaud, the young radical, would be improved. "But it's not in the script yet."

Margot gathered up her things, promising to read and to look for young girls. "Must they speak English?"

"No, no more than you."

"But you don't understand me?"

"That's only because I'm deaf."

She left, looking confused. And Preminger scowled.

Water Torture

A perfect misunderstanding was growing. When Margot cast her liquid brown eyes over the little dancers of the Café des Artistes and wistfully called them "creatures for dreaming," she evoked a lifetime of sentiment. Like Willy Holt and Eva Monley, she had a face that showed every emotion, in contrast to Preminger, whose face was *set* by wealth, power, and his own self-consciousness. While Preminger could get angry, Margot, Willy, and Eva could get hurt.

I had yet to see Preminger's temper. Of course, the stories persisted: Otto slapping a tycoon at a party; Otto finding a writer making out Christmas cards instead of working and tearing up the cards; Otto driving an insecure new star nearly to a nervous collapse. But just as often the stories had a touch of the absurd: Otto arguing with Barbra Streisand's mother years after the event, about not casting young Barbra as St. Joan.

Once, driving with Otto and Erik to view yachts, I had asked a question that made the director turn on me abruptly. If I made "private conversations" I was not welcome on the film. "What's the matter with you?" he demanded. "You used to be so tactful!" To Erik he added, "He doesn't know the way I must have things."

"But he's finding out," said Erik.

A few minutes later the anger was gone and Preminger was happily spinning stories of old Hollywood.

But by Paris, the pressure was heavier. It showed outside the screening room where Otto had seen and liked Lalla Ward's sample reel. He asked when the budget would be ready. Eva took a painkiller and answered that it was complex. She needed more time. "You know it can't be done working alone in five days." She would try for a ballpark figure.

That was it. He turned suddenly and began raging. His anger was sustained, amplified by the tiled corridor walls until it filled the ears with a gravelly ocean roar. His hand cut the air like a knife hitting a chopping block. The fingers were together, palms open.

"I don't want [chop!] a guess! [chop!] I don't know [chop!] what ballpark is! [chop!]"

The tirade continued at the hotel, interrupted only while Preminger met Wolfgang Glattes, the assistant director from Munich—a tall, handsome, correct German in his early thirties.

"Let him stay two days to help with the breakdown. Why didn't you tell me you needed more time?"

"Mr. Preminger—" Eva began.

"I can't start everything without a good budget. Figures out of the air don't help!"

As Preminger worked himself up, his face turned red, the veins on his forehead stood out like a V drawn by a shaky hand, and his lower lip seemed to cup and quiver, collecting spittle which flew from his mouth. He was roaring again, nor was this happening in some impersonal corridor, but in Suite 403, amid all the civilized comforts.

Later he would say he only got angry for effect. Well, at first sight the effect was frightening.

"I don't think we can do the film in eleven weeks," Eva said. "We'll need thirteen."

"Let *him* judge! [Meaning Wolfgang.] We've got to get the right figure. With a schedule. And a breakdown. Not imagination!"

Later he called Erik, who was rewriting in Nice. "I had a terrible shock. Eva did the budget without breaking down the script. 'This is only a guess,' she said. Look, it'll all be . . . if it happened eight weeks later, *then* it's a catastrophe."

About Margot he was happier. "At least she came prepared. But she's had her best days under President Wilson. Gershy sends his love. He's happy. He found a terrific streetwalker." Hanging up, he smiled again. "I'm very proud of him. I missed him so many years."

Given Preminger's new demand for haste, Eva had tried a guesstimate. She had made enough movies to allow trust-worthy guessing and she knew her boss's style. But he needed more. This budget was going to UA. He would be held to it.

All night and the next day, in a Left Bank hotel, Wolfgang worked on the breakdown and Eva figured.

"It's no good," she muttered, "taking Valium for breakfast and Librium for lunch. He says he knows how to make pictures. Well, I know something too!"

Next day she submitted a preliminary figure that amazed Preminger. "If you can do this picture for that price I'll give you a hundred-thousand-dollar bonus. I'm planning to make a first-rate picture." He turned to me. "You wrote down the bet?" I had. "Eva, if you can do it you're worth the money."

"I don't expect you to give me a hundred thousand dollars if I'm right."

The "bet" temporarily relaxed him. He called the front desk to send up his visitors, almost singing the command, *"Faites monter, faites monter!"* while Eva whispered to me, "This day's going to end in tears. I can feel it."

She and Wolfgang returned to work at their hotel, where brown clover marched relentlessly over the wallpaper. (In Nice the clover was blue, in London beige.) From Eva's window one heard traffic splashing through the rain on Boulevard Raspail, toward the night life of St. Germain.

The beds were covered with files as she angrily jotted figures. "Change one thing and you have changes everywhere.... We all *know* it's not going to be final.... *Exodus* was a three-hour movie shot in seventy-two days.... Now he says sixty-six days aren't enough for a two-hour movie."

Just how long it would take was Wolfgang's problem. Working for Huston, Fosse, or Preminger, this part of his job never changed. He attacked it methodically, with quiet concentration, barely looking up.

First he listed each set and what was needed on it. This information was then put on strips of colored cardboard, with one strip for each set. If a day's work used three sets, that day had three strips. All the strips could be fitted into a production board and rearranged endlessly as the schedule changed endlessly.

The information on the strips was coded by number (so that the part of Larry Martin was #1, and so on). Thus, Wolfgang could get lots on those narrow strips.

He was following long-mastered rules of scheduling:

Finish one set before starting another.
On the same location, shoot interiors together, then go outside, or vice versa, but don't shuttle in and out.
Leave a simple interior for last as a "cover set" in case of rain.
Leave the easiest shooting for last, so the crew can start packing early.

All-night shooting posed another problem. Before resuming day work, the crew was entitled to a day off, a "turnaround day." Wolfgang thus tried to bunch night work together, to avoid extra turnarounds.

But there would always be insoluble conflicts. Thus, when the *Rosebud* became available for only a week in France, all scenes on it had to be done at once, including night shooting, which added turnarounds.

And there would always be changes to ruin all plans. For example, they originally expected to shoot the nude scenes on the boat during the day and end with some dinner scenes at sunset. Then Preminger and Coop decided it would be more interesting to shoot the nude scenes at dawn, under an ominous gray sky. So they *began* at sunset and worked all night, into dawn. But the dawn didn't last long enough to finish the scenes. So they set out a second morning, but the light that day was too bright to match the first dawn. So they went out a third time . . .

Above all, Wolfgang understood Monley's Law: "Change

one thing and you have changes everywhere." For this production, he would go through eight complete schedules, shuffling strips, hardly looking up.

Back in the Plaza, Preminger gave Margot Capelier a view of his tactics, trying to close the gulf. An actor had been recommended by friends, but Preminger would offer only half what the agent asked. "I will not pay more than they get in France. His agent was so tough, I thought she'd hit me."

Margot listened glumly.

"You have no sense of humor?" he asked.

"Ah, Monsieur, I have quite a *big* sense of humor. I don't think it, I know it."

"And I know I'm making this film and if I make mistakes then *I* make mistakes. Agents have a sense of honor in the United States. Here they lie. . . . Find out what this actor got, but don't ask his agent."

"In English, I'm not very good, Monsieur, but in French you can trust me."

"*Au revoir.* Don't forget about the actor."

"He worked for Lelouch, and Lelouch doesn't overpay."

"Well, I underpay!"

As she left, he dialed Onassis. A friend had supplied the number. "You must admit I have good friends. Let's see if he's home. . . . Ari? How are you! . . . Wonderful! I'm here in Paris and I would give anything if you'd lend me your boat. Any time it's convenient. I will arrange a time according to your time. . . . It leaves Cannes and arrives at the coast of Israel. . . . Ah. . . . Ah. . . . Uu-huh. . . . Well, think about it. I'm back here Thursday. . . . I will pray and you think. If you go to Monaco and you don't give me the ship, maybe we have dinner."

Hanging up, he scowled. "I hate to ask people."

A Sense of the World

That Sunday, before Preminger returned to Nice, movie people seemed to be scattered in hotels throughout Paris. As they talked, their work merged with their memories and histories.

Judd Bernard drank black coffee and laughed about his problems. "I'll be an American if I live here fifty years. And I've always lived well. By borrowing. Scrounging. But I miss being home terribly. I have strong visions of the Sherry-Netherland and the Beverly Hills Hotel. But I'm not very popular. I make waves. I fight for what I believe. Plus I make tough pictures. That helps too!" His smile erupted. "Oh, I wish I had Preminger's problems!"

On the Champs, Preminger strolled along, savoring the city crowds and pausing to tell a Chaim Weizmann story. Someone had asked Weizmann why he wanted to relocate Jews in Israel, where there were already "too many." Why not, for example, someplace like Arizona? Weizmann answered that wherever they went, there would always be "too many Jews."

And then, as she was about to leave for Nice, Eva told about her sister's life in a concentration camp joyhouse. Out of strain, exhaustion, and the irrational panic—inexplicable to an American—of thinking her passport was lost, the story emerged.

Eva herself had been born in Berlin, before the second war, of one-quarter-Jewish parentage. When her father's brother tried to seduce her mother and was rejected, he denounced the family. Eva and her mother got away to Africa.

There, Eva was legally adopted by another family while her natural mother, a German citizen, was put in a British camp.

Thirty-four years later, Eva was reunited with her sister. When they met, Eva came up from behind and touched the woman's shoulder. "She whirled and slapped me. . . . It all poured out in two nights of talking—how she whored her way through four years in the camps, had her head shaved, her wrists broken, had worked for them and then, afterwards, embraced Orthodox Judaism."

Eva also explained that she took painkillers because, during the fuel-conserving brownouts in London, she had slipped on an office staircase and hurt her back.

And in the next breath she reflected on how she had always had all the luck. There were memories of drinking with Bogie on *African Queen* . . . helping to carry Errol Flynn to work on *Roots of Heaven* . . . eleven days in an Irish castle with Huston running his old films . . . Christmas on *Mogambo* with Gardner, Gable, John Ford, and the natives dressed in feathers and carrying Christmas candles . . . and especially an unforgettable twenty months on *Lawrence of Arabia,* living in the open, under canvas.

It was a good life. "It still is. . . . I won't let it destroy me. That's what OP is doing. Destroying me with condescension."

February 25. Among all those memories and histories, there was the lingering silence. Back in Nice, Preminger reluctantly lent me a script. I read in the Westminster, beside the window of my new, rear room, with a view of slate roofs and the yellow-umber hills beyond, now dusted with puffy clouds.

This view didn't help.

Here, among people whose emotions had been buffeted by so much of reality, a film was being fashioned that seemed indifferent to the world.

The central themes of media manipulation and the danger to Israel had dwindled. The threat had shifted mostly to the unmemorable bunch of rich girls. Their galley scene used up four pages just to show they couldn't cook. One resented them for slowing the story and taking screen time at the expense of the world.

Gone were the international reactions, the reporters, TV shows, and hysteria comparable to the Hearst case. Gone was the hypocritical posturing of the news media, whose pursuit of the story led, in the novel as in life, to their own exploitation by the terrorists.

Gone were two of the best "set pieces." As Preminger had promised, he'd cut the hijacking of the Lufthansa jet, which had established Martin, Hacam, and Kirkbane. Also cut was the arrival of the first Arab film at a TV network in Paris. In the book, the film was followed up the hierarchy of the corporation. The press reactions, the frantic VIP screenings, the dawning certainty that this was not a hoax, were handled with crisp authority by Bonnecarrère, who knew the milieu. The sequence made credible the whole role of the media.

In the script, action was replaced by reams of verbosity. The hostages' communiqués in the novel were bad enough. (Erik had actually toned them down.) But now Fargeau introduced Martin by reading aloud his role in the Lufthansa hijacking, thereby establishing Martin's Black September contacts and making him a logical man for this case. But the contacts were never used later. The whole summary could have been dropped.

Disconnected talk was everywhere, mostly in the form of character expositions. We heard how Mrs. Tardets broke down after her children were killed. We heard how the Nikolaos family fled the Greek junta. None of it mattered to the story, but, as Erik said, "My father wants everyone to be a character." And thus everyone had a story to tell.

Another weakness was the relaxed tone of the agents. In the script, they were so "busy" with a simple surveillance that they only saw a new Arab film by coincidence, while in a bar. In the book, agents from five countries flew specially to London to view that film.

The unreality was crowned by the new arch-villain. Scheidemann/Schrantz was now Sloat, an English anarchist who wanted to see mankind destroy itself—a villain out of a comic book.

Returning the script, I took a long walk, telling myself that they were still working, that there was still time, that this was still the only major film about the Middle East. Always

Preminger cautioned others, "This is not a script. It will give you only an idea of where it plays."

Yes. They knew. They both knew. The work had just begun.

As Erik said, "Oh, I'll die on the picture!"

Breaking

In the Westminster, Eva struggled toward a budget. There were more calls to shipping agents. "Two thousand kilos of freight won't be enough. . . . The list of equipment is faintly shattering." And, to herself, "You put in money for something, hoping you'll cover the holes."

At lunch, in the park, she chewed a tasteless ham sandwich while dreading her Corsican trip. "Being shipped off like a location manager a few weeks before the picture. . . . Don Siegel gave an art director two weeks by himself to find locations!"

Her budget came out higher this time. "You win your bet," she told OP.

"It's still not enough."

She could hardly believe it. "I'm so staggered in this day and age that someone says it's still *not enough!*"

The end started over lunch at the Negresco with the Corsican Connection—M. Farrago. He was well into his fifties, with the resonant, syrupy voice of an old-fashioned radio announcer. Wearing a brown, crusty toupee, waving a cigarette between his stained fingers, he had an air of impossibly fraudulent elegance. Preminger was appalled. ("How can anyone wear such a phony *rug?*")

In the Salon Louis XIV, we ate cold, stringy veal, flavored by an occasional whiff of M. Farrago's cologne, while he rambled in mellifluous French about his glorious island home.

"A veritable picture for the cinema . . ."

Eva sipped her wine and groaned under her breath. "I don't think I care to survive today."

60

She barely did. Approaching Preminger's suite, I heard them inside.

"Is there any doubt?"

"The only doubts you have are whether I should do the picture—"

"Because you don't *listen.*"

Their talk was clotted with irritation. Almost as a distraction, he discussed other matters. Ann Shetland's agent had refused the five-year option agreement. "The man is an ass." Otto happily gave Lalla Ward the part.

As for Eva, he told her, "Go now and rest a little. Enjoy yourself." Chalky White, the accountant, would start early and do the budget. "Don't redo it now."

Eva was seething. "The accountant *always* makes the budget. Chalky did it for you on *Bunny Lake.*"

When she had gone, Preminger sighed. "I don't want to be tough. She'll only break down. The important thing I say to myself in cases like this is to make a good film if you can."

Outside, the rain whipped at the Promenade, matching Eva's temper. "I've *always* had an accountant and first assistant on to help. But, God, he knows when he's been a bastard. All of a sudden he's overcharming."

Preminger held people by the force of his personality. When he flew to Paris to cast, he left behind the two individuals he had been driving the hardest. Without him, talking to each other, Erik and Eva dredged up unsuspected pain. For Eva, a few words were the final indignity.

We ate at Il Pozzo, a tiny, Franco-American miracle off the Promenade. Dinner began with an immense basket of *crudités*—raw cauliflower, carrots, peppers, celery, fennel, leeks, zucchini—with dips of oil, dill, and mustard. Then came lasagna stuffed with shrimp, lobster, and crab and baked bubbling in a hot cream sauce. It was a voluptuous, winey dinner, except for Erik who had given up stimulants for meditation. As

61

we relaxed afterward, he lit his pipe and confided that the secret of working with Otto was doing what Otto said. If Eva
didn't agree, she would be better off leaving.

By lunch next day, Eva was ready to quit. "It's like a marriage that's gone bad. You want out because you don't want in."

At the café, people in overcoats sat with their faces turned
to the cold light. She and I sank into wicker chairs.

"I'm so queasy inside . . . so shaky. That's why I like to
walk downstairs. See a bit of sun."

She mentioned a possible replacement for her who had just
quit a Bond picture: "For the same reason I'm leaving OP.
Life's too short."

The harsh light deepened the lines around her eyes.

"Can't retain my sense of humor anymore. It's not fun. Not
worthwhile. Well, I always knew my fiftieth year would bring
some great event. But this—"

We ordered wine and skipped the anemic little sandwiches.

"What about the Corsican recce?" I asked her.

"I'm quite sure OP will just tell me to get lost. I know what
I did wrong! I should have attacked him from the start. Now I
just don't want to do it." She nodded slowly back and forth.
"Somewhere for me it's just gone wrong completely."

The waiter brought out two glasses of wine.

"To freedom."

"To freedom." Foul stuff, but it sparkled in the sun.

Eva slumped forward on her elbows. "I'm confused because
I keep being told I'm confused. And I reckon I'm too good at
what I do to be haunted for six months. It's a question of pride
and dignity . . . and Papa's Chinese torture. Drop by drop, on
your head, each day, until pretty soon the brain starts to show.
Being told that you're stupid each day . . . that you don't listen. . . . There has to be someone between me and Papa . . .
someone to take the personal *assaults*! And to be there, and to
hear what he's thinking. Erik says, 'Just do what Father tells
you.' But I can't anymore. Maybe that's aging. But it's over.
Terminée!

"What should I do if he tells me to put in six weeks finishing time and I *know* it's not enough? We've got to allow a week for a week. A week of finishing for a week of shooting.

"You know, I absolutely don't think he's going to make the picture. That shows you the destruction of my train of thought.

"I'll tell you. I get a flat seven hundred dollars a week. For twenty-four hours, seven days a week. It's good for British pay—but you know how little that is in America. Why, a good first assistant in your country gets nine fifty a week!

"Well, I shall say I accept his kind offer of the other day about quitting. Pity is that I lasted this long. . . . Sidney Samuelson was so funny about him on the phone. His son rang OP and politely introduced himself as a production person. He asked if he could be of any help. Papa said, 'I am Otto Preminger—I don't need help.'"

Heading back to the hotel, Eva stared at the pavement.

"I'm too old to deal with him. I'd rather be happy and poor. Hell, I didn't do the *Kubrick* picture! I'll stay with the little guys like Siegel!"

Grimly she telexed Preminger in Paris.

PLEASE CALL ME TODAY SO WE CAN DISCUSS WHO CAN TAKE OVER FOR ME AND MAKE ROSEBUD WITH YOU. I AM SAD BUT I KNOW IT WILL NOT WORK OUT. SINCERELY, EVA.

"The really sad thing is to lose OP's friendship. I tell you, this is one of the hardest decisions I've ever had to make. But I just want to live. That's all. . . . I know it'll be a terrible scene when he calls. I shall probably break down and cry . . . and the worst of it is he'll probably enjoy it."

Eva didn't cry that night. After Preminger called, she paced her room, smoking. "He wasn't angry. You know what he said? 'You've been on the picture since January first and now when the going gets rough you want to quit?' When I offered to give back my paychecks, he said, 'We'll talk about it when you get back from Corsica.'"

Erik marveled. "Someone wants to quit . . . and he ignores it. We'll talk about it after *Corsica* for god's sake!"

Erik meanwhile faced his own problems. Cheerfully he transmitted bulletins from Paris, where his father had hired Amidou, a dusky French-Moroccan with soulful black eyes, to play Kirkbane. ("You will make this character *charming*," Preminger told the actor. "A smiling killer . . . a smiling cobra.")

But Erik could not forget the script. And he thought it might be time to bring in another writer, someone like Robert Bolt, Ring Lardner, Jr., or Gore Vidal. "Two months from now I could see where it's overwritten or where it doesn't flow. But now I can't. I need someone to talk to besides Otto, just someone to react to this material. I think it moves, it has pace, it's interesting. . . . What do you think?"

Every word opened a chasm.

So I lied. Encouraged. Stalled. "I wish I didn't know the book so well. That makes it difficult to judge." Erik was left with the choice of misunderstanding.

As he went on, I felt the trouble acutely. The script was choked with talk. "Everyone is extremely articulate. Everyone talks like me or Otto." Yet Preminger was still trying to make everyone a character, still working on love affairs between Martin and Hélène, Thibaud and Sabine.

Preminger also liked *scenes,* so the arrival of the Arab film at the TV station was still out. "Because it's a *sequence,* not a scene," said Erik.

They wanted a star to play Martin, but still had none. To make the character more "involved," they considered giving him a moral dilemma. Perhaps he knew the Arabs and didn't want to pursue them. They also gave Martin a sleeping bag for his apartment. To make him "cute."

Finally Erik seemed to be talking about another script. Was Martin "uninvolved"? Or didn't he give a damn? Was Patrice Thibaud only a "boyfriend"? Or a serious radical?

One couldn't focus on the work. *Rosebud* decomposed in

conversation until it became . . . a debate. The talk could drone across Europe in a fog of pipe smoke and cooking aromas. It was a form of nonwriting when one has lost hold of whatever seemed vital in the piece. By then one could type anything because it was all the same, all nothing.

I read fifty pages of second draft in the Westminster lobby with rain falling and cars hissing on the wet pavement. And depression deepening.

The new changes were mostly surface strokes.

They had dropped the montage of world reactions. "What would they speak," asked Erik, "German or English?"

And the boat didn't go aground. (Preminger had enough trouble just finding one to go to Israel.) Now Hamlekh and his boss were lowered by helicopter, saving the boat just before it crashed.

The big change was the "dinner scene" on the yacht. Fargeau was the guest of honor. His granddaughter Sabine organized the evening as a celebration before she and her four friends set off on a pleasure cruise. Sabine's lover, Patrice Thibaud, also came to dinner (at her urging), and the young radical inevitably argued with Fargeau. Meanwhile, the Arabs waited in a raft to attack.

In the first draft, Thibaud angrily denounced old Fargeau's exploitations, and Sabine immediately ordered her lover off the boat.

By the second draft a good idea had emerged. Thibaud boldly accused Fargeau of smuggling arms. The old man denied it but a simmering scandal was suggested, which made his later confession plausible.

In the final draft, later, Thibaud left coolly, telling Sabine to "find herself." The gun-running wasn't mentioned. Until Fargeau's confession, one didn't even know he was in the arms *business*.

The characters were sinful clichés, created as if radical chic had never happened and political beings ceased to be human beings. Yet one sought a redeeming idea in this melodrama, an effect Preminger might be aiming for: aboard a luxury yacht two bourgeois pillars, a professor and an industrialist, discussed "revolution" while real rebels waited in the dark. The Arab presence might frame the banalities of the scene, ironically suggesting the ignorance of a whole society. Or so one hoped.

"I'm disappointed," said Erik, "that no more was done this draft. But if it makes him happy, that's it. The movie's in trouble, but it'll start May fifteenth. You'll see."

More Is Not Enough

Before flying to Corsica, Eva left her version of the budget at the Negresco. It must remain guarded, since Preminger felt his financial information involved UA and so was privileged. Therefore, I have assembled data from other international film productions with similar schedules and Anglo-European crews. For these figures, averaged in 1974, I am grateful to several production sources and readily available union rate cards, rental and laboratory catalogues. The numbers reflect the then reduced cost of shooting in Europe (as against the United States), the complex organization, perhaps the overorganization, of a big film, and the mounting, relentless, inexorable pressure to spend more. Always more.

The forms varied from one country to another. But the information was the same. On Eva's thirty pages were resolved the gut questions she had been asking since January.

The schedule came first: on *Rosebud*, Corsica would take nineteen shooting days, Cannes fourteen, Paris seventeen, Israel fourteen, and Germany nine—in that order—plus thirty more for "travel, rest, and turnaround." Total: almost fifteen weeks. The estimated delivery date of the film was October 8, 1974. Running time was two hours. And, for computation, a dollar equaled 4.20 Israeli pounds, 2.50 Deutschmarks, 4.20 francs, and 44 English pence, which meant a pound was worth, then, $2.30.

The film first previewed in New York on November 22, 1974. In release, it ran just over two hours. Despite enormous problems, the only major change from early projections was for extra finishing time.

Next, the budget was summarized. Accounts below the line—excluding story, screenplay, producer, director, and leading actors (A and B accounts)—might be organized as follows. The figures, as noted, are averaged. (See page 68.)

Additional indirect costs might include the producer's office and finance and legal fees, which could add $200,000 to the budget.

These figures represent only the crudest outline. To appreciate the numbers, one must pick through a thicket of notes. What follows are notes *on* notes, highlights, bouquets for the curious. Prices are generalized and salaries given in ranges. Yet the expenses discussed were basic to big, international features. Some movies spent less on travel, more on special effects. Some spent more on everything. What you see here was the fundamental cost of lavishness.

Producers fought for years, seeking this money.

Under production management (C–1), Eva and a U.S. aide might each work for nine months, including two of postproduction. Eva's salary was low by U.S. standards; her counterpart here would have earned at least $1,250/wk. Movies like *Rosebud, Rollerball,* and *The Man Who Would Be King* would also employ *location* managers, under Eva, to arrange transport, extras, permits, catering, et cetera, in their respective countries. *Rosebud* might need a French location manager (for, possibly, 14 weeks of pre-production and shooting in France) and several assistants for Nice, Corsica, and Paris. Plus, of course, an Israeli manager (8 weeks), a German (6 weeks), and their aides.

And managers need secretaries. An Englishwoman might toil half a year on a film, typing movement orders, call sheets,

C. Production Unit Salaries:
    1. Production management & secretaries $100,000
    2. Assistant directors & continuity 30,000
    3. Technical advisers — — —
    4. Camera crew 45,000
    5. Sound crew 35,000
    6. Editing staff 40,000
    7. Stills camera staff 10,000
    8. Wardrobe staff 25,000
    9. Makeup artists 10,000
    10. Hairdressers 7,000
    11. Casting 5,000
    12. Production accountancy 20,000
    13. Projectionists 2,000
    14. Misc. studio staff 7,000
    15. Foreign unit technicians 100,000
D. Art Department Salaries 55,000
E. Artists:
    1. Cast (nonprincipals) 25,000
    2. Stand-ins, doubles, stuntmen 10,000
    3. Crowd 125,000
F. Musical direction, musicians, etc. 40,000
G. Costumes & wigs 10,000
H. Misc. production stores (excldg sets) 10,000
I. Film stock & lab charges 140,000
J. Studio rentals 15,000
K. Equipment 125,000
L. Power 15,000
M. Travel and transport:
    1. Location 300,000
    2. Studio 30,000
N. Hotel & living expenses:
    1. Location 600,000
    2. Studio — — —
O. Insurance 100,000
P. Social security, etc. 70,000
Q. Publicity salaries & expenses 15,000
R. Misc. expenses 45,000
S. Sets & models:
    1. Labor—construction — — —
    2. Labor dressing (total S–1 & 2) 115,000
    3. Labor striking — — —
    4. Labor lighting & lamp spotting 25,000
    5. Labor-foreign unit — — —
    6. Materials—construction (in S–1 & 2) — — —
    7. Properties 80,000
T. Special effects 40,000
U. Special location facilities 50,000

TOTAL BELOW THE LINE COST $2,476,000

carnets, revisions—working a killing seventy-hour week for $300 (in pounds). There were also bilingual secretaries needed in each country.

The Germans and French generally got top wages, with the English slightly back and the Israelis far behind. Thus, the German location manager reporting to Eva might earn as much as she did. (Nobody said life was fair.)

Directorial aides (C–2) included a first assistant for six months at $400–600/wk., an English continuity woman for fifteen weeks at $300–350/wk., and local second assistants— French, German, and Israeli—at an average of $250–350/wk. (The locals were eligible for overtime.) On *Rosebud*, Preminger had further aid: young "observers" who traded cheap labor for a chance to learn. He said, "It's as if I run a little film school." Past graduates included John Avildsen, director of *Rocky*.

Like many Britons working in Europe, the camera crew (C–4) made one-price deals. And what a price! A director of photography in America could command $2,000/wk. and much more if he had a "name," while in England a fine DP like Denys Coop, with major credits, would work for the equivalent of $850–1,200/wk. A crew would also include an operator ($500–600/wk.) who steered the camera through its pans and tilts, a focus puller ($325–375/wk.), a clapper/loader, and a camera grip ($275–325/wk.). The latter three changed lenses, moved the camera, racked focus, ran the auto-zoom, slated scenes, loaded film, *un*loaded it, canned it, and sent it off neatly to the lab with camera report sheets, keeping duplicates for the production. Do five people seem like a large camera crew? When they were dollying, booming, and zooming through a complex take, five were barely enough.

A top English sound mixer (16 wks., $450–500/wk.) was another bargain when even a mediocre American would get more. "Sound" would include an English boom man ($325–375/wk.) plus an assistant ($275–325/wk.) in each country (a local who got overtime).

Sound crew also contained studio engineers to "loop" (re-record unclear dialogue) and to record extra sound effects. Normally all this might take two weeks at $50/hr. in France, $100/hr. in a top U.S. studio. *Rosebud*, however, needed more time to correct its murky accents. Preminger decided not to revoice his foreign actors and summoned them back to atone for their crimes against English. Alas, the language was not readily forgiving.

Final sound costs could include three days to record the score and three weeks (120 hours) to blend (dub) all the voices, music, and effects into one balanced sound track. European studios cost $60–75/hr. A quality U.S. room began at double that.

We move past the predictable categories: a wardrobe master for twenty weeks ($350–450/wk.); two wardrobe aides in each country at $300/wk. top scale; a makeup artist and hairdresser ($325–400/wk. each); aides for everyone on crowd days; an accountant for six months ($400–450/wk.) and his assistant; and miscellaneous workers like an Israeli auditor, a nurse, and a London contact to "liaise" there.

Less obvious was casting (C–11) at $100/day, running through the picture, as compared to an American casting company taking a flat fee of $10,000 and up.

Foreign technicians (C–15) would be a burden for their overtime. Eva might add 60–80 percent to the base salaries of all French workers to cover that cost. (Night shooting alone, for the French, might cost an extra $2,000 per session.)

The art department (D) was made up of painters, designers, and a few types who simply looked artistic. Willy Holt would surely work twenty-five weeks, normally for a flat weekly fee of $700–900. His assistant might get two-thirds of that. And two lesser aides in each country would be assigned to carry out Willy's designs for turning a candy store into a photo shop, fashioning a brass doorplate, or repainting a pickup truck. There would be local construction managers (top scale $500/wk.) who built mock-ups of flight simulators and made steel vaults spring up on Corsican farms. Inside, prop buyers would supplement the furniture on locations, as when they rented $40,000 worth of Oriental carpets to line Sloat's hole in the desert.

As for below-the-line cast (E− 1)—the buzz of pilots, guerrillas, and security forces who peopled *Rosebud* without dominating it—one might guess at twenty roles costing $500/day, others at $250, and so on. The total might be $25,000– 75,000.

Stand-ins (E− 2) earned $40/day. Eva might use five through the film at $15,000. They weren't luxuries; as Coop said, "You can't light air." Preminger's observers might also do the work—but then few producers are clever enough to run "a little film school."

Doubles and stuntmen ($250/day) might work when Martin fought Kirkbane in Corsica, when a policeman beat up Patrice in Paris, and when Hamlekh and his boss dropped from a helicopter to the *Rosebud*. In Germany, two drivers could also work on a car chase. In fact, the actors did their own stunts and the car chase dwindled to a pace akin to that of two senior citizens in aluminum walkers. The film did, however, hire fight coordinators in Corsica and Paris. And the budget might include a fee for people to help the sound-effects editors record extra steps, blows, et cetera.

For crowds, Eva might guess anywhere from 1,000 to 5,000 men per day—including boatloads of tourists and Sloat's Arab hordes. At $20−40/day per crowd member, this left lots of room. And there might be another fee for *night* crowds (airport passengers, reporters, et cetera).

Music (F) was contracted. A composer could undertake to deliver forty minutes of orchestral score for $40,000. Of course music *might* cost anything. Consider a suspense film set in Germany, scored by a world-famous rock composer. His marching songs, beer-hall sing-alongs, and atonal brass so overwhelmed the little melodrama that the score was partly dropped and partly buried in the dub. The composer also did a Christmas song that didn't work, so another composer wrote a *second* song, also not very good. (Preminger had his composer on from the start to avoid such surprises.)

Costumes (G), according to the director, would be mostly the actors' own things. Eva could still earmark money for uniforms, djellabahs, and a few party dresses rented for the girls from boutiques.

Production stores (H) were things the film used up: gaffer tape, light bulbs, and still film for publicity shots. Consuming ten rolls a day (high), a stillman might spend $4,500, including processing. Yet a page of color photos in a national magazine paid *all* a stillman's costs, as measured by the price of advertising in such space. (And *Rosebud* got its page in *Seventeen*.)

Film and lab charges (I) were the Great Irreducible. Given the investment in the rest of the project, it was thought wasteful *not* to shoot a lot of film. The minimum on such a movie was 2,500 feet a day—meaning twenty-seven minutes of which three to four were expected to be usable, for a ratio of seven-to-one. Over the whole schedule, 185,000 feet of film might be shot. (*Rosebud* used almost exactly that amount.)

From that figure, all else followed. There were fixed (list) prices for film and its development.

There were also charges for transferring dialogue and music from quarter-inch tape to 35mm magnetic film so it could be synchronized with the picture. The movie might use two hundred rolls of magnetic film at $40/roll.

Once the picture was edited, the original negative was cut and assembled (at $100/reel) to conform to the final film. A fine-grain interpositive was made, from which new negatives could be fashioned so that printing would not damage the original one. A color-separation positive was done to preserve the original colors. And an answer print was made . . . and made . . . and made . . . until the producer approved a "perfect" one, which became the standard for all prints.

The overriding factor in lab costs (besides discounts) was the amount of footage exposed. Shooting *Rosebud*-style created, inevitably, a bill around $100,000.

If a director improvised—as some did, running the footage to 500,000 or 700,000 feet—lab fees (and editing costs) would skyrocket.

Normal lab charges could also include dissolves and titles. (The opulent main title of a James Bond film cost $100,000 or more.) Eva might designate still another figure for matte shots—in case the live shooting of TV and movie screens didn't work. As it didn't.

Studio rentals (J) on location might mean editing rooms— two for the production and four more after (at $25–100/wk.)— plus a fat fee for projecting partially assembled material. At first, *Rosebud* saved money by having its cutting rooms in hotels, where it got discounts. But afterward Preminger hurried. Eventually, *twelve* editors and helpers took almost a whole studio floor. Preminger then ran assembled material back and forth all day, fine-cutting with his editors in *relays*, from nine to five. The rock-and-roll (stop-and-start, back-and-forth) projection would have cost $400/day in the United States. In London it was a quarter of that.

Many items were not spent as foreseen, which only left room for the inevitable, grim surprises. I believe that Preminger drilled economy into his staff as a preparation for future mishaps. The great trick, as both he and Eva knew, was to include some provision for everything, so there would always be some headroom. It was not padding—it was realism.

Section K represented the higher levels of mania—the provision for everything. It covered equipment, which might typically include eighty cases of Panavision camera gear. The rental fees, in Samuelson's catalogue, reflect no discounts.

1 Panavision camera—Panaflex	£510.00
2 Extra 250' magazines	27.00
2 Extra 1,000' magazines	54.00
2 Additional 1,000' mags for safety	54.00
1 Panavision PVSR camera	198.00
1 Panazoom 50–90mm lens	90.00

35mm Auto-Panatar lens	48.00
40mm " " "	48.00
50mm " " "	48.00
75mm " " "	48.00
100mm " " "	48.00
2nd 50mm " " "	48.00
Moy 16" geared tripod head	28.60
Ronford Tubular tripod (tall)	5.40
Ronford " " (short)	5.40
Elemack Spyder Dolly	54.00
Lattice Jib (crane arm)	36.00
72' of Shoreham dolly track with curves	7.50
Vinten Head with leveller	24.00
Vinten Head plate	8.80
Camera Basher (light)	3.00

I leave to your imagination the cost of the additional "join-ing links, protecting mats, horizontal tie pieces, top-pad suc-tion grips, eye-bolts, wedge plates, Barneys, locking knobs, clamp supports, gelatine filters, PVSR filters, bogie wheels, seat-extension brackets, dolly-steering handles, 35v. batteries, 24v. cadmium nickel batteries, chargers, studio base plates, matte boxes, zoom controls—oh, *all* of it. The lot might come as high as $3,000 a week and arrive from Samuelson's in a blue and lilac Mercedes van weighing two tons unladen. (Van and driver cost extra.)

Denys felt uneasy later without some longer lenses, so the company ordered three, for another fifty-six kilos and perhaps $500/wk. And the budget should cover an aerial camera: the Mobius cost $800/day plus freight, travel for its crew, and their expenses.

Sound gear, like that in Robin Gregory's Delta Sound van, might run $400–500/wk. "Completeness" demanded two tape recorders, two mixers, three headphones, five Sennheiser mikes (which pick up sound at different angles), four cordless radio mikes (which the actors could wear), two transmitters, seven walkie-talkies, four bullhorns, and a radio with a mast and aerial to connect the location to the production office back at the hotel. Robin's truck also held a 35mm projector with screen, lens, amplifier, et cetera, to show rushes on location, and a 35mm transfer machine to convert quarter-inch sound tape to magnetic film, which saved sending it to the lab.

For lighting, a fitted van with more of everything, including cables, lamps, butterflies, flags, turtles, stands, pancakes, appleboxes, and sheets of acrylic window filter, could cost up to $2,000/wk. Eva dropped the van in favor of the Lee Electric trucks. But one could still assume that lighting a major film would average $1,500–2,500/wk.

Editing tools were the simplest requirement. A Movieola and 300 kilos of benches, racks, and rewinds would be available for $100/wk. or less. Three more units (for a second picture editor, effects, and looping) might be needed for ten weeks of post-production.

With $4,000 for cameras, $2,000 for lights, and $1,000 for sound, editing, and office supplies, the production could easily spend $7,000/wk. on hardware. Adding trucks (for sound, picture, electricity, and rigging) and fuel over sixteen weeks, a conservative equipment bill, before discounts, might be $110,000–125,000.

Power (L) included diesel fuel for the generator and, on this movie, the *Rosebud*'s Israeli trip. Not knowing the size of the boat, Eva had to estimate generously for it. The generator was more predictable; she knew exactly how fast it burned money.

It was on travel and transport (M) and hotel and living expenses (N) that a location picture could soar into orbit, challenging the unknowable, producing awesome dramas (off-screen) with every move. How could Eva foresee that in Corsica the company would have to charter a 150-seat jet to fly sixty people to Paris—and that it would be worth it?

Still, she mapped journeys. The cost of travel began in pre-production, with recces to Corsica, Berlin, Israel—900 francs here, 5,000 there, on and on. Plus transport while *on* these recces.

Later, during production, there was more travel. *Rosebud* might have forty actors flying to various locations. And some would return for retakes.

Thirty-five permanent technicians might also fly London–Nice–Corsica–Paris–Hamburg–Berlin–Tel Aviv–London at $800 per ticket. Some of the "permanents" would later become transients—as they left or were fired—to be replaced by a shuttling of new faces.

Another band of French workers from Studio Victorine in Nice might be sent to help in Corsica. And Studio Hamburg craftsmen could well be dispatched to Berlin. There might be five such workers. Or ten. Or twenty.

As for freight, one might estimate two thousand kilos flying with the company, plus the Mobius winging from London to Bastia and Israel. (A private guess for those Mobius trips alone was $4,000.) There was the daily sending of rushes to a Paris lab and back to locations (except in Israel, where film was locally processed). And there were visas, excess baggage, duty, and tax on duty.

All these charges only covered movement *to* the locations. Once there, the film needed vehicles and drivers. By the time we got to Israel, *Rosebud* had become a cavalcade. No audience would care, but General Motors would have been proud:

Car 1. With driver. For leading actor.
Car 2. With driver. For Preminger, Coop, Glattes.
Car 3. With driver. For camera crew.
Car 4. Driven by Israeli location manager.
Car 5. Driven by production manager.
Minibus 1. With driver. For continuity, riggers, and Israeli assistants.
Bus 2. With driver. For gaffers.
Bus 3. With driver. For observers and reporters.

Bus 4. Gone. One of our minis was missing.
Bus 5 and Bus 6. For props.
Bus 7. With driver. Wardrobe.
Bus 8. With driver. Sound dept.

There was a jeep, a 1,000-amp genny, a camera van full of equipment, a special-effects truck, two construction trucks, an electrical truck, a pickup truck, and a rackety old catering bus. Twenty-one vehicles were helping *Rosebud* on its way, but even that didn't impress one jaded Israeli. "You should have seen *Jesus Christ Superstar* here. Oy, *that* was a *production!*"

Given this orgy of fly-and-drive shuttling, given the *stacks* of air tickets, the kilos of freight, the squads of wheels, the army of local drivers, the river of gas, it was possible that movement charges on a big film could be $200,000–400,000.

And there were still "meals, hotels, and living expenses." Even for Preminger, living meant sleeping in the Plaza and dozing in the desert, a swing from champagne to cold coffee. Eventually luxury and discomfort ran together, until living was just more work.

As the tour organizer, Eva applied strict logic, assuming a daily hotel and food cost in each country, from $35 in Israel to $70 in Germany.

She plotted recces first: so many people for so many nights at so much per. A week in Corsica for two at $50 a day? Easy. Unfortunately, *Rosebud* blossomed with unexpected journeys. Preminger himself was always in motion: to Corsica for surveys, to the United States to meet with UA, to Paris to cast, to Rome to see a writer, to Tel Aviv for scouting, to London to see a yacht, to Hamburg to cast a city . . .

Then came "preparation": those workers shipped from Nice to Corsica *dwelt* there (as did the Hamburgers in Berlin) to build and paint and collect props before shooting. So many workers at so much a day: 100 men per day? 200?

During shooting, the 35 "permanent" staff members would

spend 104 days (3,640 men per day) in good-to-*grande luxe* hotels. And those locals from Nice and Hamburg stayed *on* in Corsica and Berlin. And of course the cast was present: two or three stars and many lesser lights. Strung across Europe.

In effect, the company had to entertain 6,500 or so people for a night in a luxury hotel, feed them, and do their laundry. And lunch was not included here. It was catered and carried separately as a "location expense." There was a further problem if crowds were used. By French union rules, they got a meal allowance of 18 francs: lunch for 3,000 might be another $13,000.

The party was not democratic, either. Lodging for the actors might be 50 percent more than for the others. And stars might require $200 a day for hotel space. Stars carry films after all and must *feel* stellar. A suite for one on a long shoot might run above $20,000.

Eva said the sums were "faintly shattering." All together, travel, transport, food, and lodging might cost a big movie $1 million.

Discounts would of course lower many prices by as *much* as 20 percent. But *all* figures should be increased for inflation of 10 percent a year since 1974. Certain crafts moved ahead *much* faster, coming into line with U.S. rates. And some individuals gained dramatically. Assistant director Wolfgang Glattes joined the American union after *Rosebud* and worked in the United States. From $500–600/wk. in 1974 he moved to union wages. By 1979 he would do the same work as on *Rosebud* — a seven-day week on location, "all-in"—for just under $1,700/wk.

On *Rosebud*, nothing went exactly as planned and the party was a howling success. At each location, new people fought to get in, so that Jerusalem saw eighty-one hotel rooms occupied and it was no tragedy because they only cost $14 a day. Yet, for the old hands on the picture, "luxury" grew less and less important. What was a good breakfast when one ate at 3:00 A.M. before going into the Israeli desert? For myself, it was enough to be with a woman I had come to want, and on those terms two indifferent hotels in Juan-les-Pins and Paris were home and heaven.

"I am not doing a travelogue!" Preminger insisted. But on the K'damm he told his staff that "the audience must know at once, unmistakably, that this is Berlin." That's what he was paying for: actual locations to reinforce a feeling of truth. If the drama was played in the streets and caves where it "happened," the events might seem a little more real.

Spectacle was involved too, despite Preminger's disavowal of "travelogues." He knew that rich, exotic vistas were important to a big movie and paid accordingly. Producers really have no choice. Since films had left the studios, audiences expected the world.

As Eva budgeted, she struggled to include every possibility, often in a catchall category that included the Mobius, a camera boat, location rentals, and a large sum to build a simulator. Preminger saw her figure for that simulator and raised it like a poker player. If Eva's defense was completeness, his was thinking rich. And making her think the same way. Watching them, I felt a bite of jealousy, remembering the scrimping on my own low-budget films. I knew from the first day that one was under-budgeted. That would not happen here.

Preminger built into his estimates the freedom—the luxury—to change his mind, even to experiment a bit. The only question was how he would react if Rosebud fell seriously behind. If all defenses failed. Would he speed up, compress, cut? With complete control, he alone could make all the plans and numbers work. Just as he alone was liable if they didn't.

Eva left the budget at the Negresco and headed for the airport to meet Willy Holt and fly to Corsica.

"Christ, it'll be good to come up for air. . . . This is the best part of filmmaking. Seeing new places. Vamonos, chico!"

RECCES

Back to Nature

In thirty minutes, a 727 flew from Nice to Bastia. They were thirty minutes that carried us beyond Preminger's scrutiny and into a more primitive world.

Bonnecarrère had written of Corsica after living there. He knew the *bruccio* caves, the highways cut into cliffsides, the isolated airfields set against mountain vistas. But Eva and Willy had to see it for themselves—10 million square meters of it.

Between them now one felt sparks of expectation, a smoke of ambition rising. What they found on this trip was *their* contribution, their mark on the film.

They could be tireless, as Eva had been on *Lawrence of Arabia:* "The one movie I've worked on that I'm really proud of . . . twenty months searching for the right color sand! Picking up a hundred meters of track and moving it in the heat. At one point we were getting twenty-eight seconds of film a *day.* All those people like Guinness and Tony Quayle came for two weeks and stayed three months." She called David Lean, the director, cold and demanding. "But thirty-eight of us lasted. I had two birthdays on the film."

"Excuse me, ex-kuh-yewwze-*me!*" Each syllable throbbed as Farrago bounded toward us through the empty terminal, his overcoat draped around his shoulders and a Gauloise Bleu clamped between his fingers. Late and flustered, he patted his peruke to make sure it was still on. Indeed, it rose from his brow like a thick dark mulch, divided in two around a bald crown and hung in curls at the neck over his own gray fringe.

Outside, his rented Simca bucked like a palsy victim as he

80

shifted gears. In reverse, it didn't work at all. Eva and Willy were appalled. But, like the car, they could only go forward.

Farrago led us along the coast to a deserted hotel that shared in the scruffy gray sadness of the town. It was cold in Bastia, cold enough for sweaters and large brandies at the local bar. In the gritty twilight, one or two dogs crossed the Place St. Nicolas near the docks, accenting its open, dun spaces. At night, the men argued in a Franco-Italian dialect, playing cards and drinking "myrte," a myrtle liqueur. On the walls the name STROMBONI was spray-painted. They said he was a patriot, a fighter against France for Corsican independence.

Next morning at six, cold and coffeeless, we went to see the ferries come in. Preminger wanted an opening shot to pan Bastia, then pick up Hacam coming off the boat and follow him through customs. But where to play the scene? With the freezing wind flailing their scarves and jackets, Eva and Willy studied the harbor and the lumbering boats. Most of their bows lifted on hinges like amphibian jaws, letting trucks and cars roll out from Nice, Toulon, and Marseilles. Willy photographed everything, but the background was open sea. No Bastia.

They persisted. Near the dock was a huge white customs chamber with an oval, wooden luggage rack in the middle. The room was a no-man's land created by artists of bureaucracy for the pleasure of making people wait. One imagined the Arab workers here, passing uneasily in their shabby clothes.

But what about the city?

Willy found an answer on a side dock, where a tiny shed could be dressed as an outdoor customs office. The camera could pick up the passengers disembarking and dolly with them to that "office" in one move.

Beyond, visible in an extreme angle, but *visible,* the old port of Bastia rose like a sandy wall from the water. As they watched, the sun broke through, burning off the last morning mist, framing some clouds in a rim of peach fire. It might have been a hill in Tuscany.

"Fantastic!" cried Eva. She almost skipped to the car. "We've got the first shot. We'll do it at eight A.M."

After fixing that shot, they went in circles, trapped in Farrago's Simca, with towns passing like a movie montage: "Speloncata . . . Renucoli . . . Santa Reparata . . ."

For the Arab compound (the Tardets farm), Farrago thought they wanted to see vineyards. So they saw vineyards. In one, a band of Algerians peered suspiciously at us: a silent man with a shotgun, a girl with rotten teeth, an idiot son.

"Every family has a sad story," said Eva.

At another villa, an ex-paratrooper presided, while exchanging tender glances with the owner's son.

Everywhere we were offered wine. Farrago always drank, as the vintners toasted "Mon Capitaine!" Lurching to the car, he finally bellowed "Capitaine is my Christian name!"

By noon the Simca stank of wine and Gauloises as it careened over the mountain roads. Farrago drove with one hand on the wheel and one on his wig, belching profoundly.

At one vineyard the car sank in mud. As we pushed it, great gobs of muck flew up.

"Impossible!" cried Eva.

Beside the Tardets compound, they needed Locci's farm, home base for the Israeli commandos as they prepared to assault the Arab stronghold. In the script, it was an oil mill. So they looked for oil mills, though not a single *olive* ever got on screen.

Eva felt pure dread. "There isn't *time* to be looking at oil mills. Nine weeks away is the *film*!"

The car got stuck again.

"We have nine weeks to prepare *five countries*!"

Suddenly they found three farm buildings on a dead, rocky plain, a scene of desolation like an Antonioni vision. The main building had a huge, stone pit for grinding olives and an attic of musty, beige shadows, perfect to house the commandos. Willy tested the attic floor, checked the angle of the sun with a compass. But nothing could be chosen without first picking the Tardets location.

In the waning afternoon, Eva and Farrago went to appraise some hopeless hotel rooms. "You look at these places from the outside," said Eva, "and think, Marvelous. Next day you go in and they're small, ugly, crappy, and expensive."

Willy meanwhile waited outside, slumped in the Simca. It felt like the end of the line: sunset on a knob of rusty rock, with gulls wheeling overhead and a sting of brine in the air. Willy speculated, "I think maybe we find the Tardets place behind Nice. Two weeks here is difficult. I don't know . . . carpenters, painters . . . maybe they get tired here."

As often happens on a movie, strangers tried to help. We had retreated to a tiny Île Rousse hotel on a street the color of dust. Supper was a boardinghouse affair with the Captain downing *pastis* and lustily recounting his OAS activities—and his resulting prison term.

I had to get away: down a silent street, across the town square, to a beckoning bar. The handsome woman tending it was obviously restless. She brought me a myrte, and poured one for herself. For want of something better, I asked about farms in the area.

Soon others drifted in and listened patiently to my lame French. A thunderstorm started, its lightning stabs throwing the whole coast into dancing relief. The men in the bar clearly wanted to give directions. I asked them to wait *cinque minutes*—five fingers held up (count on a tourist to be graphic)—then bolted out in the rain to find Willy and Eva, knowing the men would wait and that the barwoman and I had said our last words.

Next day, we followed directions, bucking over a rock-strewn road at five miles an hour, beside an antique rail spur. Finally Farrago parked amid the rocks and led the way, a hundred yards down a tamped-earth road, to the compound.

It looked tropically hot, as if the yellow walls had absorbed a hundred years of summer heat. The first building was an ancient chapel, once a jewel box, now peeling and scabrous with its interior stripped bare.

From here, a flight of cracked, stone stairs led down to a dusty courtyard and the main house, with living quarters and cellars. And what cellars! Made of stone and timber, they had Roman arches and bats clinging to vaulted ceilings. Workmen with lights showed us past six-foot-high wine casks, through the atmosphere of a dungeon.

Parallel to the house was a long, rambling stone shed, its interior sealed pitch dark by heavy, indoor shutters.

Between the two buildings—the house and shed—lay a cobbled yard surrounded by sullen stone walls.

Behind the whole complex, ancient palm trees shaded a garden. Farther off were the mountains.

Willy saw at once: the Arabs could film the hostages in the chapel and put the simulator in the workshed. And the whole *area* was alive: the house, the rough stone floors, the bare, plastered stairways, the tiny bedrooms with carved furniture—every scrap of it was right. The farm was a unity rooted in the island. In blood ground.

Even the old farmers were perfect: strong as bulls, rolling in fat, their faces the color of caked earth.

There was some chatter about the farm being "too picturesque" or "a little Hollywood," but it was the movies and one had to say something. When Preminger saw this, he would want it.

The island had finally offered everything: the Locci mill, the Tardets farm, the Bastia harbor. And one unique locale: the Desert des Agriates, lying between Bastia and Île Rousse, rose in tower shapes, a vision of gnarled, weathered rock that swept down to the sea. Somewhere in those stony whorls Hélène would be set free.

You few who have seen the film and know how the sets were used, don't judge people harshly for being optimistic in those early days. The locations were imprinted with real life. If anything could have nourished *Rosebud*, it was those sets, working on the imaginations of the director and actors. Passing through that stark customs office, any good actor would feel an alien's anxiety. Seeing a radio in the Tardets kitchen suggested the isolated terrorists listening for news about themselves. And Hélène's awakening at dawn in the desert, to her first sunlight in weeks, could be a cutting mixture of exhilaration and desolation.

The settings offered more to the film than the vision of any one man and would challenge, perhaps expand, such vision. One hoped Preminger would see them soon.

Flying back to Nice, I found to my surprise that I missed him. Four days of off-season gloom with M. Toupee had yielded some large sights and a feeling of camaraderie with Eva and Willy. But no fights, no explosions, no passion. Not even wit, as a substitute for passion.

"Gershy," he would say, "you are so easily bored."

At the Negresco, Preminger was delighted with Willy's photos. Shooting would start in Corsica; they would fly there next week to set locations. And Preminger wanted as few changes in the sites as possible.

"The whole idea of shooting on location is to make it real. Would you *build* a hotel room like this?"

"Certainly not," said Willy.

"In the cheapest new hotel you wouldn't find such closets. But that's what makes it real. . . . Eva, did you pay Farrago?"

"No. The poor man was so tired afterwards he could hardly walk."

"It's because of his heavy *hair*."

The First Good-bye

Saturday, March 9. That weekend Eva made it clear she was leaving.

And a new production manager packed his bags in London. Graham Cottle had worked for months to start his own film, *Good Morning Midnight*, based on Jean Rhys's novel about a lonely woman. Glenda Jackson, Jean-Louis Trintignant, and Joe Dallesandro would star. Graham had already produced *Triple Echo* with Glenda. But that film was only moderately successful and loneliness wasn't selling this year. Graham had invested £20,000 of his own developing the project, only to see his major backer drop out. "So much of the time one sat home waiting for the phone to ring." He was glad when *Rosebud* called. He needed it.

In the purple twilight, Eva and Willy strolled to dinner through the flower market of the old city of Nice, where workers hosed down the street.

Eva sadly defended Preminger, citing his liability for budget overruns, his need to hurry and worry even after building so many safeguards into the budget. Such was the price of his creative freedom. (That same freedom would prove costly to producer-directors like Norman Jewison and Francis Coppola when *F.I.S.T.* and *Apocalypse Now* went over budget.)

But Eva also defended herself. "He amuses me, he charms me . . . yet I just don't want to work with him. And at the end he had grace. I give him that. No questions about why I quit or harshness. He just said he knows how to say good-bye because he's said it already to two wives."

Across the city Preminger mused. "I think she honestly felt it was too tough a picture. Possibly there was something personal. I didn't feel it."

And next morning, Willy Holt waited for her replacement. "It's very hard for Eva, no? She is happy and she is not. And she does so much work! I think it will be very hard for the next man. . . . Preminger is looking all the time for fear in a person. When he see fear, that's when he move."

Fear was a theme that took him inevitably back to the camps. Quietly he told how he spent weeks at hard labor, until the Germans heard he was an artist and tested him by having him paint a picture. They took the work away—he waited all day in suspense—then an officer came and wanted more.

"It made life easier."

From then, in each new camp, he took the dangerous step of asking for paper, gambling that he could prove he was an artist. Confronting fear.

Graham Cottle stepped out of a taxi looking as if he were joining friends for a week at the beach. He was young and fit, with bright blue eyes, dark hair slicked over a high, bony forehead, and a toothy grin.

Like Eva, he was a talker. Behind corporate seriousness and crisp flannels, he harbored a sly, self-deprecating humor. While Eva made her points with a machine gun, Graham used a stiletto. But while Eva was a co-adventurer with her crew, Graham was "management."

A photo shows one murky room in the new Westminster office during the few hours when Eva and Graham were together.

It was Monday morning. They sat across a library table scarred with cigarette burns. On the table were notes, contracts, and the production board. Graham read. Eva slumped. A square of sunlight crept along the floor between them, until, moments later, Eva exited, summoned by an implacable stage manager.

"Now everything's as it should be," she said. An accountant was coming, they had an assistant director, and an office. "And Papa's got a young man to handle production who'll do it his way. One likes to think it'll all be easier because one did the strong thing and left. And it will. . . . We all got the schedule nailed down last night. It's what I wanted. Start in Corsica, come back here. The end'll be changed a thousand times but the beginning's set."

No. The beginning changed a thousand times too.

"And I'll be in London this afternoon . . ." She spoke to me with only a hint of wistfulness. "At least I've met you and Willy . . . I mean, you're friends one hopes to see again and again over the years. You know, when I started *Black Windmill* I never thought Don Siegel would become, well, a friend for life. But he is. And that's what it's all about, isn't it?"

Corsica: Take Two

The director and his key staff had thirty-six hours to see the Corsican location. Preminger shot through the arrival gate to confront M. Farrago.

"Well, what do we do first?"

Farrago started a long answer. Preminger cut him off.

"I didn't come here to dance with you!"

As the gang piled into two cars, Wolfgang nodded to me. "You're going to write a long, long book."

Preminger exploded into a set. In Bastia, he strode from ship to ship, gesturing, palms up, palms down, pulling and tugging like a man moving furniture in the air, while his staff raced to make notes and keep up. And it was as if the first recce never happened, as if Willy and Eva had found no "opening shot."

"For the first shot, we want to play titles. . . . I want to combine the church and that—" he pointed to the old city on a hill—"that *castle*. . . . We turn the Mobius around . . . and pick up Hacam coming off the ship. . . . And there is another possibility—"

Pens stopped. Poised.

"We put the Mobius on the boat . . . shoot as we approach the town . . . then come down and see Hacam . . . from an angle that doesn't show the crane." He told Farrago, "Find out if people are here."

People?

"We need extras coming off the ship. Three hundred Arabs. Four to five hundred people all together . . . with suitcases."

He lined up a second shot. "A policeman checks passports outside. We'll see the boat behind. It will work well."

The customshouse—that stark, white building—was empty. "We need a crowd here . . . and outside. . . . We follow Hacam—but you need lots of light here. I wonder if it's worth it. We could have the customs *out*side . . . could use the parking lot. . . .

"And we need a shot in the street as he mounts the bus. We have four good shots. With beauty. If it's not enough we put *you*, Willy, in front of the camera. *Allons!*"

As the afternoon sun reddened, the cars wound uphill to a sweeping view of the port. Everyone got out to look.

"But the angle is too—*far!*"

They all dashed back to the cars.

Higher up on terraced hills the sun shimmered brilliantly through the tiny leaves of the olive trees.

"We're six minutes ahead. A *good omen.*"

Near the Desert des Agriates, the cars waited behind two shepherds and a flock. "What a marvelous character the place has. . . . But the light is going."

89

At the Tardets farm we could barely see into the caves. The farmers brought a light downstairs, which Wolfgang held up in the dim, wet stillness.

"Yah!" said OP. "It will be very good!"

As the entourage headed upstairs, he called back down to me, in the rear, "Gershuny you are always in the way!"

Outside, the twilight was turning cold. Wolfgang gave Preminger a vest to wear against the chill, as they set off.

On the road, with a raw wind cutting through the open windows, Preminger looked at Locci's mill and signaled to drive on.

We ended in a tiny Île Rousse bistro, a possible location for a scene, where Preminger toasted the German woman tending bar. *"Nasdrovya!"*

The jukebox played a German song. The director laughed. "A Tyrolean jukebox. No one can have quiet anymore."

Everyone sagged against the bar as Preminger talked about Oskar Werner, who might play a role. "But at the last moment he would want only a star part. He's a wonderful actor. You saw *Fahrenheit 451*? Interesting . . ."

Then Farrago caught his eye. Preminger had a teasing look. "Does the Captain understand English?"

"Oh, very well . . . especially Eva Monley. The sonority and clarity of the voice . . ."

"Ah ha. A question of sex appeal."

"No—"

"You understand Ted. Perhaps here is also a question of sex appeal?"

"Absolutely not!!" the Captain was outraged.

"Gershuny, you think that bar girl is attractive?"

"She'd make a nice hostage."

"Ha! I will miss you." He looked around the club; it reminded him of a famous bar in old Berlin, the Triangle Club, where naked girls sat with the customers, drinking champagne. "Berlin is a city obsessed with sex. For the bar scene this place is perfect. A Triangle Club without sex."

"You know," said Graham, "he's not Hollywood at all." Added Wolfgang, "The man is really cultured, he knows everything—and he's very *funny.*"

Next morning, we were on the road at eight, driven past a blur of Corsican scenery and the silent gravity of the sparkling sea.

"Definitely May twenty-ninth! Graham *Brodt!* Half the unit should be here May twenty-second. . . . Margot should find faces. . . . There will always be difficulties, but we definitely start May twenty-ninth!"

With small changes, the farm would play itself.

The workshed was ideal. "Willy, do as you suggest. Have bulbs hanging . . . put the simulator in here. . . . The *charm* of the simulator is that it isn't a major thing."

In the house, the cellars were splendid. The girls' dungeon only needed bunks and a steel door.

"You want to sleep here, Gershuny?"

"It's a little damp."

"You want realism, you'll get it!"

Upstairs, he stressed that they must paint the bedroom. "Otherwise Mrs. Tardets is unhappy about the rooms and not her dead children!"

Locci's mill. Perfect. "Don't change anything."

"He's in such good humor," marveled Graham.

And I watched him, a man in his late sixties, scampering up a shaky ladder to the attic, jumping on the rickety floor to test it. Outside, a smell led him to three little pigs in a pen. "The smell is sexy . . . for pigs. You know, Mastroianni said he can't make love to U.S. women because they shave. . . . Now, Gershuny, I think of love, I think of you. *Allons!*"

Wolfgang held out a hand to help him off a rock ledge—and Preminger refused help, as always.

Driving to other sites, the director was already restless. He liked only the first ones, which would let the troupe stay in Île Rousse without moving.

Already he questioned the need for the Mobius in the harbor—meaning it was *out* in Corsica.

Already he looked ahead to Germany. Could the Frankfurt scenes be done in Hamburg?

At the rate he was going, the island had no chance to affect him. The demands of time, money, and his impatience separated him from the landscape, forcing him to superimpose *his* need on the settings rather than be stimulated by them.

To Preminger, the wonder was finding the Tardets farm. "You know, I spoke to the author and he *invented* it!"

It seemed never to occur to him that the island had suggested that farm to Bonnecarrère.

Guesswork

Back in Nice, Preminger prepared to fly to London to see a yacht—*The Brave Goose.* Graham cornered him for a fast conference in the Negresco, a replay of one of Eva's inquisitions, a litany of the same dates, names, boats, and questions.

Seeing that Preminger was still undecided in many areas, Graham gently muted his own fears and doubts, even when the director claimed they would only need the yacht in France for a week.

"Did you say—ah—*one* week?"

"How long do you think?"

"Well, in the cross-plot it's fourteen days."

"No!" Bang. Like a guillotine. "Do forget, I've cut some material."

"Well, I suppose we'll wait for Wolfgang's breakdown."

Graham's tact was a virtue. Seeing that he was less prone to argue, Preminger casually confided as he had never done before.

"Look, my real worries are not the boat . . . but questions about the dialogue. The characters. I'm going to get someone to help Erik. I've contacted a man who is very good and fast. You see, I know what I want. There are so many places. Take the galley scene: there is no girl today who doesn't know how to cook—here we have four girls who don't. It's not right. So we will have only one girl who doesn't and the others will make fun of her." He was also worried about developing some of the characters, especially Sloat. From a Jewish mystic to a neo-Nazi to an English anarchist, the villain was changing again—to an Englishman whose family had been blown up in the King David Hotel. "It'll work well . . ."

Preminger's departure gave Graham and Wolfgang a day to work on the schedule. They struggled like two Anglo-Saxon Talmudists, shuffling strips, droning in cryptic phrases, guessing at the unknowable.

"The Ajaccio road . . ."

"He's obviously not going there . . ."

"It's simple . . . *any* deserted road."

Things rapidly got simpler.

"After Cannes it's easier," said Graham. "We haven't seen the locations."

They were almost done when Preminger returned from London with Chalky White, the accountant—and with a guarded view of *The Brave Goose.*

The yacht was modern, it would look big in Juan-les-Pins (its summer berth), and the price was right. But there was one little problem.

I felt Graham and Wolfgang tense for the blow.

It seemed the boat was chartered for the time they planned to be in Israel. Since they couldn't switch the charter, they had to switch the country. Preminger saw it as a break. They would end in Israel instead of Berlin.

"It's cheaper to buy Israeli pounds to send people back home. Even without the boat I'd want to do Israel at the end!"

But he still had not given up on Hochbaum's boat, even if he lost the *Goose* by waiting. "I am an optimist! Wait till you see the Israeli coast with Hochbaum's monster! It will be worth it!"

Graham and Wolfgang went to lunch in shock.

"We have to switch Berlin before Tel Aviv."

Graham smiled morosely. "I was racking my brains this morning. I could see he didn't want to answer questions. Especially detailed ones. The only big one I could think of was: Shall we put off the film till next year?"

They laughed in the face of disaster.

"Disaster?" Chalky White's voice boomed across the café. "Old boy, I've worked on a long list of them! *Nightwatch, Pope Joan, Judith.* Mostly all I've *done* are disasters."

As the gloom thickened, I thought again of Eva Monley. She alone hadn't needed the money. The others, to some degree, *had* to hang on. And so they rationalized about duty ("finishing the job") and cultivated a sense of humor, transforming the film into a bizarre escapade—already a myth: Days with King Otto.

Of all the company, only Preminger himself was truly cheerful. What the others felt never bothered him. He seemed insulated by his impatience, his indifference, his imperial control. What good was the trepidation of his staff, anyway? They couldn't help with the real problems.

Paris Blues

March 20. Most of the staff set off on a major recce to collect actors, locations, and *things*—to see the problems firsthand.

94

Chalky White stayed behind to make what Preminger called "a complete budget. I don't want a guesstimate!"

Preminger signed a few blank checks for him—in case of emergency. "For some reason I trust you. How foolish can I be?"

"Once I had a million-dollar check and didn't abscond."

"How foolish can *you* be? Here, don't lose these. Lock your door. Gershuny comes in the night." I reminded Preminger that I was going with him.

There was one last shout at the people building his villa: "Tell my lawyer he is the biggest disappointment of my life! The electricity doesn't work! The phone isn't in! I have things to do!" As he hung up, his rage vanished in a smile. "I wasn't really mad. But I spent my whole day yesterday waiting for things that didn't come. God, am I glad to get out of here."

It would soon be April in Paris, and Preminger arrived at the luxurious Plaza Athenée to meet the most beautiful young women in Europe. He should have enjoyed it. Instead, he groaned.

"If everyone speaks with an accent, we'll drive people from the theater."

What he wanted seemed simple. The women playing the hostages had to be actresses—"Not a chorus line!"—who spoke English without being English, so as to retain some ethnic character. And they had to be young.

But the beautiful young women spoke no English. And the experienced ones with good English were too old. There was no bridging his idea of realism and the facts of reality.

Women fluttered or swept in, wearing jeans, velvet suits, safari jackets, mantillas, frilled blouses, jump suits, and fake fur. It was a fashion show of haute couture and cheap chic. There was straight blonde hair, short coppery bobs, clouds of wavy chestnut. There were kisses of eyeliner, discreet to the point of invisibility. And there were masks of maquillage, faces hardened into porcelain icons. Beauty broke in waves over the room.

Until they spoke.

Even the names were musical: Arielle Sonnery, Ludmilla Mikael, Laurence Monaghan, Marie-Christine Adam, Ann Deleuze, Claude Jade, Laura Duke, Dayle Haddon, Sonia Petrova, Jane Birkin, Veronique Jannot, Marianne Eggerix, Anicee Alvina, Sylvie Meyer, Pascale Rivault, Valerie de Tilbourg, Nicole Calfan, Virginie Thevenet, Virginie Billedoux, and more—all Margot's "creatures for dreaming."

At night one saw them in a string of local thrillers, romances, and semisoft sex films. Often they were nude, decorating second-rate movies with first-rate bodies. Next morning, they turned up at the Plaza trailing erotic possibilities.

Until they spoke.

"She is in the Robbe-Grillet movie entirely naked and has a beautiful figure!"

Margot introduced them, and Preminger formed an idea immediately. Thus, Isabelle Huppert "looked like talent" even with dirty fingernails.

Others he dismissed quickly. "It's sad when you're twenty-two to be told you're too old."

Another girl had starred as a nun in a sex film.

"Trop Jewish!"

But wasn't her grandfather supposed to be Jewish?

"If you all like her, *you* hire her. Put her on the cover of your book, Gershuny. The more I see of your taste in women, the more I see your problem."

Inevitably he didn't want the "older" actresses like Ludmilla Mikael. Yet, at twenty-three, she was someone people might pay to see, with a rangy body and strong features framed in wild brown hair.

She had worked for seven years in theater and films, but what mattered was how her hands diagramed sentences in the air and her huge eyes danced when she smiled. As Hélène, she would have been a perfect chaperone for the debs. But Preminger wanted another deb.

"What have you done? Professionally. I don't ask about your private life." Coaxing them to talk he often asked, "Are you a good actor?"

"That's not for me to say," answered Isabelle Huppert.

And Patrick Floershein, a small man in a scruffy flyer's jacket, shot back a surly "No!"

Preminger laughed for ten seconds. "That's a *wonderful* answer. The first time I ever heard it!"

He was hired immediately as a *Rosebud* crewman.

Some of the young, attractive actresses had no film. So Preminger sent them into the bedroom to study a script and then read.

A blonde spoke with her hand over her mouth. "She was not even *nervous*. Talented people are always nervous when they read."

Sometimes he forgot they were *in* the bedroom. "Read what you want," he finally told one actress.

"I did."

He slapped his forehead in exasperation. "Aloud!"

Then she spoke—in a dialect hauntingly like English.

At first he was calm. "Look, if all these girls were good, we'd have too many. Be patient," he advised Margot.

By the second day his own patience was gone. One girl said she was twenty. "You were twenty when you were supposed to be here. Now it's a half-hour later!"

He looked grimly at his appointments list. "We're in very bad shape."

"Now I know what you want," said Margot.

"If it doesn't exist, *you* must play the part."

With agents he had Negative Patience, telling one burly woman, "The *next* time you're late, you can forget you know me!" She was so surprised she almost swallowed her cigar.

Calling his old friend in Paris, Anatole Litvak (director of *The Snake Pit, Anastasia,* and *Night of the Generals*), Preminger proclaimed, "I am a prisoner."

The problems were exaggerated because he didn't know some of the French actors. Actually, only close followers of French films would have. But Preminger *asked.*

"If I hurt their feelings by asking who they are, too bad!"

"They will *talk!*" exclaimed Margot. *"He can't treat actors like this!"*

She didn't know he "treated" everyone the same.

Sometimes, from boredom and impatience, he turned to teasing. As Graham said, "It's his way of showing he likes you."

For Margot, who only half-understood, it was painful. Preminger pointed at her and asked Isabelle Huppert, "Do you know that twelve years ago Golda Meir looked exactly like her?"

"I admire her," Margot answered tartly, "but I don't like to be treated *comme ça.*"

"Doesn't she look like Golda Meir?"

"Yes, but I told you I'm not a great woman and it's not my fault I'm ugly!"

Preminger was trying to lighten the tension, but finally tears brimmed in Margot's eyes, in front of her actors. As Eva had said, it was like a bad marriage, erupting in public.

He could not know why actors kissed her or how many she had helped. But one day Wolfgang and I got some idea. We drove with her to Studio Boulogne, outside Paris, where Jean Gabin and Sophia Loren were making a film. She was sent to ask Gabin if he was interested in playing Fargeau.

We entered past a commissary, where everyone knew and greeted Margot. She got directions and we followed in her wake, toting her satchels, through a dark maze of scenery. Suddenly we saw them—waiting between takes, at a card table lit by a single work lamp. Gabin was reading a newspaper, Loren knitting.

Wearing a plain yellow dress (for the movie), Loren was both more slender and fuller bosomed than one might have guessed. Her arms and face were pale cream, topped by a dark froth of perfectly careless curls. When she looked up and saw Margot, her eyes opened in a wave of warmth.

Gabin reacted at the same time, setting down his paper and breaking into a poster-sized smile. His face had massive grandeur, like a florid, limestone sculpture of pouches, bags, and jowls.

If there were *no* movies, one would still have stared at them. And they rose together, calling, "Margot—!" Gabin's voice was a coal-dark growl, Loren's silvery. Calling through the dark, they drew out the second syllable so "Margot" became music. *Cher Margot. Cher Margauxxx,* and the *x*'s were kisses.

They sat for a few minutes at the card table, littered with scripts, yogurt, and knitting, talking about *Rosebud.* Gabin simply didn't want to work in English.

"But you should do it," Loren said with a laugh. "Maybe you'll win an Oscar."

He paused. "I did two films in Californee . . ." The word was exaggerated: *"Cal-ehh-for-neee,"* as if it were Timbuktu and too, too far.

"Maybe," suggested Margot, "you could do it in French?"

"No." He bent forward and patted her arm. "You tell OP I am touched that he asked . . . but it's too much work."

Margot kissed the stars again and started back into the dark.

"I told Loren once, 'I can't *dream* what I would have done with your face."

Over lunch, she talked of casting in the dire tones Eva Monley had once used.

"I don't know what he's doing! I'm fighting second by second to be not too nervous. . . . I can play a game, but it's immoral. It's a joke. . . . These girls are eighteen only because that's the way this kid writes it!" (It was also the oldest age when they might conceivably start a cruise without boys.)

She knew Preminger had his own problems with a rush of unfamiliar faces. But that just aggravated the major problem.

"Only a few actors speak English well. And they are scared to death, even big actors. And our director is not finished with the script. . . . If you give actors new lines at the last minute— *hey, hey!*"

Besides the language problem, Preminger himself "terrified" the actors. He must learn, Margot announced haughtily, that "the French people are not Zulus!"

Next day he summoned her into the bedroom. She returned looking astonished. "Now he wants me to stay for *the whole picture!*"

The Girls Most Likely
Amid the confusion, they groped.

Margot found an actress to play the lesbian photo-shop owner in Berlin. She spoke her lines to men with slow-burning contempt.

"It's good," Preminger told the woman. "You underplay. If we get together on salary, you have the part."

"I don't know whether I can make her lesbian. . . . I've thought about it."

"What do you mean? Did you try it?"

She laughed.

"I take back that question."

Some performers were bringing film.

"Don't get too much," Preminger warned.

Margot assured him: one reel per actor.

"Vous avez le sens d'un ange."

"I'm not an angel. I'm Jewish!"

"All angels are Jewish! You want another drink?"

100

"I'll collapse."

She couldn't afford to. Evenings, around six, she and Wolfgang took the sample reels from the Plaza to the screening room, typed the order in which they were to be shown, gave a copy to the projectionists, and dashed for coffee.

Relaxing a moment, she reflected on "The Grand Voyagers," Wilder, Zinnemann, and Preminger, who had all been born within a year of each other in Vienna. "So Austrian . . . but they had success. And it's touching. *If* you can be touched by Prussian *cholérique*!"

By eight, Preminger would arrive and settle into one of the modular leather chairs in the screening room. "This is very dangerous after dinner." On his first visit, he decided the rich fathers could view the Arab films here.

The lights would dim, the curtains open soundlessly. And then one felt the uncertainty, the awesome handicaps of a director on foreign soil, guessing about unknown talent.

There were French films dubbed into English and English dubbed into French. And there was silent film. All useless.

He would wait fifteen seconds and then start a mounting volley of questions, his voice rumbling more and more irritably in the dark.

"Who is this girl? What is this movie, Golda?"

"She pretends to be raped," answered Margot.

"Does she speak English? If she could talk to me on the phone, we'd see—"

Pencils scratched in the dark.

During a love scene, he growled, "This man could also be a girl. Look at his breasts."

The actress didn't speak.

"Why do they bring a print where she doesn't *talk*?"

"Monsieur, the girl had only three hours to arrange it!"

"Is this a new film?"

"No."

"Successful?"

"No."

Dialogue began.

"This is English dialogue?"

Wolfgang turned it louder. English it wasn't.

"Now, which one is she?"

"The student."

There were dozens of students.

"What is the name of the girl?"

"Virginie."

"What?"

"Verr-jhee-nee!"

"What did you say?"

"Virginia!" shouted her agent from the back.

"Golda, what's wrong? Didn't you sleep last night?"

"No, Monsieur, I was playing at the Crazy Horse!"

"So! You are really Ursula Picadilly!"

"Exactly!"

"Hah! Golda, I love you. I'll adopt you, okay?"

"I have to think it over!"

From this chaos Preminger made two discoveries. One was genuine.

"For three years I've been trying to help her!" Margot said of the woman who shall be known as Betty Berman.

She came from Third Avenue in Manhattan, modeled in Paris, had some checks from home, but no parts. Tall and slightly gawky, she talked too much even when trying to be discreet. ("Oh, I never tell my age . . .")

Reading Sabine's big speech, wearing denims and a jacket with a picture of the Eiffel Tower on the chest, she looked less a French heiress than a Scarsdale princess kidnapped from Bloomingdale's. Discovering that the Arabs would hold her for a year, she collapsed in synthetic tears, begging her grandfather, "Tell them to kill me."

"Very good," said Preminger. "You will play one of the parts."

"Really?!"

"Yes."

"Then I can *really* cry!"

Said Preminger later, "She has an extraordinary, direct, self-created impact. She'll play Sabine."

In contrast, Isabelle Huppert at twenty seemed almost stolid. Her outfit obscured her face and accented a wide bottom.

"Take off your hat," Preminger ordered. "And the scarf."

Beneath strawberry hair, she revealed a spatter of freckles.

"Already you look better. Put this down, Margot. She could play only Hélène. Sabine is serious. Hélène has life."

Driving home from the screening of a French TV movie in which Huppert had portrayed a stolid peasant with a wide bottom, Preminger asked for reactions. The silence in his rented limousine was embarrassing. No one wanted to challenge him, yet, whatever life he saw in her, neither Wolfgang nor Margot nor I could feel it.

"Well, you are all wrong!" Next morning he told Isabelle she had the part. "I liked your performance very much!"

Later he explained, "The charm of these girls is that they are not so pretty. A bit . . . *pudgy!*"

Truly, in those days Preminger only needed to give and get support from one person. When Erik appeared, dressed for an evening out, Otto beamed. "He got a *tie!* Erik, I could smell your jeans—but I love you. That's the problem of a doting father."

Roman Holiday

Next morning the banks, the taxis, the Metro, and Air France were all on strike. I thought of returning to New York, but my energy was on strike too.

Preminger asked if I was coming to Rome. Indeed I was, hoping to witness his visit to a possible new writer. But I witnessed nothing. When I asked to go along to the man's villa, Preminger refused. I had wasted the trip.

After the assignment was declined, I encountered Otto and Erik on Via Veneto, where the director greeted me robustly.

"This man is everywhere. A spy."

Sitting alone at a Veneto café, watching American actors on Harley-Davidsons buzzing the tourists, I felt a very foolish spy at best. The confusion, the teasing, the invisibility that sapped one's pride, the travel and unraveling plans, all made it harder each day to go back. Yet, when I thought of leaving, I wondered how this movie would ever be made and was *drawn* back.

Rome was even busier than Paris, and more like Old-Hollywood-on-the-Tiber, a crossroads of high serious and Higher Selfish, culture and shlock, artists and whores—an appeal to all of one's favorite weaknesses.

Preminger's suite at the Grand Hotel was the largest he'd had on the film so far. A phone with six buttons summoned waiters who came ... slowly. One explained he had been eating.

"The people here are so charming," said Preminger.

He had *come* for the people. Little by little he was gathering his flock. To him, Rome *was* people. And some reached heights of professionalism.

Annalise Nascalli-Rocca, his costume coordinator, was an old pal of Eva's and even looked a bit like her, with close-cropped gray hair and no-nonsense pants. Preminger was delighted with her crisp, authoritative manner, just as he had been delighted at first with Eva.

And Raf Vallone, who had played in *The Cardinal* for Preminger, was now a possible George Nikolaos. "Can he play a Greek?" Preminger asked Erik. "Let's not discuss it but listen to him."

They saw that night an actor who had mastered the demands of his ego and could laugh about it. "I lived in Beverly Hills six months, and my first U.S. picture was *Harlow*. It seemed so important then. . . . Now I don't even remember the name of the director."

His conservative blue suit accented the craggy good looks of his middle age. He carried himself with courtliness and a hint of swagger. "We're both fighters," he told Preminger. "It's the only way to live."

Sitting in Taverna Flavia, while the papparazzi milled around outside, they talked of *The Cardinal* and how Vallone had helped Tom Tryon in the lead.

"Ah, what a time!" Vallone laughed. "Seventy-five takes! For a scene where Tryon is walking. Finally he is getting the idea of his monologue. All *I* have to do is agree once. And I think, my God, now *I'll* start to make mistakes. And now he's a successful writer. Well, he didn't want to be an actor. He wasn't comfortable."

"Then why did he take the part?"

"Ooh, la la, *what* a part!"

Himself a director, he talked of Shakespeare and his favorite play, *Coriolanus*. "What a *conception*! A man who makes his own great moral position! Even when he comes back at the end against Rome, after defending it heroically, he *knows he is right*! And when he wants to be Consul and he cannot ask for the votes of the citizens! He cannot *speak*! It is the same as Cordelia. . . . It happens to *me* in school. I collect for some charity. And a boy have to give me some money. And he *say* he give it. But he don't! And is a trauma for me! I *can't speak*! . . . Shakespeare was the greatest. He has an idea, then he is into another. . . . It is best to be deep in a light way."

After the meal, the owner put a dozen different liqueurs on the table. Outside, as Vallone and Preminger left, the cameramen descended. Otto bent over and kissed Vallone on the head, only partly clowning.

For such evenings, one stayed on.

March 24. On his final Sunday afternoon in Rome, Preminger met with Debbie Berger, a young actress up for the part of the German hostage. She was accompanied by her agent and a friend, Crystal.

At seventeen, Debbie looked vaguely German, with long blonde hair and pillowy breasts threatening to spill out of her nylon blouse. Her voice, however, was totally American, thin and high. She suggested a slightly jaded cheerleader. But neither she nor her agent said much.

That left Crystal, a tall black woman in her late twenties wearing the international-hip uniform of jeans, Afro, and silver jewelry.

"Oh, Mr. Preminger," she asked, batting her eyes, "what sign are you? . . . Sagittarius?! Oh, you notice how when you said it the ash dropped off my cigarette?"

She slipped off her shoes and tucked her long legs under her, telling of Debbie's impending debut in a new Marcel Carné film. The agent said Carné had the reputation of a French Preminger. But Crystal knew better.

"Oh, no! You're not a monster like Carné! People are afraid of you, but you're very gentle!"

It amused Preminger at first, even when Crystal made it clear: Wherever Debbie went, she came too.

"This woman is a bodyguard!" said Preminger.

"Debbie was given to me when she was twelve. You'll always find me where she is."

Right. As I left, I saw friendly Crystal exiting the hotel with one hand clamped on Debbie's left buttock.

Little by little, *Rosebud* was collecting its people. *Andiamo!*

Truth and Beauty

If Rome was people, Israel was things—things strewn over deserts.

At Ben Gurion Airport, Preminger met Coop, Cottle, Glattes, and Holt, who had flown in from Paris. They all drove west through the night, past a few lights, a solitary bus, sentries at a crossroads. The country and the streets of Tel Aviv offered a huge, humid, salt-scented darkness.

In another anamorphic suite, a Howard Johnson–Tropicana fantasy in rattan and plastic wood, Preminger explained his needs again, cataloguing hardware.

In my room, I passed out without undressing.

By seven next morning, the drivers were waiting outside the hotel. Nearby, along the empty beach, there wasn't a yacht in sight. "Don't forget," said an Israeli, "we cannot compete with the French coast. This is a country at war."

Work and war. One's heart sank before the distance to be covered, even in that tiny country. The joy finally seeped out of the project there in Tel Aviv. Days began at dawn and ended after dark, in the director's suite. The script had spread locations over the country.

And most sites had to be filled with military gear.

"Army and official help are the most important," said Preminger. Graham had a whole shopping list: a plane or helicopter for ten parachutists (raiding Sloat), a small plane for Martin (visiting Sloat), a helicopter to lower Hamlekh onto the yacht, another copter from which to hang the Mobius for aerial shots, a coast guard boat, a camera boat, fishing boats, a military observation plane, et cetera.

By Israel, the physical demands of the film had taken over. The momentum was irresistible.

Preminger told Graham, "Make all deals in advance so they treat us like business people. We are not tourists!"

Yet he catered to the tourist instinct in his audience. The director craved "true" places—reality—preferably with "beauty." If he had a choice of locations, he took the more picturesque.

In Israel, his job was legwork: the search of an aging man driven over a boiling landscape by the need to fill a screen, when all the while he had problems with the script and when body and spirit must have called for rest. It was a show of integrity. As producer, he did his utmost.

Thus he studied all the ways a yacht might really be discovered. There could be shots from the tower in the Haifa Navy Yard and from the Mt. Carmel observatory.

"There are no firm rules! If there's a high point in Akko, we'll have a shot there too!"

Preminger now returned to Akko fifteen years after shooting some of *Exodus* there. He brought with him his usual sentiment: "I forget the whole goddam picture. I have a gift of forgetting."

He led his panting aides up the clocktower to a view of minarets and the open sea. "This is excellent! We can't do better."

And the sequence clarified in his mind. The yacht would approach and cut the nets between two fishing boats . . . the helicopter would fly over . . . the two agents would come down. There would be shots from this tower, from one in Haifa, and maybe from one more.

And it didn't matter. None of it. In the film, there would be *no* fishing boats. *No* towers in Akko, Mt. Carmel, or Haifa. And no regrets. The last thing *Rosebud* needed was more scenery.

They drove to the Judean wilderness, descending to the desert and Sloat's hideout.

Leaving Jerusalem, they passed the battlements of the old city and a tour bus belching exhaust. On a country road, they ignored soldiers with guns on their shoulders, thumbing rides. Beside the road lay rusted tank hulks, relics of 1967.

Gradually the landscape dried and roughened. A single Arab tent flapped in the distance. Yoram Ben Ami, the location manager, said that by June the earth would all be brown. "From the sun."

And by August, when they would shoot?

108

"You will not stand in the sun. You will always look for shade."

Now all vegetation was gone. Rock and sand and cliffs stretched in the distance.

Near Kum'ran, not far from where Jesus was baptized, Yoram finally brought us to a location he had used on *Moses*. It was the single most impressive sight on the film: a network of chasms set in an endless vista of bare, gnarled cliffs; a main valley winding into others, between the wrinkled hills. Looking down at this total, spectacular desolation, this image of earth untouched by human history, we were silent. Here one could understand falling in love with the desert, as one might love the absence of human voices or a vision of healing death.

Preminger spoke first.

"Beautiful. . . . Here you believe a man feels he's safe."

It was exactly what he wanted. And like the towers of Akko, Mt. Carmel, and Haifa, it was never used.

The driving seemed endless, with time and energy bleeding away. Up front, Preminger fussed, commanded, lived his movie. "The minute I get in this car I feel sleepy."

"Shows you how comfortable it is," said the driver.

"Ha! That's one for you. I always sleep well. But never enough."

Wedged in the rear seats, the staff grilled him all day for answers. What car for Sloat? What uniforms? Should they build the whole hideout?

By evening the problems wore tracks in the brain and the voices merged into the One Voice of the film. "We use extras for soldiers chutists in clubs look in Shin Beth arrange Arab village need small genny in the desert . . ."

Certain words became . . . caustic. Like "Mobius." "We need it when the *Rosebud* arrives in Israel . . . for the men coming down from the helicopter . . . and for the parachute raid . . . hang it from a helicopter and follow the chutists down . . . use it next day on the boat . . . do the two together . . . make a deal . . ." Deal. Deals. Dealing. Endless.

Preminger tolerated no distraction now. Once he saw me make a note. "Gershuny, don't ask questions! *There can be no private conversations!* When this book comes out, someone else must write the epilogue because you'll be dead!"

Meanwhile, at the hotel, the phones started failing.

"Good morning," he told the operator there. "I wish to make a difficult call. Last night we almost had it. . . . No, don't call me back—" But the operator had disconnected.

"The connection to France must be bad," said Graham.

"They haven't *made* it yet. . . . Hello, Operator? Try another number in Nice. . . . No, *not* Tel Aviv! Nice, France!"

Next he tried Tel Aviv. "Look, darling, it's *here*, so connect me—" She hung up.

Again: "This is becoming an emergency! When I ask for a number *I'm not a tourist!* . . . It's not possible! Yesterday I *spoke* to this number!"

Graham watched with a small, wry smile. "Have you noticed a certain tension has developed since Nice?"

In a few days we saw Tel Aviv, Haifa, Akko, Caesarea, Jericho, IBM offices, tennis courts, Olympic pools, the outside of the Shin Beth, docks, mosques, prisons, citadels, and wastelands. We saw a whole country—from the outside—because, finally, we *became* tourists who knew the surfaces of the world and avoided most contact with its people.

Yet Preminger tried to reach out.

He listened as Yoram Ben Ami, the thirtyish, feisty location manager, told of interrupting *Moses* to fight for six weeks in a tank battalion.

And, on the last day, Preminger went to see a film of Josef Shiloah, a Jewish actor who might play Hacam. Said one Israeli,

"He speaks English and is very good. . . . Cold. Shrewd. For a heavy, very good."

The audience in the packed screening room held up their own movie to let Preminger view his. Later, he hired Shiloah in the street outside the screening room, while a woman called to him, "I hope you win an Academy Award!"

He thanked her and shrugged. "Too many people there don't like me."

Finally, his deepest contact was in the memories of the Israelis. Director Baruch Dinar told the famous story of the crowd scene in *Exodus*. Preminger had cajoled thirty thousand people into paying to be in it by selling them lottery tickets. The prizes were trips to New York for the opening of the film. And the drawing was at dawn to keep them all night. "I tell you," said Dinar, "he is a *great* producer! And a great friend!"

While Preminger dined with officials, the crew ate together and began to know one another.

Over kosher beef flanken, boiled dry as shirt cardboard, Denys told of operating the camera for Oswald Morris on David Lean's *Breaking the Sound Barrier*. As a boy, I had been spellbound by a scene in which Ralph Richardson, playing the inventor of the jet engine, demonstrates one on a block; it revs up with a demonic shudder. Showing barely repressed glee, Richardson takes out a handkerchief, lets it go—and suddenly *it isn't there anymore*. It is sucked into the jet so quickly that it seems to disappear.

"He used a real rocket bed in the place where jets were developed—De Havilland's at Hatfield. I remember the thrill all through my body when the engine started. There was just room to dolly. Flames poured out the back. Richardson was like a maniac—and it showed on screen—when he realized all that power was actually at his control."

As for David Lean: "He impresses what he wants so vividly

and clearly in your mind that there's never a question of one more take for safety. You know when you've got it."

In Israel, with so many choices made, Preminger was starting to be committed. The days when "nothing was set" were over. He was heading toward August in the desert. Dates and contracts had settled in his wake like so many fire doors sealing off the exits.

And still there was no word about the script.

As we left for Berlin, I felt uneasiness give way to a little stab of panic.

Chase Scenes

Germany would be the scene of a wild goose chase as Martin tried to find Sloat by following his couriers. The trail was to begin in a Frankfurt art studio, lead to a Berlin photo store, and be broken when a courier dropped a film-processing receipt into a mailbox and disappeared. Martin and Schloss (the German agent) would then stake out the photo store and follow another messenger when she picked up the processed photos— only to lose her as she entered East Berlin. Discouraged, they would go to a bar and there, quite by chance, see another Arab film on TV.

Said a staff member, "You could drop Germany and not lose a thing."

By Berlin, one recce was like another. There was the inevitable big suite in the Kempinski, dressed in coral silk. There was the inevitable hustle as a beefy salesman flashed a shark's smile. "Mr. Preminger, you here for a film? Delighted."

Someone muttered that in the war "they were all Nazis."

And there was the inevitable sense of dislocation. Coop and Cottle arrived a day after everyone else, having scouted Israeli labs.

They had gotten up at four in the morning for their flight.

"Well, you chose this profession," said Otto.

Graham grumbled, "I'm starting to wonder what my profession is. . . . Idiot?"

As always, the excitement was in prowling the city with Preminger in search of "character," braving his hail of teasing and impatience.

Even if people didn't know him (like the Japanese who whispered that he was Hitchcock), they knew he was somebody—barreling ahead with his leather greatcoat flapping.

He stopped at the Kaiser Wilhelm church, a bomb-scarred tower of black stone with a new chapel of mournful midnight blue, a memorial to war and troubled conscience.

Immediately he wanted it for a background and sought a photo shop nearby. But a real one had no view and another would be hidden by trees. Then he saw the candy store.

It had the right location, view—everything. But it also had two thousand chocolate nougats in the window.

"Mr. Holt, can you re-dress it? Let them close at two on Saturday and we'll shoot on Sunday!"

En route back to the hotel, he saw a mailbox where the courier could drop his photo-store receipt. As the pieces came together, Preminger was ebullient, not even minding when I asked if an English type might play Martin—say, Peter O'Toole?

"Absolutely not." The part was written for an American.

At twilight everyone but Preminger went in search of another mailbox with a "better" view of the church. Which set the stage for our last, jolly night.

The Kempinski served an enormous buffet dinner with a standing rib roast and an array of salads. We were half through it when Preminger burst in, with his collar open, followed by Graham and a captain, waving a hotel tie.

Otto raised both hands to get us up.

"You've got new locations? I want to see them. I started to undress—I even had my tie off. Let's go!"

Denys produced a director's finder and we started up Kurfurstendamm, seven abreast, with Preminger holding the finder, its silver chain dangling.

"The problem with the candy store, Otto, is that you don't see the church," Denys explained.

"I will *show* you that we see the church. How does this finder work?"

Denys turned it so the view was horizontal, like the screen. "With the new location we'll see more church."

At the candy store, as a crowd gathered, Preminger explained again.

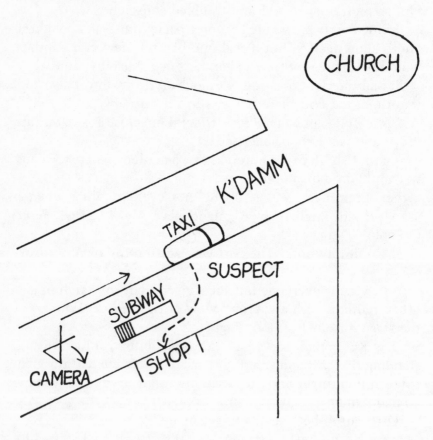

"We pick up the taxi as it drives up. Pan as the courier gets out . . . follow him to the shop . . ." He would even pan across a subway sign saying *K'DAMM*. The church was in the background.

"But Otto, you won't be able to see the whole church—it's too tall."

"So I *don't* see it! I am not doing a travelogue! We *feel* the church. That's enough. You don't go to Paris and put the Eiffel Tower in every shot."

"Otto, you really should see the other location—"

"So show me. Let's go!"

It was a mailbox, under a concrete bridge. Escalators led up to the overpass.

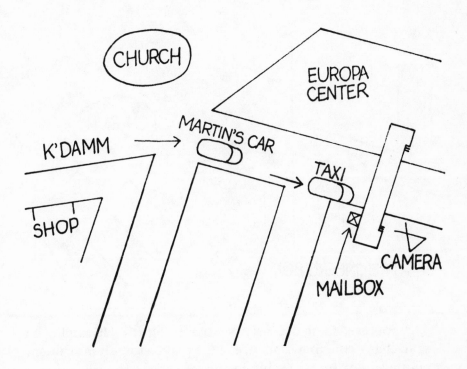

Coop, Holt, and Glattes explained that the cab would stop, and the courier get out and dismiss it. As Martin's car followed into frame, the spy would drop his photo receipt in a mailbox and disappear up the escalator. The church could be framed beneath the overpass all during the action.

"We will hold on the church too long!" Preminger said. "If we pan with the spy, up the stairs, we lose Martin and Schloss. Then I have to cut back to them for their reaction. It's not good! Too busy! Does anyone know where that thing goes?"

"It's just an overpass, Otto."

"Then he's not lost! They can still follow him!"

"Well, but you can assume—"

"You can't spoil the scene just to have the church in the frame! I want to see the mailbox we saw this morning!"

Back they went.

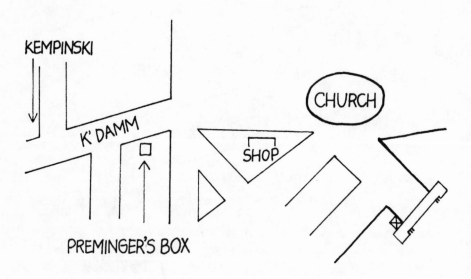

"You see, there are twenty ways to do it!" He might, he said, change the first sequence at the photo store so the camera pointed *away* from the church and save the landmark to use as background here.

"But that's not good," he decided. "Everybody—at least everybody in Europe—knows the church *is* Berlin. So I want to shoot the church early to identify Berlin."

Suddenly the problem evaporated. "We can hang a mailbox *anywhere*! Willy, you and Wolfgang tomorrow go and find another place for it altogether."

It was midnight when they returned, too late to finish dinner.

In the hotel lobby, Wolfgang let his shoulder bag slump down on a bench.

"You know, really . . . it's no life."

Old Dreams Like Old Soldiers

The last stop was Paris. It was April Fool's Day. Preminger returned to the Plaza, singing lustily to his lawyer on the phone, *"D'accord . . . d'accord . . ."* and enjoying a stream of visitors who often came with gifts.

A publicist had found "Martin's apartment." It belonged to an American writer. "Fabulous," said Preminger. "A view of Notre Dame . . . books . . . photos—ideal! The apartment of an intellectual!"

Willy Holt displayed photos of more sites, including "Fargeau's office"—a marbled, mirrored, gilded suite in the Chambre de Commerce. Preminger loved it, as he loved the way the photos unfolded into wide-angle panoramas.

"Masterly!"

But most of all on this trip there were actors bearing the gift of themselves.

"He has a habit of crucifying young actresses," Coop said. Yet they flocked in, along with waves of would-be Arabs, Jews, sailors, yacht brokers, terrorists, tourists, mothers, and whores.

An agent said, "The book was a best-seller. He's making an international film. People would kneel at his hotel to get a job!"

"Even a *bit!*" Margot told Preminger. "They all want to be in the film because of you!"

"They will change their minds."

The main problem was remembering who was who among the actors and those who were just a "look"—like the pale woman with dark, mad eyes for Mrs. Tardets and the fat man whom Willy called "not an actor but a silhouette."

By the end of a day they blurred. Preminger was not just seeing actors. He was being shown the whole French cinema, the Paris stage, the faces of the street, and the women of Europe.

No one knew how much work was being wasted.

Some of Margot's faces were delightful—an old "Corsican driver," a regal blonde "girl friend," a noisy "tourist family."

Yet, in time, the driver's part was cut to almost nothing.

The girl friend was out before the shooting.

And the tourists were out afterward.

And nothing moved in a straight line.

On the phone, Raf Vallone agreed to play George Nikolaos without reading the script.

Preminger then almost hired a French actress for his wife. But an hour later he wanted an *Italian* one, to match Vallone's accent. "So people will think they're *both* Greek."

And then he realized that at least one parent should look like Isabelle Huppert (their daughter).

So, what he really needed was a chic, strawberry-blonde, freckle-faced . . . Italian.

By now, Margot had come to enjoy Preminger's teasing, knowing that if he liked people he often showed it by making them miserable.

And what a pair of hams they were! From the bedroom, Preminger shouted on the phone, "Keep this architect out of my reach or I'll kill him! . . . Two years without toilet seats!"

While Margot stamped around the living room muttering *"Merde, merde, merde!"*

She finally had to speak. "Monsieur, can I say something which tortures me? I think the lines Huppert has to say . . . I'm scared to death that someone who doesn't speak English can *hurt* the picture! Her first two films were simple. But Huppert isn't a good actress. Her English is weak."

"That's why I want rehearsals. I thank you for warning me."

"If you decide a girl works, she will be good. She will die, but she will be good."

"You don't know how many people are bad in my films! Jean Seberg was terrible—but she lived! Huppert was good from the start and she will learn English! . . . You did a good job. Why are you arguing?"

"I'm not."

"Did you drink at lunch?"

"Five! Bloody Marys!"

"Oy, Golda, Golda. . . . I will miss you."

"Me too." She glowered. "I will miss you."

"I won't call you Golda anymore. I only tease you because I like you. Would you rather I *didn't* like you and didn't call you Golda?"

He dealt with actors exactly as he did with aircraft, landmarks, cameras, and crowds. Negotiating himself, and being horribly pressed for time, he still tried to prove he didn't *need* what he wanted.

He rebuffed agents. "The most I'll pay is five thousand a week. No profits or deferments. Call me tomorrow!" Click.

And he showed Margot. "When Betty Berman's agent calls, *I* will make the deal."

"Monsieur," she snapped, "I would only like to be there when you talk. I adore to learn!"

"When you negotiate, you must take the risk to lose."

The agents understood all too well that it was a buyer's market. Dick Dassonville at William Morris had worked hard on the film after hearing about it from Preminger's French publicist. Later, someone at UA tipped off a Morris agent in California, Lenny Hirshan. "A memo was sent worldwide. . . . We read the book and broke down the characters immediately. Even then Lenny suggested Alan Bates and Cliff Gorman for Hamlekh."

Now all his work came to this: "I try to keep the deal going, to get an offer . . . and not have Otto get furious."

His associate down the hall, Anne Correa, had the crisp, professionally attractive look of many women in the business. But as we spoke she nervously tapped red fingernails on a red cigarette box.

To her, the business was "very cruel. Worse than for a man. Because you must cope with everything. OP is just one more stone in my work. He has no time. It's Speedy Gonzalez."

When they all met, Dickie was of course charming. And Anne was knowledgeable.

But Otto got what he wanted.

For Fargeau, it was either Claude Dauphin or Charles Boyer. "They both have advantages. Dauphin can be hard . . . and with Boyer you would believe his love for his granddaughter."

He told them what he would pay for five weeks of shooting plus one extra, if needed.

"*Basta*," said Anne. "What about Raf Vallone?"

"Tell me what you think."

"No, I'm without defense—"

"He was so nice on the phone."

"All I can do is give you his quote." Which she did.

"Look, don't become now a Shylock." He offered a compromise.

They agreed.

Then he told them his terms for Betty Berman. "With five-year options."

"Oh my God!" exclaimed Anne.

But they agreed.

"I went four years without acting jobs. Hibernated for one year. Paris was my last chance."

Now Betty Berman found that *Rosebud* justified all her years of self-absorption. Giddy with joy and relief, she sat in a café, spilling out the story she wanted so hard to conceal, about Paramount almost persuading her to take the part in *Goodbye, Columbus* that made Ali McGraw a star.

"Don't tell Preminger—it makes me too old."

One heard from her the actor's fantasies of being sought— and the desperation beneath. Lately she had been offered pornos. "They wanted me to make love in an elevator. And I asked myself, What am I studying to be an artist for?"

Getting the part of Sabine was not, however, a total surprise. "My astrologer *told* me! She said by twenty-eight I'd be a star, meet the man of my dreams, and live happily ever after. She's pretty good! I'm gonna have to go back to her!"

As the film came to life during that spring in Paris, there was one other person for whom it was magnetic. Paul Bonnecarrère could not stop thinking about it even when his thoughts were painful.

He might have been his own leading man: tall, fortyish, husky-voiced, with a face like the late English actor Jack Hawkins in his prime.

Paul had been a paratrooper in Vietnam and a foreign correspondent in Algiers for the Marcel Dassault magazine, *Jours de France*. For seven years he "had some fun and cost Dassault some money."

Dassault could afford it. He was a hugely wealthy airplane manufacturer and the model for Charles-André Fargeau.

After three nonfiction books, including one about the

French Foreign Legion, *Rosebed* was Bonnecarrère's first international success. He created the plot alone, then friends introduced him to "the little Hemingway girl. She helped a great deal. She did research." Her name would appear on the cover in America.

Paul explained how friendly foreigners often helped French writers with tax problems. One master of thrillers had sold all future royalties to a Swiss corporation in which he owned stock. The corporation collected royalties at a lower tax rate and paid the writer a salary. A Frenchman might have a foreign "co-author"—say an American—who collected U.S. royalties, paid U.S. taxes, kept a service fee, and put the rest in the Frenchman's U.S. account.

As we talked, I could feel something tearing at him. And it wasn't money. He had a heart condition and tried to cut down on his smoking by steadily sipping Coca-Cola. Tensely, he insisted that before anyone called him about a movie it had been "the dream of his life" that Otto Preminger make *Rosebud*. *"J'aime beaucoup les films de Preminger!"*

He would not have written the screenplay—he hated to intrude—"Yet I think of nothing else! I dream of the work at night! I would like *nothing* better than to see the whole film rising. I *love movies*! All my life, every day since I was five, I have gone. Sometimes three a day!"

Walking to the Plaza, Paul shrugged off Preminger's temper. "Next to Dassault, I promise you, Preminger is an angel!"

But upstairs, after polite greetings, Preminger motioned me into the bedroom. Standing six inches away, face to face, the angel exploded in the whole show—the veins, the spittle, the red eyes—telling me I lacked all tact, had no business inviting people up, et cetera, et cetera. Returning to the living room, I was numbed. Soon Bonnecarrère left. And thirty seconds later Preminger's thoughts were elsewhere.

Flying back to Nice, there are fragmentary memories of the last hours in Paris.

It is afternoon at the Left Bank hotel. Wolfgang sits on his bed with bombed-out eyes fiddling with cross-plot strips, knowing he'll have to redo it all anyway.

Outside, steady rain.

The concierge tries booking a flight to Nice.

"Air France is the worst," mutters Wolfgang. "Twenty minutes they play music on the line."

A screening that night is chaos. Film breaking. Sound fading. Actors dashing up with reels. Agents fumbling in the dark.

"Mr. Cottle," asks Preminger, "where are you going?"

"To phone Israel."

"What's your hurry? We'll do it later."

Graham slumps back into his seat. Preminger orders the next film, which goes out of focus.

Wolfgang whispers urgently into the intercom, *"Faites le point!"*

Suddenly a face jumps off the screen: Yves Beneyton, in his mid-twenties, intense, with a scruffy goat's beard. On the phone he demands ransom after a kidnapping, then slams the instrument down. The film breaks. But the whole room knows. This could be Patrice Thibaud—Thibaud as he was in the book, anyway.

At the Plaza, later, they hear of Georges Pompidou's death. Preminger remembers, "He sat in my box at the opening of *The Cardinal*. He was a man without much personality."

That's how everyone feels. Ground down. Unable to see past the film.

In Preminger's suite, he hands out new scripts. When I ask for one, he answers no, I showed one to Anthony Quinn, I'm a traitor. What is he talking about? Who cares?

Wolfgang and Graham slump in the elevator.

"God, it's been the longest day . . ."

"And the phones not working . . ."

"We really must find another hotel . . ."

"We must . . ."

No one can work any harder. The vast material *glut* of the

production has swollen to fill all time and consciousness. Preminger cannot turn now to script problems. But they wait. Oh, yes.

Upstairs, he misses his wife and twins, who are coming from New York. He will surprise them by joining their flight to Nice in Paris.

He calls Erik in Nice. "Don't tell them I'm on the same plane . . . okay, darling, good night. Sleep well."

And so time stretches out.

The days seem interminable as we travel . . . Nice to Paris . . . to Corsica . . . to Paris . . . to Rome to Tel Aviv to Berlin to Paris . . . to Nice. On April 4, Wolfgang and I return to the Westminster. The heavy wooden shutters open to a familiar view — orange slate roofs, TV masts, the mountains in the distance, dusted with puffy clouds.

It feels like home.

SORTING OUT

The Desk Set
In Nice, Preminger and his staff began "sorting out" the deals made on the recces into something beyond notes on paper napkins.

The staff had grown with the addition of Graham's new production secretary, Barbara Allen, a woman of just over thirty, slender, blonde, and plain at first glance—pared down to efficiency by her work. But, like all the Englishwomen on *Rosebud*, she *talked*. Soon her humor showed and her eyes brightened with sly, feline mischief. A brisk secretary who spoke fluent French, she engaged her boss in a continuous, wry sniping, like Preminger and Golda.

"I didn't even like Graham at first on *Triple Echo*. Now I think he's lovely."

As the work piled up, so did the uneasiness.

Barbara hinted, "You should read Huston's new film [*The Man Who Would Be King*]. It's wonderful. I almost worked on it but did this instead."

"A hundred and eighty-five pages of synopsis," was one verdict on "this."

"If you or I went to UA with that script," said one aide, "we'd be thrown out on our ears."

Soon the rumors began. A staff member furtively drew me behind a curtain in the hotel lobby. "I spoke to William Morris in Paris. They've heard from London that it looks very bad for this production. It might collapse."

While the mood darkened, the office filled with a multilingual nerve-racking babble. And Preminger's teasing was turned on me.

I was not working on his movie. I took up a chair. I was the "traitor" who had shown a script to Anthony Quinn and now recorded Everything. In short, I was a sitting duck.

Each time he entered the Westminster, I braced for a going over.

He asked if I was coming to New York with him over Easter.

"It depends—"

"You make conditions?" He told the others, "He used to follow me around like a little dog."

Sitting across from Wolfgang, I handed him a paper. Preminger growled, "You let *him* see papers?"

Finally he told me to get out of his office while he did some "personal business" with the staff.

Later Wolfgang said, "It's a joke. Or he's made a joke of it. They aren't discussing anything at all."

It was obvious I wasn't welcome, so I took a long, angry walk along the seafront, thinking that Eva had been right all along. ("Day by day," she'd said, "it's Papa's Chinese water torture.") And Preminger would go on until I took the hint.

"At least he recognizes you're alive," said Graham. "I don't inspire any reaction at all."

The staff tried to cheer me up as we met at 2:00 A.M. on the shadowy, silent staircase of the Westminster. Complaints swelled in a bleary chorus about directors who sooner or later "lost their magic," were "phonies," and "only as good as the people around them."

It was no one's finest hour, but it helped to share the woes and to see the others struggling too—on a film they barely cared about.

"As if I give a shit," said one.

The next evening, Graham mentioned a friend who had recently worked for Preminger. "I slightly looked down on that person at one time. Now I'm doing the same job."

It was Saturday night in Nice. "Yet here we all are talking about the man!" exclaimed Barbara. "We've got to leave the office by six-thirty every night! And on Sundays be on the beach so he can't reach us when he calls! He probably thinks it's a great giggle that we care so much!"

No. He probably didn't think about it at all.

Monday the work resumed: a mass of calls, contracts, and memos. And I returned, thinking that if Preminger wanted me out, he would have to say so.

The yacht broker phoned, quoting a price for the *Goose*— plus fuel, plus the move to Israel, plus the owner had to meet the stars and be able to buy a print of the film.

"I'll accept!" said Preminger. "We will have the boat, the berth in Juan—take it! I won't fool around!" He would wait no longer for the other boats.

Graham called back hesitantly. "I'd hate to blow the deal in front of you."

"Be very firm. Your voice and all."

They bargained until Graham covered the receiver and asked, "Can we put him up in Israel if he can't stay on the boat?"

That tore it. Preminger seized the phone, telling the broker, "Stop this chiseling! We won't show him Israel! And he's rich enough to pay his hotel! Or you pay it out of your commission!"

For the father of the American hostage (Senator Donovan), Preminger had a brainstorm: John Lindsay. A call was placed to Zermatt.

"John, what is your decision? . . . Skiing? You think only of skiing? . . . You will never get anywhere this way. The best you can do is become mayor of New York or some other small city." The dirctor dropped some names of actors who might play the other fathers.

("What's his wife's name—?"

"Mary—")

"Give Mary my regards!" Hanging up he grinned. "He didn't say no. He's afraid of news stories, he doesn't know what he'll do yet, but . . ." he savored the impact ". . . it would be tremendous."

Again they plunged into the maze of co-production. As a U.S. film, *Rosebud* would recover all the French value-added tax (TVA) it paid. As a co-production with a French company, it would lose the tax but gain a subsidy.

Chalky White was even then tallying all the funds the film would disperse to French citizens so the government could decide if the project actually qualified for "co-production status."

Was it worth all the effort?

I sought the answer from my friend the Film Doctor. An Englishman of prudence, he prefers his anonymity, at least outside the such favorite London cafés of the film crowd as White Elephant and Les A.

We met in a bar near the Plaza. The Doctor had a girl with him from Guy Laroche.

As usual, he looked grandly Falstaffian: a large, ruddy man with long silver hair, dressed in a blazer and a jaunty, checkered ascot. Beside him, Coralie idly stroked her copper bangs.

I broached the topic of the night.

"Ummm. Dodgy . . . "

"We shouldn't bore Coralie."

"She's never bored. They invented mirrors to keep her busy." He patted her sleeve as she scanned the crowd.

"You've been part of some co-productions."

"For the subsidy, naturally. Aohh, Gaowdd!" His Golders Green accent rumbled over the din. "Film's in a bad way all over the world. So governments subsidize production. The money comes from a tax on *all* movie tickets."

Coralie was becoming engrossed in her nail polish.

"If you're British and you make an English national film *and* it plays in England, the government grants you an additional sum (from the Eady Fund) based on your share of what all English films grossed that year. The rish get richer, don't you see? If your picture is a hit, you, as producer, get an extra hundred or hundred and fifty thousand pounds. A nice little packet . . . . You can do as you like with it. Spend it on nail polish."

He smiled for Coralie. "The problem comes when you try and get nationality. What *is* an English film? Or an Italian one? The rules are clear but the facts, well—"

"Elastic?"

"Highly. There was a film shot in Italy. I can't say which one because you'd put it in that notebook and then we'd all be in the soup. I may go back there someday." He stroked Coralie's hand. "I can only say this film had two huge stars— married then—that's all the hint you get. The money for their film was all dollars. But the American producers bloody well wanted the Italian subsidy.

"So they co-produced with an Italian company. Dodgy part came when they had to show that twenty percent of the money for the film was in *lire*. Plus all the services, the cameras—all had to be Italian. Well, it wasn't so! There were bodies around that never showed on the books. And dollars! Aohh, Gaowdd! Dollars kept in boxes. Real lockboxes, stashed in offices at the other end of the studio, way the hell and gone."

"What about the books!"

"The *books*!?" He looked dumbfounded. "The books were *cooked*! Any non-Italian bodies on the film were hidden. Paid out of external accounts. Paid in dollars. The U.S. company had to conceal those people.

"They even paid overtime to the Italian crew in dollars.

129

Handed over the bloody bills behind the set. That made the budget look smaller so the twenty percent in *lire* became smaller. The less money the U.S. company had to pump into the Italian one, the better they liked it."

"And it worked?"

"Aoh, Gaowd! My boy, it was a *fye-nan-chill* achievement! Mind, it wasn't easy. Italian inspectors came round unannounced. The books had to be ready at a moment's notice. And of course the company paid someone in the government to tip them off just before the inspections. The spy would ring up just as the inspector left the office. The U.S. people ran like rabbits—one man took the dollar accounts to one end of the studio. Another took the dollars—the cash—to the other end. Just left a handful of *lire* on the table . . ."

"All that for a little subsidy?"

"Thirteen percent of the gross in Italy! And the picture was a big hit there! Huge payments."

"What about the Italian co-producers?"

"Aoh, Gaowd! *They* were keeping *three* sets of books. One for the tax inspector . . . one for themselves, which they kept altering for their own benefit so no one could understand them! Finally the U.S. producer called in a big American firm and they got it sorted out. That was the third set." He lit a Cuban cigar and puffed deeply.

"Mind, not every co-production is cooked. But once in a while there's a masterpiece. Take a famous English picture, some years ago. Marvelous adventure. I can tell you—in the privacy of this lovely bar—that everyone who's ever bought a cinema ticket has heard of it. They got English nationality, and maybe thirty seconds of the whole two-and-a-half hours of film was shot in England. Ninety-nine percent foreign made. In a desert. Employed thousands of foreigners. Before they finished, they had to make the producer an English resident. But it worked. It was a masterpiece."

"The film?"

"That too."

As Coralie watched a young man at the bar, I rose to go.
"Will you be at Cannes this year?" asked the Doctor.

"Maybe. I'll try."

"Don't know why I bother. It's just a habit." He smiled at
Coralie. "Aoh, Gaowd, I'm too old to change habits now."

During that long April of "sorting out," the truly explosive
dramas came over shipping.

Graham and Barbara collaborated with shipping agent Max
Seeburg on "unalterable lists"—"carnets"—of all the equipment to be taken through foreign countries. The carnets were
then deposited with the English Chamber of Commerce,
which arranged that the gear could pass through foreign customs without the payment of duty or a cash bond. In effect, the
Chamber guaranteed that goods would not be shipped abroad
duty-free and then sold.

The catch was, they could not *change* the lists.

They could only make *all new ones*.

Meanwhile a new schedule was creating interlocking problems. They would start in Corsica but not leave there until
they could use a big ferry—unless that conflicted with later
dates.

If they had to leave early, on a small ferry, they would have
to take smaller vehicles.

And thus they would have to redo all that sacred and unalterable lists.

"Why look at the worst?" asked Preminger. "You must always look for the best!" That day he cheerfully asked—for good
reason—if they might start in Juan-les-Pins and *then* go to Corsica. Graham bit the bullet, swallowed, and said he was 80 percent sure they could.

I knew then. Between Preminger's optimism and Graham's
dour precautions, they were in it together to the end.

"Please, it's Mr. Cottle speaking. . . . Not Cocteau! C-O-T-
T-L-E!"

For Graham, the days were a continuum of jangling phones, cold coffee, gelid pastry, and nagging questions.

What about extras in Corsica?

Electricians in Hamburg?

Hotels in Berlin?

Deposits in Juan?

Vehicles in Paris?

Were seventy francs a week enough for laundry?

Barbara snorted, "It is for me. Just because you're a dirty beast—"

For comic relief, the Corsican Captain submitted the highest expense voucher Graham had ever seen. "Ah, well, into the pile . . ."

The office by now was a clamorous terminal as papers piled up and department heads hustled through.

"God!" exclaimed Graham. "The director is going to New York, my art director is in Paris, the casting director is in Corsica, and the cameraman has a commercial in London and can't leave!"

"Are you going to collapse?" Barbara asked brightly.

"Oh, I do on all my pictures."

Before leaving for New York, to show the budget and script to UA as a courtesy, Preminger gave directions.

"Be firm . . . be strong . . . be strict."

Surely he set an example, pulling together paperwork.

About the actors' contracts, he told Graham, "The girls can co-star. Let the lawyer say 'position at my discretion.' "

And "actors must be available for looping or we have the right to revoice them."

Minor actors would sign and return Margot's "letters of agreement." "Not that I'm scared of losing them," said Preminger. "There are always others."

And so on, through a recital of controls.

He took Wolfgang's latest schedule—"It looks quite reasonable"—and picked up Chalky's budget.

132

"I think we're high," said White later, "but on this film we'll need every penny."

Finally, Preminger gathered up the photos of the four European hostages he had cast. "I need them. The only face I remember is Golda's."

For a moment he stared silently at the glossies: Isabelle Huppert, Lalla Ward, Debbie Berger, and Betty Berman. Then he smiled. "They really *are* pretty.... See you all after Easter!"

He left them numbed by his confidence. Chalky was reminded of *Exodus*; at the start of shooting, Preminger had announced the date the film would premiere.

The accountant lit a little cigar, inhaled deeply, and savored that memory.

"It took balls."

Gone with the Wind

During the next week in Nice they all grow closer, having no choice. As much as tax tables and co-production, this too is the life of the film—this final respite before the juggernaut.

They are in a foreign legion for creative nomads and everyone finds ways of dealing with the loneliness.

Someone suggests the healing power of infidelity. But it's not for Barbara. She won't endanger a solid relationship.

"He'd never know."

"He'd know and *I'd* know. So I'll just have to disappoint that queue of fellows waiting every night on the steps as I come home." She laughs and blushes beautifully.

Everyone finds ways. Lunch on the beach becomes more than a meal as the women of the city sunbathe.

Chalky White sits down to an omelet at an outdoor café, watching a topless beauty on her stomach, exchanging kisses with a boy. When she gets up and dresses, in white stockings and a jumper, she's a schoolgirl of thirteen.

One rainy afternoon, as Wolfgang walks back to the Westminster, a brunette with torrid eyes falls in step with him. He doesn't notice, so she strides ahead and wheels around to face him.

"Don't you know? When a woman smiles at you you're supposed to say something."

Gradually they remember this is a resort hotel.

Easter brings unescorted women: a Dyan Cannon type from South Africa and a big Dutchwoman with heavy, diamond earrings. Mme. Hollandaise is enchanted with Wolfgang. At lunch she smiles like a lusty alligator. At night, moaning through the halls, she knocks on his door. He opens it to see her grinning, one hand working inside her kimono.

One Sunday the staff runs to the beach lest Preminger call—and finds the whole city there already. It's a congress of topless bathers, sprawling families, American teens in backpacks, all crowded on the fringe of pebbly sand. Above, the baroque hotels on the Promenade sparkle in a light so bright it hurts hungover eyes.

Wolfgang and I watch the women, who sometimes watch back. A beauty of twenty, motions to me from not far away. Soon I'm sitting beside her, as she explains with a notebook and pencil what she wants. The first words she writes are "femme" and "homme."

Mostly, however, the crew turns to each other. It's a crash course in friendship, among half a dozen English-speaking castaways.

Graham worries about "making my first costly mistake."

And everyone fears a terrorist raid.

"Oh, God," cries Barbara. "If I'm going to be shot, please not for *this* script!"

On Barbara's birthday, we jam into a tiny Lancia and drive along the Grand Corniche.

"No, it's the Middle Corniche," says Barbara. "Everything about this film is average."

We drive to the African Queen in Villefranche, to eat bouillabaise and drink rosé and watch the street lamps shimmer over the black water of that tiny harbor.

As if comparing battle scars, they trade stories of other films.

Chalky remembers a sadistic production aide on *Lawrence*. "David Lean was wondering what to do, staring at a line of Arabs in the desert, when one of them fainted. The production aide said, 'Don't give him *cold* water. That's for Europeans!' The person was banished to Morocco."

Directors fascinate them, like caricatures evilly distended by their reputations and their father roles.

For Wolfgang, there was the man making a period picture who announced that the horses would never trample the peasants. This man *knew* horses.

"I *still* get letters with medical claims."

David White tells of a director who kept a virtual slave. "Stephen carried the script open to the scene. Stephen took off his boots at night. The man was always yelling, 'Steeeeevyn!' That boy sold his soul to go on location."

The scorn is unmistakable. "They con people into giving them money who think they've still got the magic."

Perhaps in search of magic, I go to a grand cine-palace built for tourists to watch splashy spectacles. As the supply of such films dwindles, the theater caters to nostalgia: there aren't fifty people there to see *Exodus*. For me, it's a private screening. The movie illuminates Preminger so brightly it's like the Easter light—it hurts.

The French print is dirty, jumpy, scratched. Dramatically it's slow going at first, as though characters are coming into a languid first act. Movement is perfunctory. The staging dwells on unbroken dialogue scenes treated like playlets, with the camera only moving to follow the actors.

History is merely background. The State of Israel is pro-

135

claimed before thirty thousand extras (waiting for their raffle at dawn). Preminger doesn't dramatize the cheering throng, he simply *presents* it, shooting down from a balcony. It's enough that they are *there*.

The past isn't shown, only discussed. Thus, Sal Mineo tells how the Nazis used him as a male whore. What we *see* are his feelings as he breaks down.

Preminger's cinema is verbal—even literary—full of motives and psychology, miles from the visual shorthand of TV, with its quick cuts, hooks, and grabbers. His slow pans and wide views tie the characters to a landscape, creating the rhythms of a processional. Each shot moves the story. The *Exodus* sails past its English blockade in one stately frame.

"My father wants everyone to be a character." Finally it happens. Dalton Trumbo's screenplay has made them not quite real, but more than icons. Having gone through so much with them, when Jill Haworth dies or Paul Newman reacts to the death of his Arab friend, we are moved too.

As the lights go up, the tiny audience applauds.

(When I tell Preminger I've seen the film, he snorts. "You have nothing better to do?")

The last night before Preminger's return, Wolfgang drives everyone up the Grand Corniche, through the lilac-scented evening. He is taking us to a legendary restaurant, La Ferme, which David Niven led him to on yet another picture where the menu was better than the script.

As if to forget tomorrow, we chatter and gorge on cold pork loin, tiny, chestnut-flavored sausages, huge steaks, brandied pears, chestnuts in double cream.

Returning to Nice, walking upstairs in the hotel, Barbara stops and listens to the laughter of the others below.

"Crickey, we're so close now. Such a family. And everyone *likes* one another and gets on nicely. And you *know* that six months after this is all over we'll meet in a bar or somewhere and it'll be as if we never knew each other. We're all lost souls on location. We need each other ever so much more. . . . But it ends when the picture ends. You ought to call your book *Gone with the Wind*."

On the Beach

"Gershuny, you missed the whole book!"

Preminger was back with a fresh crisis. The film was due to start in six weeks; they were about to visit Corsica again—*ten people were going*—*and still they had no star*.

Preminger had seen a young actor in a film who could play Martin. For the public, it would be a new face—an interesting mixture of raw-boned vigor and Yale intelligence. But UA wanted a star. The situation was a bit like *Anatomy of a Murder*, when Preminger dropped Lana Turner over a dispute and hired Lee Remick. Columbia Pictures had been furious.

"But stars don't matter. Talent and performances matter!"

Another problem was that the actor was unavailable until June 15. And *Rosebud* was supposed to start two weeks earlier in Corsica.

Preminger could delay there . . . if he could delay using the yacht.

Or he could start in Juan-les-Pins. The actor had only two small scenes there, and they could be shot later, elsewhere. All Preminger had to do was get the yacht a month *early*.

Summarized this way, the choices seem almost rational. But they were sweated for four days. Everything was affected: carnets, ferries, the yacht, the location rentals, even the selling concept for the picture. "Bloody everything."

After leaning toward a Corsican start, Preminger settled on May 29 in Juan-les-Pins. That "final decision" cut to the boiling center of ego in which *Rosebud* lived.

"I prefer to start in Corsica," said Graham. "Instinctively."

"Are your instincts good?"

Barbara answered quickly. "Yes!"

"But we're here," said Otto. "Somehow it's more logical if you're here to *start* here." He grew thoughtful, listening pos-

137

sibly to his own instincts. "Suppose Corisca *is* more difficult. You know the unit better by then. As we get older we all change. Coop gets more subdued. I get wilder! . . . Also, suppose one of the girls is no good. In Juan we have time to change." He laughed. "Everyone will say I've now got a chance for *five* flops in one picture."

He knew the real problems.

They would start in Juan on May 29 — for the young actor.

But movies don't go in straight lines. Next day we heard that the actor was out.

It was a dark, desperate week as agents called to excuse their clients, explaining tactfully how so-and-so was feeling "down" or wanted to stay on his island and "do coke" or was *really* interested in directing.

One agent was brutally frank about a small part. "You could get anyone off the street for fifty pounds to play it. You don't need better with those lines."

Feeling the worst kind of rejection, Preminger was feisty. Now he considered making Martin English. And they were also changing Sloat again. "We're giving him a new motive. He ran four times for the House of Commons and lost. Now he hates democracy."

During these dreary hours, Preminger casually mentioned that he had sent a script to Robert Mitchum. Everyone immediately became enthusiastic.

Among the disillusioned, the cynical, and the fatalistic, Mitchum was a big favorite.

"He has a wonderful, caustic humor," said Graham.

"I'll offer him the part. But he's a friend. I can't get *out* of it." So he called Beverly Hills, remembering how good Mitchum had been in *Angel Face* and *River of No Return*. In the mid-1950s.

"Bob, how are you!?"

He practically had to shout across the Atlantic.

"Did you read my script? What do you think of it? . . . In a

way you're right, I'm afraid. Would you be interested to play
Martin? . . . With whom can I discuss business? . . . Bob, I hope
we'll get together." Click.

Preminger was delighted. "He likes the script very much
except for Sloat. I said would you like to play Martin and he
said, 'Why not?' Such a funny man."

Immediately he called New York with instructions to
phone Mitchum's manager and then UA. "They will have to
put up more money. It's outside the budget. I expect your call in
an hour." Click.

The Mitchum news came just in time to buoy them up for
Corsica. Department heads were flying in for a recce there to
make "final decisions."

"Golda, you look wonderful!" said Otto.

"I am but nobody knows it."

"Ha! How is Farrago?"

"He says he's a liberal. He doesn't know he's anti-Semitic."

He laughed, indulging her completely. "She does look like
the real Golda. *And she takes me seriously sometimes!*"

So did Willy Holt. Before the departure, he hurried to show
Preminger a "modest café" where the Arabs bribe a *Rosebud*
sailor in a men's room. But Otto hated the location. It was too
"elegant"; a seaman would never go in.

Instead he suggested public *pissoirs*, leading the staff from
one foul chamber to another until he came upon a bewildered
worker urinating.

"*This* has character. But I want a place we can *see* something!"

The Frenchman blushed and flushed.

"We must look and look and look? *Allons!*"

In Juan, Preminger finally found the Las Vegas—a sleazoid
café in Formica and neon, jammed with electric rifle games and
featuring a seedy rear lavatory.

The pinball joint was as big a hit as Mitchum, maybe for

some of the same reasons. Graham loved its "irony" and Erik exclaimed, "How I wish I'd thought of it!"

An elated Preminger then led the staff out to the sun-splashed breakwater, to illustrate the taking of the yacht. At night, the treacherous *Rosebud* sailor was to light a cigarette as a signal. An Arab on a light tower would relay the sign, blinking his flashlight to his men on a raft . . . then jumping down to meet them.

But *could* he jump?

"Gershuny, make yourself useful!"

Earlier, Preminger had asked if I could act. I had said yes, and this seemed like the audition.

"Now! Jump!"

It happened without thinking—an act of faith. By sheer luck I landed in one piece.

"You've got a part! I didn't realize you were so athletic!"

Believe me, Otto, neither did I. But the production fever had begun. Truly, I wanted a part.

VISIONS AND REVISIONS

Corsica: Take Three

Fear broke out here; they tried to do Corsica in a day and a half, driving from set to set with sixteen auto doors opening and slamming shut as everyone raced after Preminger in a musical car act.

"I don't understand," said an aide. "He runs around and we're supposed to chase him?"

Amid the running came a growing dread, arising partly from not having the leads: Cliff Gorman was uncertain about doing a TV show, Topol was also doing TV, and UA was "considering" Mitchum.

Worse yet, Preminger was still changing his mind and leaving a trail of revisions. Even now, at the end of April, nothing was quite set.

"If we get Mitchum," he said, "we can start anywhere. Even Corsica!" The mind went limp.

On the recce, his own rules were an added strain.

"No private conversations" meant that people could talk only to Preminger. And no one could stand in his view. When he suddenly turned to study a reverse angle in a cramped attic, we all scattered like panicked cockroaches.

It was embarrassing and funny and maybe also necessary.

In thirty-six hours, Preminger did an astonishing amount of work—checking airports and jet planes, recruiting and dismissing extras, speaking at meetings in perfect "minimum

Berlitz," selecting angles at the farms, deciding to build a stone wall around the Tardets place for added isolation, choosing a cove for a motorboat scene, choosing a site in the desert for Héléne to be freed. But at his pace, the locations became a blur. Even Preminger got confused. "He asked me today if I'd seen Israel," said Denys. "It's always like this around him."

A joke, a joke. The mind staggers upright and walks from the scene of the accident, disclaiming knowledge. The heart is an innocent bystander. I have seen a share of films—both hits and misses—being made. This was not so far from average.

Each department head was absorbed in his own problems. Margot had trouble finding Jews in Corsica who looked Jewish enough to suit Preminger.

"Golda, this man is a Slav! In Vienna, the first people who *hit* Jews looked like this. . . . There are so many Jewish actors. At worst I put *you* in trousers. Or let Gershuny play it!"

Privately she grumbled, "By the end of a film, his unit must not give a damn! You've got to have five or six people in *love* with a film to make it work."

The Jewish question came to a head in the Bastia harbor, where Margot suggested looking in a synagogue.

Preminger slapped his forehead with a laugh. "I give her credit! She tries!"

But then she wanted to advertise for all Jews to *report* there.

"No! Absolutely not!" He was shouting so loud that people crowded onto the ferry decks to look down at the excitement. Preminger roared. "I want people who are naturally—*effortlessly*—Jewish! Like— Like—" He looked around for a revelation, looked from Wolfgang (pure Aryan) to Graham (Celt) to Erik (blue-eyed) to Willy (nearly a Catholic icon) to Farrago (hopeless) to me. And settled. With a shout:

"—*like him!*"

From that moment I was sure enough of a part to start worrying.

Willy Holt had trouble keeping up with the changes. When Preminger no longer wanted the Tardetses' bedroom cleaned up, Willy was astonished.

"But Mr. Preminger, last time you say—"

"If I said it, I take it back. Now they don't get money as in the book. They are prisoners. They are hopeless."

More changes revolved around the flight simulator. In the book, the girls were freed in Corsica but were convinced they had been *flown* there after being drugged, blindfolded, and shaken up for hours in that simulator. Later, Martin realized the trick because the hostages' ears hadn't popped as they would have in a light plane.

Standing in the shed where the simulator was to have been placed, Preminger again changed his mind. Instead of a "home-made" mock-up, he wanted the actual Singer simulator.

And he wanted it outside, in the light, where it could be seen and the hostages would *feel* the air through their hoods. All the art department had to do was clear out a hundred chickens from the yard. It was like moving two thousand chocolate nougats in Berlin.

At the airport Willy expressed doubt that there *was* a simulator in Paris.

"So call New York! If you see the real machine, you believe it. Unless we make this very real in every detail it becomes *lousy*! They will say, 'Oh my God, this girl is *stupid*!' This is a question where we should not worry about spending money and get the best there is!"

Is Paris Burning?

The hunt continued at the airport in Paris, where Willy showed him a simulator that didn't move and wasn't a Singer.

"Look, when I say I want to see something, I want to see it! This is *lousy*!"

Willy answered in rapid French, and Graham stepped in.

"He thought the Singer was too high for the barn. He—ah—didn't realize you'd do it outside."

"He was *there* when we decided! He doesn't understand when I speak, and vice versa."

From his Paris hotel, Graham grimly phoned Barbara in Nice.

"We're trying to find flight simulators. . . . He lost his temper. . . . Disastrous morning, I'm afraid."

The hotel filled with French aides, including Raoul Baum, an assistant director who had served Truffaut and Buñuel and looked like a rabbi waking from a blissful sex dream.

"Raoul," asked Graham, "what do you know about simulators?"

Raoul smiled, waiting for the punch line.

There was a brief truce in the "Nikolaos flat"—which was really director Anatole Litvak's elegant, duplex penthouse.

He and Preminger were old friends and now met like doges, with the crew at a respectful distance. Small, white-haired, and immaculate, "Tola" gossiped with Otto and showed the view of the Eiffel Tower from his airy terrace. The boxes of spring flowers on his railings echoed the Dufys in his living room.

Tola had also employed Willy Holt on his last film.

"Otto, I tell you Willy is the best man in the world."

As they parted, the directors bent forward and touched cheeks.

Then the hostilities resumed.

Still seeking a simulator, Willy led them to an "industrial park" outside Paris. A sign announced AVIONS DASSAULT/BRE-GUET AVIATION. Fargeau country.

Inside a modern, windowless building, they came abruptly into a spectacular space at least five stories high, with scaffolding around the walls to accommodate viewers. Under bright, white lamps, at once theatrical and functional, a black training cabin—the whole cabin—was poised on huge, hydraulic jacks.

Danger signs flashed and the structure started to move, as a powerful throbbing traveled through the jacks, through the concrete floor, and through our spines. The whole cockpit, modeled like an immense, black bullethead, shifted from side to side as if buffeted by winds. Inside, someone said, there was even front projection.

For a few seconds, Preminger imagined this in his film. Then he shook his head. "No. It *really* is too much."

By now he had to reach an understanding with his art department or get a new one.

He spoke calmly to Willy and his assistant. "About the simulator . . . I must explain. So you know I'm not just stubborn."

They gave him their complete attention.

"The whole story depends on the audience believing the girl thinks she is flying. . . . It must be so: that I sit in a theater and think, goddammit, I would be convinced *I* was flying. . . . Now let's forget the past. A misunderstanding. If I misled you, I apologize. *You* should have lectured to *me*. Now go to work a little harder!"

It didn't help. In a suburb, Preminger and Graham negotiated for a police station, which the French staff thought he would never get. After all, public policy was against such usage.

But Preminger's French publicity wizard, Georges Cravenne, had set up the meeting—as he had found Martin's apartment—and had tipped off William Morris at the birth of the project. If *Rosebud* had a gray eminence, it was this balding, carefully tailored, middle-aged man who looked down an aquiline nose with sad, shrewd eyes as if nothing could surprise him. He knew some history, some personal tragedy—and he knew how to play the telephone even in France so as to wring music from its black heart.

145

The French production staff moped about outside the station until Preminger emerged, victorious.

"You offer them money for a charity or widows—and you'll get it!" He gestured to the Frenchmen, in baggy trousers and rumpled jackets. "I don't understand your attitude!"

In the car he asked Denys, "How many suits did you bring?"

Coop laughed. "You're right, Otto."

"People must fit into the environment. I don't give a shit. But the people we need—they don't want to see dirty hippies!"

Returning from that single, small victory in the suburbs, Preminger learned that Cliff Gorman was "out" and Isabelle Huppert nearly so. It was as if his film was hemorrhaging.

Isabelle sat in the Plaza looking heavier and worrying about her option contract.

"Miss Huppert," said Otto, "my advice is to marry a rich man. . . . It should be clear I *can't* exercise the option if you're already working on another film."

He fretted later. "I don't like a girl her age so concerned with money."

"Monsieur," Margot cautioned, "Huppert gave up a picture for this."

"At the worst I'll pay her off. I visualized her like a ball . . . like the new lamps in my villa."

Finally he realized he had enough troubles and hired her anyway. "But tell her to lose weight!" He even admitted her point about the contract and told his French lawyer to alter it.

May 1. The start date was four weeks away and he still had to find two stars, cast a German city, scout some key locations, and supervise a major rewrite by a new writer, already hired and now working back in Nice.

As he packed for a flight to Hamburg, he told Margot to relax and order a drink.

"In time of crisis I have one philosophy. It can only get better."

On the plane, I recalled the times it had been better, the moments when it seemed there was some life in the film, when it looked as if this juggernaut of revisions might somehow *work*.

It happened once in a Corsican attic, amid balls of dust and bars of sun, as Preminger acted a Jewish commando. He entered from a far door, creating a silence with his own concentration. He "saw" the Arab bunks, where the men lay unconscious from "sleeping gas."

Or were they faking sleep?

The commando was bald, nearing seventy, with a sports jacket and a Gucci belt—ludicrous yet real through the force of his imagination, an old man transformed into a twenty-five-year-old paratrooper, moving toward a fancied bed. The staff felt his adrenaline as he handcuffed one imaginary Arab . . . came closer to camera . . . cuffed another. Still the Arabs slept. He pushed a door open . . . peered into another room . . . stole out . . . leaving his audience suspended, silent.

Another morning, the caravan stopped in the Desert des Agriates. On that blasted moonscape the air was so clean it scoured the lungs. The sun over the water was a pearl disc in a gauzy, gray sky.

Denys said, "Even hazy like this it's a terrific background." It would be "marvelous" to shoot at dawn.

"You want to make problems?" asked Preminger.

"No . . . but it would look fantastic. Fantastic."

As Hélène woke up and walked to the road, the camera would crane up to reveal the surrounding desolation.

"Golly," said Erik later, "there are some good sequences in this film. . . . I wish I liked the whole script as much as this part."

Driving away, I thought how much they wanted to believe. How quickly belief faded. How everything was subject to revision.

Closing Time

The recce in Hamburg was organized as if to prove again every weary national stereotype. The scenes there may have read like a wild goose chase. But this goose chase was going to be efficient.

Arriving in Hamburg, everyone was handed a schedule (see pages 150–51.

The German staff, chosen by Wolfgang from Studio Hamburg personnel, was clearly dedicated to efficiency. As Preminger stepped into a slight drizzle, an umbrella was automatically lifted over him. As he asked about an elevator, location manager Rudolph Hertzog whipped out pictures of *six*.

And everyone got a note from Studio Hamburg:

"Welcome in Hamburg! [We] hope that you feel in good hands with us."

In good hands. . . .

Hitchcock had said that directors must use what is characteristic of a location, what everyone knows of it. In Switzerland that would be Alps and chocolates.

What then was known of Hamburg?

It was the major city of northern Germany: six square miles of docks leading to the Nordsee; population almost 2 million; the new tunnel under the Elbe, a marvel of engineering; St. Michael's with the great spire and the world-famous organ.

Hamburg was Studio Hamburg, a complete production facility. It was beer everywhere in the city, a belch of sour air from every tavern as its doors swung open. It was business, buttoned faces, immaculate streets, and sex corraled in the Reeperbahn—the inevitable, true, magnetic north for every punk teen-ager, for sailors off the docks, and for busloads of tourists come to ogle the live shows. And Hamburg was the sex clubs, Madame Pompadour's and the Amphora, 50 marks for membership, more for champagne and the Thai girls naked on the customers' laps—but no charge at all if one performed on stage, where it was always amateur night and a pensioner shuffled up for his once-a-month slow-motion debauch, while blond bouncers patrolled the exits.

Hamburg was the brothels of Saint Pauli with dark pavilions at street level, partitioned into a maze, girls leaning in the shadows, men cruising, peeping, stalling with shaky smoke. It was 25 marks for a half-hour in a clean room with a clean girl, all checked, state certified, vomit on the sidewalks but never, never any sex without a prophylactic.

Hamburg turned desire into real-estate speculation, while one wondered at the soul of a nation that could create "Eros Centers."

Of course none of this was in the script. The city simply replaced Frankfurt, which Preminger felt was less interesting, as a background for the first half of the German chase. Martin would watch an art studio until Sloat's unsuspecting courier left it, then follow him to the airport, on his way to Berlin. At best Hamburg would provide incidental graces, like a museum full of primitive art, from which the agents would conduct their electronic surveillance of the studio across the street. The rude totems would contrast with the TV gear—as the rough Tardets farm might contrast with a sleek flight simulator—to give the film a hint of style and design.

Again, on a bridge, the courier could leave a taxi going one way, dash downstairs (as part of his normal evasion), and drive off the opposite way. The camera would show the docks of Hamburg as background, for the movie's one wide glimpse of the city. Hello, Elbe, and *auf Wiedersehen.*

While Preminger studied the autobahns in a lead car, trying to beef up the courier scenes, Graham leaned back in another car and let it all roll by—his boss, his worries, his feelings—all of it.

"There are eighty pages of new script. Snap, crackle, and pop."

They stopped. Preminger gave orders. They drove on.

SOON TO BE A MAJOR MOTION PICTURE

"R O S E B U D"

An Otto Preminger Film

Reconnaisance trip   Hamburg and Berlin 1. - 3. of May 1974

Hotel in Hamburg: Hotel in Berlin:
Loews Hamburg Plaza   Hotel Kempenski
2000 Hamburg 36   Berlin 15
Marseiller Strasse 2   Kurfürstendamm 27
Telefon Nr. 040/35 10 35   Telefon Nr. 030/88 10 91

Location: HAMBURG AIRPORT (DAY)
                 INT. Lobby and Message Board (Sc. 108)
                 INT. Locker Area and Mens Room (Sc. 109)
                 EXT. Airport and Parking Area (Sc. 110)
                 EXT./INT. Van (Sc. 111)
                 (EXT./INT. Airport (Sc. 113, 134)
                 (EXT./INT. Martin's Car

Location: PARK AT BISMARCK MONUMENT (DAY)
                 Adress Länder Allee / Ost West Strasse
                 EXT. Streets and Park.
                 EXT./INT. Car (DAY)
                 Sc. Nrs. 120 part, 121, 122, 123, 124, 125, 126

Possibilities: STADTPARK AT PLANETARIUM
                 Hindenburg Street / Saarland Street

Location: SIERICHSTRASSE 20 (DAY)
                 INT. Schifflerstr. (Sc. 113)

Possibilities: Schäferkampsallee 30
                 Schlüterstrasse 63
                 Mittelweg 151
                 Rothenbaumchaussee 91
                 Beim Andreasbrunnen 8
                 Haynstrasse 1

150

- 2 -

Location: AUTOBAHN NORDERSTEDT - FUHLSBÜTTEL (DAY)
             EXT. Entrance Road to Autobahn
             Access Road to Airport
             INT./EXT. Car (DAY)
             Sc.Nrs. 127, 129, 130, 131, 132

Location: MUSEUM FÜR VÖLKERKUNDE, Hamburg 13 (DAY)
             Rothenbaumchaussee 64
             House Opposite, Rothenbaumchaussee
             EXT./ DAY,/ Sc. Nrs. 112, 114, 117, 120
             EXT./INT./ DAY./ Entrance Museum (Sc. 115)
             INT./ Day./ Museum (Sc.Nrs. 116, 118)

Possibilities: DAG Haus
                Karl Muck Platz
                DEUTSCHES SCHAUSPIELHAUS
                Kirchenallee 30 - 41

At 5 P.M. there will be at our disposal a screening room at
Studio Hamburg. We will be able to view light tests and a
Pilot-training-film in which one can see two flight simulators.
(Unfortunately at this time we only were able to get hold of
a work print and one mix tape.)

The location list for Berlin will follow.

[signature]

Hamburg, May 1st 1974

151

And Graham recalled how Otto hated their current hotel. *"Every time he sees me he talks about it."*

For an hour they stopped and started.

"He came down this morning saying 'I waited fifteen minutes for an elevator.'"

In the end, none of it mattered. They found a new hotel. And there was no autobahn scene. When the production finally reached Hamburg, there was no time for it and probably no need.

And nothing moved in a straight line.

During this restless shuttling, Preminger also met the actor Helmut Griem, who might play the German agent Schloss. Griem's dedication was a sudden reminder of what all the preparation was *for*.

Physically, he was somewhat like a young Oskar Werner. Blond, fine-boned, and obviously intelligent, he spoke swift, perfect English with only the slightest foreign overtone—a flavor of cultivation.

Griem cared about his work and about his meeting with a director who was flesh and blood with movies. He explained his own recent film career: after playing the German lover in *Cabaret* he had been set for *Good Morning Midnight* until it fell through, and then lost the lead in *The Odessa File*.

"I was okay with the director and producer, but Columbia worried about an all-German cast sounding like a dubbed movie. So they got Jon Voight. . . . I hurt and left my friends in the theater, giving up parts for nothing." His voice took on a passionate lucidity. "I love the theater in Berlin. But when I'm there I feel the sadness of the city . . . it's like a city amputated."

That night Griem read *Rosebud*. Next morning he sent a note declining on "political grounds."

And the caravan rolled on . . . to a dead end in Berlin, at the Wall, where the courier would slip into the East and the agents would be unable to follow.

The staff toured the checkpoints in a rackety minibus, studying movies, history, and their yawning disconnections. Preminger rejected sites that were too modern: "These I'll use when I shoot an *East* German film!"

As they rode into twilight, a bearded, poster-face glared down at them. Preminger asked who it was. "Castro?"

"Ché."

"Who?"

A chorus sounded. "Ché! Ché Guevara!"

Ah.

At sunset they found what he wanted.

A canal with willows hanging over it led to an intersection where the Wall stood, blocking the elevated tracks and streetcar rails. Beyond, in the East, a deserted train station was boarded up, its towers chipped by shell blasts.

Desolation built up in woeful detail: random signs about leaving the American sector, a closed kiosk, feeble light filtering under the elevated three tubs of memorial flowers.

It was too real; one could not disconnect here. Unlike the other sites, this place *annexed* history to support the film or mock it.

Next morning Preminger quickly chose a mailbox and a bus stop near his favorite candy-photo store, to avoid extra moving by the troupe.

And that was it. The recces were done. Like the figures in the chase, they could go no further.

As on all the tours, they finished early and waited restlessly in Preminger's suite. He went to call Erik while the others made halfhearted small talk, picking over the same worries, knowing how little they had to say to each other.

Only the newest worker, Rudolph Hertzog, claimed that he really wanted to do the film. He explained quietly, "It will be like going to the museum . . . before the doors close on this whole world."

THE STAGING AREA

Just as the elegiac mode threatened to take over, the plans somehow all came together in Nice, with three weeks left until the start of production.

First, Preminger got his actors, with the help of forces beyond his control.

Cliff Gorman, having waited vainly for several projects, including the film of his Broadway hit, *Lenny*, now agreed to play Hamlekh. Erik expressed the general delight.

"He is really a . . . *superb* actor."

With Mitchum the problem was more complicated. If Preminger wanted a star, he needed more money from UA. Of course, for one of the Golden Dozen—McQueen, Redford, Nicholson, et cetera—the studios would cheerfully pay a one-to-three-million-dollar salary, huge percentages, lavish expenses, and so forth. But the top stars were not easily available.

That left names like Mitchum, who might get one-to-three-quarters of a million, several thousand a week in expenses, and, usually, a small share of the producer's profits after the distribution company had recovered two or three times the cost of the film. Such actors generally didn't command a large audience on their own. "Let me put it this way," said Erik. "If you come with a script and Mitchum, it'll be read with more care than if you come with a script and McQueen. Then your picture is *made*."

Preminger had three tasks: to persuade UA to pay extra for Mitchum, to persuade Mitchum to accept his offer, and to persuade himself that he wanted Mitchum.

"You see, everybody has an opinion," said OP. The new writer felt the actor was too old. But for Otto, "Fifty-five looks young. . . . With the girl falling in love with him, his age is *good*. He thinks it's silly, but she practically rapes him."

He was already persuaded. Next was UA.

"Remember this when you do a picture. It's easier to ask for money at the start."

All filmmakers reread that quote. One can make a movie without knowing what an actor's "objective" is or the tricks of the zoom lens. But one must grasp the price of "end money." Often it is loss of profits, loss of control, loss of the film.

Preminger understood this perfectly when he called UA in New York. "Tom, how are you? . . . Yes, I can hear you very well. . . . Don't talk about Gorman. It'll come out Wednesday in the trades."

There was a preliminary diversion: "For the lead, what would you think of Sidney Poitier? . . . Like most Jews you're a racist. . . . Oh, I'm only kidding! You really think I would ask you otherwise?"

Circling in, he told them he wanted to keep control of Mitchum's billing. "I'll tell his agent that I can put his name under or over the title. Leave it to me. But it will be in first position."

Then the heavy blows were struck. They spoke of money. "I have to travel. . . . I have lots of actors. . . . How can I help you? I'm not sitting here lazy. . . . Look, you have to give me—" He named an additional amount. "Are you so poor you want me to finance UA? . . . I bring pictures in on budget. I don't come crying to you later for money. I have to be realistic now."

And so he was: realistic, calm, direct.

"I make you one more concession. . . . " He rounded down

the amount he was asking for so that a bit more of Mitchum's price would come from the current budget.

"Or let me take a young actor. Not a star. *You're* the one who wants a star. . . . You're silent. Call me back if you want to think. You're costing me money. . . . Tom, there are no miracles. You're talking to a partner, not an enemy."

It was done beautifully. Preminger even smiled.

"Amazing, this business. Saturday they didn't want Mitchum and now they're trying to talk *me* into taking him."

Meanwhile he cabled Cliff Gorman, who had called with worries:

UNLIKE A STAGE PLAY, A FILM SCRIPT IS ONLY THE RAW MATERIAL FOR THE DIRECTOR AND ACTORS. CONFIDENT WE CAN WORK IT OUT SPLENDIDLY.

In a few minutes UA called back, asking Preminger to come down again by the same amount as before. Again he was calm and direct. "This is a big picture and we have seventeen locations. More money I don't have. You shouldn't ask me. It's really not fair."

There was a little pause. Then: "Fine! Write me a note and I'll call tonight. I don't want to miss him. . . . I'll tell him *I* decide on billing and it's nothing to do with you." Hanging up he beamed. "UA accepted. Now I must get Mitchum."

That proved the easiest. He told the actor's agent, "Say you leave it to me whether his name is above or below the title. . . . What problem? . . . I have more experience with UA. . . . You don't deal with UA. You deal with Sigma Productions. If there's trouble, it's my trouble not yours. We start in France. He will have a lot of fun."

Thus Preminger had a star on his own terms.

He even confirmed his start date in Juan-les-Pins. It was May 29, though others argued for starting earlier. They worried about finishing in time to catch a big ferry to Corsica. But

Preminger was worried about getting done too *soon*. "You'll sit and have nothing to do!" he told Graham. "We start on the twenty-ninth! And what if I go over? You won't throw me in the ocean. Having new girls and a group half French and half English and half Chinese you must *allow*!"

All the elements were coming together but the most important one.

"It's out of date, the girls are lacking . . . there's no action . . . too much unbelievable dialogue . . . and no reason for them being on the yacht. Not alone, not without dozens of boys. . . . I can't believe it."

That was no critic. That was the insurance broker on the film.

Preminger, meanwhile, worked privately on revisions with Erik—and the new writer, Marjorie Kellogg, hurriedly summoned from America. She was the author of both the original novel and the screenplay of Preminger's 1970 film, *Tell Me That You Love Me, Junie Moon*. Now we hardly saw her, but her boss seemed pleased.

"Marjorie wrote some good things," he said. In one scene, the German girl flew in with her father on the family jet and persuaded him to let her land the plane. "It shows how they spoil the girls. It's a nice scene." Nice enough to order the plane.

In the Westminster, Erik was smiling as usual.

"I'm so close to it now, all the lines look alike. One's as good as another. All I really know is that in three weeks all those people and all that equipment will be here and working. I'm getting more and more like Otto. I remember it's only a movie." He flung out his arms and shrugged. "So why should I worry? It's not worth getting panic stricken about! Otto works wonderfully in panic. I, on the other hand, react by flinging papers in all directions and going blank! Look, I've got to go. I'll see you."

During this time, Marjorie would appear briefly in the production office—a solid woman who quietly handed Preminger her pages and left. Her four-week deal was nearly over. Preminger was already calling agents about other writers.

"For a dialogue-polish job . . . just dialogue."

I finally lunched with Marjorie at a beach café two minutes from the hotel and her typewriter.

"I've never worked so hard in my life. Otto knows I'm fast, and that's what he needs now. Those girls will arrive and he has to shoot soon. There isn't time to sit and wait for the muse."

She was strong and middle-aged, with her large head framed in short, dark, gray-flecked hair. The whole formidable image suggested, somehow, a woman who had come through pain and remembered it.

"You made a long trip here . . ."

Her voice was almost a whisper. "I'd come anywhere he asked. He's a wonderful man. If you want to learn, he'll let you watch everything. The only thing he can't stand is incompetence. That's when he shouts."

Since *Junie Moon*, she had written, among other things, a screenplay based on a novel of her own, which she hoped to direct. "I could have sold it five times to television, but I'm going to wait. You can do that when you're not hungry."

Over lunch, Marjorie sipped wine and stared across the beach. "I saw *Junie Moon* again before I came here. All the same things were wrong with it—but I still thought it was awfully good. It really wasn't distributed right. Movies get hurt so many ways. And I worked on that screenplay a year! I lasted the whole project with him, beginning to end. I'm proud of it . . . and the film was such an experience! He has incredible energy, like all creative people."

A French waiter passed in tight blue pants. "How do Frenchmen make their asses so small?"

"It's the pants."

"Are they all so small?"

I had to laugh, and Marjorie smiled into the sun. "It's nice to get out. I've been working on those five girls. In the old script they arrived in one wave. Five people you didn't know. I broke it up and had them come successively. It takes longer, but they have faces now. There's someone to care about. And he seems pleased. . . . It's easier to work with him if you remember he's the boss. The wonderful thing is that he *knows*. He says, 'Marjoreee, that scene vill not vork.' Just like that. And he's *right*. If you really want him to, he'll explain why. And you can't just tell him you like a scene because it feels right. That's when he blows."

I had one troubling question, and Marjorie herself moved toward it. She most wanted to tell the story of what happened to the girls in captivity. "But it's a long film already. . . . " She didn't have the room.

So I asked her, after so much work on the hostages, would they become like Mrs. Tardets's children or Martin's Black September contacts: a trail leading nowhere?

"Well I did a scene in the caves that showed a little society being formed. But I have to go back to teaching. . . . " She was sure Preminger would keep working on the girls.

I wondered what more could be done, and my doubt must have showed.

Abruptly she asked, "What do *you* do in films?"

I told her about having directed three.

"That's what I want to talk about! You could help me. What was your biggest problem?"

I had answered that before, with no swelling pride. "I compromised a lot. It was either do something half-right or don't work. So I did 'something.' "

She stared as if expecting more. But there wasn't any more, just the small talk of good-byes.

In the Westminster doorway I kissed her on both cheeks and said I would call her in New York. After the film.

By now one was accustomed to good-byes and to the refrain that would haunt the picture. Preminger was boss. The others did what they could. And it was that time when one realizes that for a while there has been no time.

"Golda, I'm talking about money. . . . Money. *L'argent!* . . . You have an especially difficult telephone."

By now all the calling, traveling, and endless *disquisition* had produced results—or at least distractions.

They had John Lindsay. They had the Chambre de Commerce—at below its asking price. "What do you expect?" said Preminger. "It's the Chamber of Commerce."

They had "Lady Carter": Adrienne Corri had been in *Bunny Lake*. "Cottle, shall I take her without seeing her?"

"I don't think you'll be disappointed."

They even had help on the way—aides from New York.

But they almost lost Isabelle Huppert over the options again. OP was ready to drop her. "Suppose a girl has a big hit? Why shouldn't I profit from it? Faye Dunaway paid me a fortune to get out of hers. And Seberg was upset because I didn't pick *up* hers. . . . Cottle, why so depressed? Everything is going *well*. We have our two leading actors!"

They had Isabelle too, later. With options.

They also had competition. A major director wouldn't let go of a crewperson who was still needed for two or three weeks of shooting on the director's latest masterpiece.

Cables flew back and forth.

"Dear X——," Preminger dictated, "I spoke to the crewman this morning. You're obviously not informed by your production office that they told him . . . your film would be finished by now."

X—— answered that if a worker left before the end of a job it was a "weakness of character."

Preminger rejoined that "it's no weakness of character to want to work." He nevertheless offered to release the man from his signed letter of intent if the man *himself* asked.

160

X—— said the man never would. But would Preminger please refuse to take him?

No, Preminger would not go back on *his* word.

And so, when *Rosebud* began, the crewman was working on it. And when it ended, X——'s masterpiece was *still* shooting.

They were even close to a simulator. The art department could still build a rude platform or the film could rent a GAT (General Aviation Trainer), which looked like a small plane.

Graham preferred seeing Holt's homemade machinery.

Not Otto. "I won't risk something *built*. . . . And the GAT looks like a plane. Why are you against it?"

"I think you'll make more of it with Holt and the technicians."

"I don't want a *set*. I want a GAT!"

The question simmered into the night, with the mimeo cranking away in the bathroom and Barbara typing new crew lists.

"Cottle, you're a businessman. Look at me. These people sold two hundred and fifty GAT's all over the world. . . . *You're* in love with the unknown. But the GAT I've *seen*. I know the movements are right."

"Here's the info on prices."

"*That's* what I want." He studied the numbers. "It's quite clear if you said you were a World War II pilot who wanted to open a flying school for retarded children, you would have gotten it for a tenth the price. But we're in cinema. And that comes higher."

It was clear there was no more time when the crew started appearing—and, disappearing.

Pierre Flambeau, a special-effects man, was to arrange the sleeping gas, pumped by Israeli commandos into the Arab farm through the plumbing. He had bought a distillery's worth of pipes for a demonstration behind the hotel, in a dirty, gloomy parking lot. Now everyone gathered to watch the pot-bellied man, who worked with a cigarette clamped in his mouth. They were nervously aware of the delay as he sweated over a pipe.

"You must take some liberties," offered Preminger. "Make it go faster."

Pierre suggested Preminger could cut.

"We could also have a big sign—'Come to the next performance.' It has to be faster. Discuss it with your wife and children."

As Pierre wrapped a freezer unit around the pipe, Preminger's patience ran out. "This is not effective!"

More drilling. Sparks.

"No good! I don't accept this! It'll be a week in rehearsal!"

He stalked out of the parking lot, with Cottle at his side, angry at the waste of time, his hand chopping the air. "Not professional . . . I want a first-rate special-effects man . . ."

In the office he looked balefully at me. "And if the actor who has to play the part is so clumsy on *his* first rehearsal, he'll have to go back to his room and write his book." He sighed. "I'll never forget Gershuny, this sad, dreamy-eyed figure in black writing in his notebook. . . . Now, Cottle, go pay off this man. Everyone thinks I'm hard . . . but I won't be forced to cut where I don't want. You have an excuse. Say I'm crazy and don't know what I'm doing. I love it when people say bad things about me."

Graham rose, looking troubled.

Preminger remarked, "Whoever said English people are cold doesn't know anything. Cottle is one of the sweetest men I know."

"Holt," said Graham, "thinks he himself is responsible."

"It's not his fault and it's not mine." Later Preminger told Willy, "Pierre isn't the right man. That's my opinion. This business is a question of opinion. . . . I might be wrong, but I must do it my way. . . . If a picture is a hit, I take the credit. If it's a flop, I take the blame. And we should buy champagne and celebrate because the problem happened today and not in shooting. . . . Now go and smile!"

At this stage, when Preminger wanted something, he spent whatever was needed. Already the crew was scattered over Europe like confetti. One heard of a flight simulator being packed in Lansing, the art department building a wall in Corsica, Annalise Nascalli-Rocca combing the boutiques of Nice for clothes, Yoram Ben Ami in Israel coaxing the army, five actresses getting on planes, and second assistant Raoul Baum hauling furniture to the new office in Juan, sweating with a smile over "my first work for Mr. Preminger."

And now they sought "a first-rate special-effects person." The Englishman, Cliff Richardson, had worked on *Exodus*.

"Isn't it funny? I can *see* him in front of me. . . . Cliff!" Preminger shouted into the phone. "Do you remember me?"

Cliff Richardson and his son John would fly in from London immediately.

Exodus

Suddenly they were all moving to Juan-les-Pins. Files were packed. A "movement order" was circulated, showing the way to uncertainty. Preminger himself was glad to go. He opened a washroom door in the production suite and groaned. "In my office in New York I have a bar. Here we have a toilet with a mimeograph."

The company straggled into the Westminster for a last drink.

"So they change the script. . . . There were *five* scripts on *The Last of Sheila*."

"If you could do *Charge of the Light Brigade*, you can do anything."

"That wasn't the worst."

"There's always a worse . . ."

"One move down, nine to go . . ."

On the rattling bus to Juan, seeing the heat haze over the water, I thought the film had touched so many lives that it had finally tapped the larger confusion—the dizzy uncertainty—of all movie life.

It showed in Graham's wife, Anna, who had come to Cannes hoping to revive *Good Morning Midnight*. A poised, civilized woman in her early thirties, she had worked ten years for director Tony Richardson. Through the continuing dramas, Anna was the grown-up who held things together and now had to do even more on her own project.

An artistically ambitious version of a Judd Bernard movie, it would rise—if at all—from a heap of rights sales and the bitter memory of the major backer who had dropped out when he heard the budget had risen a bit.

Said Graham grimly, "Anna and I'll open a tea shoppe in Saint Ives rather than go through that again."

Now a new backer was involved. "He's risking a lot," said Anna, "and he's asking a lot." Indeed, Graham and Anna would be lucky to make back their development costs and a modest fee.

"Why am I sort of bust, do you think?" wondered Graham. "Maybe I should be tougher."

Uncertainty tainted that May.

Leaving Nice, I wrote to my wife, "Days go by. Your silence is complete. The concierge shrugs. *Pas de poste.*"

One of her last letters answered: "I plod on as always. . . . I'm getting frantic to do a play . . . but I can't get one. . . . Very sad. I paint a lot."

I wrote to her about the confusion of the film.

She replied, "I have managed to go through life and remain a virgin. It was a hard struggle and you certainly helped. . . . Funny, I never thought I was fighting for sterility. . . . But I fought hard and that's what I'm going to get. I now find it kind of interesting to be alone."

Then nothing.

JUAN-LES-PINS

The Girl Can't Help It
And then we arrived. And scrambled. The center of activity was the Astoria, a modest, white, five-story efficiency shelter for tourists. In the coffee shop and the tiny lobby, everyone saw and knew everything that happened. Up in the motel-moderne rooms one heard, through the walls, *more* of everything: nightlong traffic, liaisons, fights, tears.

It was the same in the cramped production office, off the parking lot. Every surface there reflected noise like an animal howl.

Preminger and his close aides stayed at the Helios around the block. It was more luxe, but it too opened onto a street of mopeds and sports cars whizzing off for heavy fun.

Partly in self-defense, I found a deserted hotel with a large, white room overlooking a garden. Off the lobby, a reading area with scuffed sofas was like a memory of Nice during February rain.

Three blocks from the troupe were the beaches. Twenty minutes away, on foot, was Port Gallice, home of the yacht. You could know the whole town in that walk: a lazy, sunny, toy town of green parks, gardens, white façades, and fluted, deco street lamps. For dinner there was the Juana, a hotel dining room on a terrace, above a moonlit garden, or a tiny Vietnamese restaurant with clear, fragrant bowls of angel-hair soup. At dawn were solitary walks along the water, stopping for coffee and pinball at the Las Vegas, then going on to work or to sleep.

"Shall I be honest with you, Mr. Richardson?" asked Graham. "The farm hasn't even *got* running water."

It hardly mattered who was speaking as the voices became the One Voice. "Find out if he wants the guns in Juan we need towels for the boat the sunbathing transistor radio sun cream a makeup case—"

Amid this cacophony the actresses arrived, some as if to a vacation, others to a torture session.

Kim Cattrall, fresh from acting school, seventeen years old, discovered by Preminger's staff in New York and approved by him there to play the American hostage looked numb with nerves.

Isabelle Huppert came a day late because of a Paris college exam. Graham muttered, "There's always something with her."

Betty Berman brought a new, less ethnic name: Betty Alison.

Debbie Berger was guarded by Crystal.

And only Lalla Ward seemed ready to work. "I'm good or I wouldn't be here. But there are hundreds of girls as good. I'm just lucky."

The first night, Raoul drove the women into Cannes for a look at the film festival crowds.

"To be an assistant director, it's not a career. So I will direct. I *must* direct! . . . Look, an angel!"

Swerve.

"There are a lot of names on the screen, but you always know it is Preminger's film."

Stall. Start again.

"I hate to drive. Last year I was almost killed. For Bresson."

In Cannes, Betty Berman-Alison led the rush to "friends" ("He's head of *worldwide* production!"), while Lalla sat in the Blue Bar, letting things come to her. "If anyone asked me, I should be very pleased to say I'm here having an *orange pressé* and doing a film for Otto Preminger."

It was amazing. Normally the troupe would have studied these women for some glimpse of the future, with that hungry curiosity which haunts all films.

But instead they watched Crystal.

Tall, sinuous, jangly with jewelry and pseudo-knowledge (astrology and vibrations), she was everywhere, insinuating herself, insulated by sublime vulgarity.

"How *are* you, Mr. Preminger?" she cooed from the rear. "You are a bodyguard?"

She laughed, but when he ordered a slight trim for Debbie's hair, Crystal asked, "You're *sure*?"

"When I say it, I mean it. Crystal, will you watch them all?"

"I don't want to make problems. But I paid my way here. Debbie's seventeen years old—"

"If she doesn't like it, she doesn't have to do the part."

"I'm sorry! I didn't know! Good-bye." She stalked off, then stalked back to apologize.

To Preminger she was funny as she purred, "I'm not afraid of you. . . . Are you positive you have to cut Debbie's hair?"

"I'll make sure it's nicely done. Wolfgang, find Sassoon or some other giant of hairdressing."

("He's amused now," said Wolfgang, "but wait.")

Crystal began campaigning to move to the Helios. With Debbie.

And Graham exploded. *"We're* in the Helios only for the direct lines."

She also asked to come to the press conference in Cannes.

"Yes," said Preminger, "but you must not get all the attention."

She batted her eyes in an impersonation of innocence. "Oh, *why* would anyone pay attention to me?"

When she discovered that she wasn't moving into the Helios, she sent Preminger a letter:

"You told me a lie and it's not nice."

He tore it up. "She's not funny, and we have bigger problems."

She camped outside in the parking lot, watching, lynx-eyed, until he emerged.

"Now she wants to come to the boats! Shall I throw her in the water?"

They drove out to a concrete quay and up to a cabin cruiser. After some jostling on the plank, Crystal complained, "Wolfgang pushed me!"

"I don't want to discuss it," said Preminger.

"Well, I want to!"

"You don't know me. There's no exception for rudeness. I can't negotiate for that boat if you're lying on it!"

"I'm not a kept woman!"

"For kept women," he answered sweetly, "I have the greatest respect. It's the best life."

Graham winced at the comedy. "He's loving it. He knows it irritates us."

Next day he told Graham to "do something" about her.

Barbara Allen described the denouement. "Crystal was crying in the hall. She wanted to go on a wardrobe trip. Somehow there was almost a fight with Wolfgang. Somebody turned to Graham, who said Wolfgang had carte blanche to deal with the situation up to and including recasting the part. . . . They just can't get through to Crystal. She's on another plane."

Crystal cornered me against a hotel wall as I waited for a ride to Cannes. "I know you're writing a book, so I can't tell you what went on today."

She smoked through a holder and her nylon blouse was half-unbuttoned. "You look so different from Rome—so tense."

"I've been working hard."

"Tell me, what *sign* are you?"

Oh, God.

"Do you mind if I talk to you? Does it bother you?"

"I don't want to miss my ride."

"I guess you'd mind if I came along."

"It's not my car."

"Well I hate to see you so *tired*. You've been really working hard. And so nervous."

Where was the car?

Suddenly she began a kind of aria about her ward. "She's such a beautiful, lovely, special person. Do you know what I told her father when she was three? I said I want half of her. He laughed, but I told him I was serious. So he said only if you take very good care of her. I promised . . ."

"I have to go, Crystal."

"You don't understand—"

"Get lost, Crystal."

"I do not want her to be with *any* official business," Preminger announced. "You can't imagine the trouble she caused. . . . And she is so *easy* to see through."

The Croisette

A staff member was driven to Cannes by one of Preminger's young observers to arrange for a press conference at the festival. There the five "new" actresses would be introduced.

The city was bedlam: hot, bright, and jammed. A parade of antique autos touted a movie and drew a throng of tourists along the Croisette. For Preminger's observer it was an epiphany. "I've never seen so many breasts!" One model rode topless in an open car; another, wearing overalls with no shirt, handed out leaflets.

The aide trotted to the Carlton, that great white plaster-pile blazing in the Saturday sun, that Hustler Heaven where cars inched up a driveway, past the terrace café, into a mob of photographers and TV cameras.

In the lobby were booths and directories. Every distributor

had a suite or a room or at least directions showing how to get to him. A huge billboard proclaimed *Murder on the Orient Express*. Beneath it, Tony Curtis strode by, looking paunchy in studded denim pants.

Publicist Georges Cravenne's second-floor suite was full of aides stuffing publicity envelopes for a movie in the *marche*, the market of screenings all over town where producers hawk their wares to distributors.

Preminger's man sank into a velour sofa beside Cravenne, from whose eyes all expectation seemed drained, as if, long ago, he had *invented* press conferences.

He ordered like a litany: bilingual releases, telexed invitations to the top sixty journalists (who sometimes ignored mere letters), an interpreter, drinks, canapes, a hand mike, chairs, and a possible "entrance" for the girls.

Though all reporters were equal, *France-Soir* and *L'Express* would get interviews before the party.

The American was shocked. "Won't that put off the others?"

"Not at all."

"You're the boss, Georges."

After the conference, there would be a photo session on the Palais roof. It was a stage overlooking the city, the harbor, the sea, and, in its distant home-berth—like a tiny beetle suspended in azure, like the furthest prize in the whole grand hustle—Hochbaum's yacht.

All the girls had to do was live up to the setting.

Erebus

It is one week to shooting and Preminger arises at five-thirty in his villa. He says, "The sun is like a red ball over the water. From my balcony it is unreal . . . the ocean like a lake. So quiet. . . . If I could speak French, I could be happy here."

No one else speaks of happiness.

It is one week to shooting, and the office static is deafening. Everyone walks around with clipboards and lists and mushrooming anxieties until the voice of *Rosebud* thickens into a great, polyphonic, a cappella wail.

Annalise: "I'll stop talking because I can't say anything!"

Willy: "He say leave everything, he has no money. . . . I think the big economy is in three weeks if *I* stop."

Graham cheerfully dreads everything to come.

"But you wouldn't want to work in a sausage factory," says Barbara.

"Yes. Here there's always something to keep the adrenaline going."

It is one week to the start of shooting and the script is being mimeographed. "It's a little better . . . maybe a little more life . . . maybe overdone." No one knows. And more changes are coming.

It is a week to the shooting and every prop has to be "approved"—guns, knives, luggage, clothes, watches, china, rafts, signal lights, cigarette lighters, candles, strawberries, blue jeans—the revenge of the material world on minds that can shut out nothing.

There is paper everywhere.

But the actors' contracts haven't come yet. Preminger shouts at his French lawyer, "If they aren't signed, they're not insured!"

And one actor's heart makes him possibly uninsurable— hence unemployable.

It is a week to the shooting and they are still calling potential "fathers."

"Rex, this is Otto Preminger speaking! I read in the Nice paper we're neighbors. . . . Come to dinner. See how a man can live without furniture. . . . OK! As long as you're here, can you play a scene? One has nothing to do with the other."

It is one week to the shooting and ads are appearing. A spread in the "trades" announces UA's new products, including *Rosebud*. Preminger is not impressed: "As usual, done with no imagination at all. And you can quote me!"

It is a week to the shooting and the experts are getting to know Preminger.

By now, Denys understands OP's visual demands. "Not documentary, but not pretty. Not false. If a scene is lit by one light, then it's lit by one light."

And Willy Holt makes a hands-off gesture about the simulator. "It will be very beautiful with a little chicken . . . a piglet."

It is a week to the shooting and Preminger sees he isn't communicating with his costume woman.

He tells Annalise, "You are not going to get me to okay embroidery for the sailors' shirts! You bring this up five times already!"

Preminger sees the girls much like his own daughter: young, fresh, well-bred. Annalise sees them with faults to be minimized. She doesn't want Lalla to wear trousers.

"That's nonsense!" He has *hired* her in trousers.

Later he fumes: "All these long discussions. This rigamarole! And I just want to *do*! . . . I don't say she is bad. *I* am difficult. I am used, when I see a dress, to say I don't like it."

Fed up, Graham tells her just to buy a certain costume. "Go ahead, Annalise, go ahead! *I'll* wear it if he doesn't like it!"

It is a week to the shooting and *new* experts are revising the old work. Special-effects man Cliff Richardson is a wiry, white-haired Englishman with an inventor's delight in the way things work and a lifetime of major credits.

Quietly he demolishes the old plumbing scene. He has solved the problem, experimenting in his garden with a simple procedure—simpler than before, anyway—in which "sleeping gas" is pumped through an open ball-float valve ("like in a toilet").

"I took the liberty of rewriting the dialogue . . ."

Preminger is delighted. "Go to Corsica, go to work! I will see it on the set!"

It is a week to the shooting and all the careful transport plans suddenly break open. Two trucks are stopped on a French road; the drivers have no copies of their carnets and there is "extra material" on board.

Graham shouts long-distance to his French shipping agent, "They won't just confiscate the extra stuff. They'll confiscate the lot!"

It is a week to the shooting and the last straw comes as Graham questions Captain Farrago's massive expense account and the Captain cables his resignation.

Graham stuffs the cable in his mouth and eats it.

It is a week to the shooting and Preminger's U.S. man shrugs off everything that has happened so far. "You haven't seen any of the big talent yet. Or the big problems."

It is a week to the shooting and Preminger has barely heard the girls read when he presents them to the press in Cannes. At bottom, that convocation of hacks, flacks, and buffet-whores is content with a simple non-event. *Rosebud* is about media exploitation, but this is as close as it gets to exploitation.

On the dais, Preminger lists his absent stars, then brings on the girls one by one, ending with Lalla. "I guarantee you will like her."

The questions are the same as in every interview.

"Is it a co-production . . . ?"

"And what part does Mitchum play . . . ?"

Says an aide, "You're lucky, really, if they just spell the names right."

Finally, up on the roof, framed against the palms and flapping banners and the heat haze, the girls, Erik, and Otto stroll in line toward fifty yelling cameramen.

"Look at us . . . pretty pretty . . . the walk . . . the chapeau . . . the same order . . . *regardez* . . ."

Shutters whirr. Click, click, click.

For a moment they are all together, all looking happy. Click.

It was a week to the shooting when all the guesses, language problems, and noncommunication of four months came to rest in rehearsal. It started in the back room of the Astoria coffee shop, with the girls sitting at tables as if at the Last Supper.

Preminger was clearly not an acting teacher. He simply told what results he wanted. *How* they were achieved concerned him as little as how Denys powered his lights.

Especially, Preminger wanted the kind of personality acting by which a John Wayne or Paul Newman becomes ever more effortlessly and naturally himself. "Just say the lines," he told the girls. "It's so *simple*."

Criticism was sharp and specific.

To Lalla, who dished with her mother about their respective boyfriends: "Father is old and tough, so you're on her side. . . . Like you'd *gossip* with a friend."

To Debbie, coaxing her father about the plane: "*Flirt* with him. Appeal to him. Then after he agrees, you've got him. Suddenly be matter of fact. 'We approach from the west.' "

Said Lalla later, "He's so much better than I thought! So accurate. . . . He says 'It's so *simple*,' and he's right."

He never spoke of spines or beats or motivations. Instead he told Kim, who had some dialogue about a spaced-out bike trip, "Say 'hash' clearly. Either the word is important and you speak it clearly or it's unimportant and we'll cut it. Every word has a right to live." Again, when she greeted Thibaud on the boat,

Preminger said, "*Expect* him to respond. It's as if you said, 'You must have heard of me, we're all in the group.' It's all *there* if you *think*."

Gradually one saw why he liked the new material. It reflected *his* style, vindicating, if anything, his "auteurism." Thus Kim *teased* Thibaud, inviting him on a cruise. "Be a kept man for a few weeks."

Sometimes the teasing blended into a flirty challenge, as in Isabelle's lines. Said Otto: "I don't like to read lines for actors"—but when she didn't understand, he carefully acted one, with a mischievous twinkle, becoming . . . seventeen.

He read aloud, he explained, he directed, he encouraged. And nothing happened. Already the work had gone wrong.

Kim Cattrall's shyness was at odds with the glib hash-smoker Marjorie had written.

Debbie Berger was quiet and dreamy, unlike the flirty German girl.

Isabelle Huppert was as independent and sexy as Hélène, but her English needed practice.

Lalla Ward was English, pretty, and upper-class. But this actress who read Thomas Mann during her breaks was playing a culturally benighted twit. When Lady Carter asked about the name of the yacht, it was Margaret Carter who made the classic reply, "Something to do with a film, I think."

As for Sabine: "I've written her very fragile," said Marjorie Kellogg. Considering how the part was played, it didn't matter what was written.

From the first day, when OP told Betty Berman-Alison to drop her Lucky Pierre accent, one felt her panic growing—felt, too, the deception of her acting teachers.

Her troubles started with her first line. Carrying groceries to the boat, she actually *brooded* over forgetting something.

"Butter . . . ?" A moment later, seeing her boyfriend Thibaud, she embraced him violently, almost knocking over the observer who was reading the part.

"Don't *think*!" cautioned Preminger. "You said you don't grasp Sabine. This is just a girl with a rich grandfather. You're just there."

"Thank you."

"What's the trouble?"

"I don't know, sir."

"Don't call me sir. It's so *simple*. Just *be* this girl. Don't think of your anger. Think of the scene."

Quietly he arranged to interview another actress from Paris.

The rehearsals moved upstairs to a lighter room as Betty's mood darkened.

"There's no excuse for this. Even Lee Strasberg wouldn't tolerate it."

"You're right."

She embraced the observer so hard he forgot his lines.

"You must be a twin of the girl who read in Paris. . . . You talk mechanically before you feel it."

"I know the lines, sir."

"That is *wrong*."

"It's horrible, I know."

"Don't put secrets into everything. . . . When you say 'butter' the whole audience will *cry*. And 'darling' you say like you'll beat him."

All her acting lessons had brought her this.

"You were brilliant in Paris. . . . That should give you more assurance. It's like when you swim. Don't *think*. Throw yourself into the water. Stanislavsky didn't sit and say this character was born in so-and-so, eighteen years ago. Brando— he doesn't do this anymore. Once you act, it is *you*! . . . It's so *simple*! Just visualize yourself in the situation . . . and say the line."

Imagine. And experience freshly. It was pure Stanislavsky.

He warned that if she didn't improve he might get someone else for the part. The other girls listened in embarrassed silence.

Afterward, Betty asked in disbelief, "Is he really looking for another actress?"

As rehearsals dragged on, one wondered more and more how the scenes mattered. Who cared about these girls, their boyfriends, their "dynamite hash"?

Preminger of course. He was a man who smiled at children in the street. Seeing a baby in a sound studio he laughed and asked, "Are you my friend?" And the women of *Rosebud* were also children.

He wanted the audience to like them—for their youth if nothing else. In the galley scene, when four girls prepared supper while Sabine made love in her cabin, Preminger felt the action should bubble along, the dialogue overlap. "You're all gossiping and bragging. It's the beginning of life, in every way."

As wrong as he had been about Betty Berman, he was prescient about Isabelle.

He assigned one observer to be with her "night and day" going over pronunciation.

When she flew to Paris for a day to finish another film and returned late, Preminger stormed at her lack of discipline. But Isabelle was tough and confident. She yawned, saying she'd gotten up at 5:00 A.M. for a flight back, then shrugged off his anger.

Gradually her weight dropped—at what cost?—and her charm came through as Preminger stressed the humor of the part.

When the character "didn't see how" she had forgotten anything for dinner, Preminger explained, "She doesn't see how *after spending all that money!*"

Isabelle sat fiercely concentrating, her arms folded, a sweater around her shoulders, sometimes chewing a bead necklace as corrections were dunned into her.

When they came to a line about "Bretigny Airport," Preminger told an observer, "She'll teach *you* how to pronounce it." And so she did, with a sudden flushed smile.

But the "rich kids" still didn't matter and the performances were mostly lifeless.

In the cave scenes, Preminger stopped Betty Berman-Alison. "She's *afraid*! Again," he ordered. "The whole scene!"

Again and again.

"We're starting to shoot next week. So far it's dismal! You can all do it! . . . I don't do this because I enjoy it. There are many other things I'd enjoy."

It was hellish with Betty.

In bed with Thibaud, she insisted on his staying to dinner. "Be strong," Preminger urged. "She has an idea!"

"Okay, I'll do it strong."

"Don't put it in a category. *You!* Betty Berman—you changed your name unnecessarily—*you* are the girl. And don't be coy! You care!"

"Begin again! You've learned the lines by heart and you're not thinking them. And your self-pity doesn't impress me. You're holding us up! Begin!"

She finished her big speech, screaming and blubbering. Preminger was silent for a time, his lips pursed, staring holes in the floor. "When you did it in my office it was moving. This is all phony . . . all on the outside."

"It doesn't feel outside when I'm shaking."

The kindest thing to say was that her acting was bad. The

cruelest was that she was being herself and it wasn't attractive. Perhaps the truth was a little of both.

In the office, he told Graham, "We have watched her self-destruction. It's sad. . . . I already have in mind the girl who played Piaf."

Three days before the start of shooting he signed Brigitte Ariel.

Betty Berman was already passing into oblivion. "Just announce that Ariel is added to the cast. Say whatever Berman likes . . . she resigned . . . anything. It's sad how this girl lost everything. But it's partly that I must have a French girl in the part. I'm sorry for her. But it will also mature her."

Next door, two aides were rejecting all offers from *Playboy* and others. "The girls are better off waiting than just sitting there with their legs open."

"The magazines are always looking for fresh meat."

Brigitte Ariel looked perfect—for playing Piaf. A tiny, waifish, birdlike creature with a husky voice and a gritty independence, she dressed like a child of Woodstock out of Saint-Germain, sporting hennaed hair, pitted teeth, black fingernails, clothes of lace, Lucite, and denim, thin wristbands on even thinner wrists, with the whole arrangement mounted on four-inch platform shoes.

"I'm very pleased to work with you," she told Preminger.

He said they would make a virtue of her slightness.

"She's beautiful," said an aide later.

"She's very well proportioned," said another.

"You have learned what to say."

And what did Preminger see in her? "She's very funny . . . and she wanted to do it." She had come down on price, and he in turn had waived his options. "She's so *intelligent* in the way she talked about the script."

To write a history of some enterprise is to suggest it has some underlying order, however great the surface confusion. But on *Rosebud* Preminger can make right choices, wrong choices, any choices. Things simply *will not work.*

It is three days to shooting and Room 602 is crowded with actresses, observers, and script supervisor Angela Martelli, an English gentlewoman, calling cuts and cues like a polite sergeant-major, as Brigitte and Yves Beneyton begin to rehearse.

Yves is tall and thin, with hair to his shoulders and a faraway look. He has been brilliant in his filmclip. And many actors start slowly. Yet . . .

Preminger stares, cupping his chin in his hand.

Beneyton is distant, hushed.

Preminger folds his hands in a gesture like prayer.

Brigitte meanwhile gives "frail" Sabine a sultry, smoky voice and a rich accent.

"It's very good, but you must work on your English."

At lunch a doctor declares that her sultry voice is the result of flu.

"You want to go to bed?" Preminger asks her.

"Never. Who wants to be in bed alone on a sunny afternoon?"

She lights up a cigarette.

"Is it good for you to smoke?"

"Oh, yes. The doctor said three packs a day."

Meanwhile, Beneyton refuses an English coach. His wife will help instead.

In the elevator, Preminger wants to be optimistic. "I'll work with them. . . . I like his mildness. The dinner scene will be even *more* reasonable. I *like* Yves Beneyton!"

The door opens to reveal Betty Berman with her bags, head-

ing for the airport. In a spasm of embarrassment she pulls back
from the elevator and walks down.

It is two days to the shooting and the doctor announces that
Brigitte has mononucleosis. Preminger sees the bright side. As
a captive, she will look really weak. "It will be *good*."

It is two days to the shooting and the hairdresser is scouring
her henna, the makeup man stripping her fingernails, Annalise
going over her wardrobe, and a dentist whitening her teeth.

Says Preminger, "Better too many than too few!"

It is two days to the shooting and some problems are sorting
themselves out. The actor with a troubled heart is insurable,
the yachtsmen get T-shirts without embroidery, the shipping
agent gets the trucks out of bondage (paying a fine), and even
Captain Farrago gets back to work.

Graham grumbles about his expenses. "He's done more ki-
lometers than you and I in a lifetime."

"Deduct the doubtful expenses from his last check."

It is two days to the shooting and Preminger calls a meeting
of sixty crew members in the coffee shop.

"Good morning, ladies and gentlemen. I'm glad to meet you
all. . . . The main purpose is to let you ask questions. If any of
you feels his equipment is not sufficient, tell us. . . . No questions? Then go to work!"

It is two days to the shooting and the arrivals become an
avalanche.

Preminger laughs about one worker. "Kubrick told him 'I'll
see you in two weeks,' meaning he wouldn't be able to work
with me."

Adrienne Corri (Lady Carter) comes from London with
a designer dress bought hastily as a costume. "It cost a *bomb*,
darling!"

181

The young composer, Laurent Petitgirard, appears with ideas of full symphonies "when the world gets the news. . . . For the world, a very *big* sound!"

But the "world" is Julian Pettifer, an English TV commentator playing himself, who strolls in and tactfully asks to Anglicize his text. Mostly he cuts and adds authenticity, referring to "BBC 2" and "The News Special Studio." (Starting in December, from a montage of international reaction to the Arab films, the world, the media, and the news have all shrunk to this one man, with his one speech.)

It is two days to shooting and revised schedule number four is being revised.

Two days and Denys prepares silent camera tests of the women. Says Preminger, "We already *know* they can't speak English."

Two days and I walk out to see the *Rosebud.*

In the dockside parking lot, rigger Mickey Murchan unpacks his errant truck. "They thought we were smuggling hash." Instead, it was four whiskey bottles.

Mickey has a beer belly, a Saint-Tropez tan, and a boozy Irish charm as he tells of Black September threats on *The Last of Sheila.* "Had private guards right behind the director. I know if it happened here some of us wouldn't work . . . the clapperboy would be afraid to open boxes of film."

It is two days to the shooting as one walks farther onto the quay, into a blistering afternoon of white light, green shore, and coruscating sea. Here one forgets the production office and the endless talk of actors—Yul Brynner, Kirk Douglas, Hardy Kreuger, David Hemmings, Malcolm McDowell, Peter O'Toole: actors too old, not available, too expensive.

Here one forgets the revisions and cuts, as Preminger lays out scenes like the dinner introductions, when Fargeau meets Patrice Thibaud and the girls. Immediately Preminger cuts a page. Out go the carving, the wine pouring, the social chatter. It ends as Patrice declines to carve. Before shooting, Preminger

182

cuts that too, so it ends with a girl offering pâté. But he hates her reading and finally cuts *that* in the editing.

Walking to the *Rosebud,* one forgets it all.

With that boat, Preminger has finally gotten lucky.

To its English crew, *The Brave Goose* is a seagoing instrument, a hundred and fifteen feet long, top speed twelve knots.

To the owner it might be a dream boat, irreplaceable under $1.5 million.

To a cynic, it is "a hole in the ocean to pour money into."

But to the camera it will be perfect: not the biggest or the most famous, but the sleekest, most elegant. Looking at it, one forgets the troubled attempts to make the girls into characters. One forgets that *Rosebud* is less a novel than a suspense *mechanism,* subordinating character to plot—unlike Preminger's best work, in which the ultimate pleasures are precisely those of character: Dana Andrews and Clifton Webb adding up to one perfect lover in *Laura;* James Stewart and Ben Gazzara conspiring to defend a lie in *Anatomy of a Murder.*

One dismisses the idea that Preminger has no characters to grasp here, that he has miscalculated. Instead, one looks at that beautiful vessel, that irreducible logo of the story, and allows oneself to hope for the best, as one did in February, riding into London.

With a day and a half left, the girls and Yves Beneyton line up on the steaming quay for the "test" of costumes, makeup, and who knows what.

It is the crew's first real introduction to Preminger. He shouts at one aide that there is no smoking on his set and at Annalise that there is no talking. Even if this *is* a silent test.

"Roll it," he orders, then tells the first girl, "Walk in . . . talk, smile . . ."

She enters and pauses in confusion. "What would you like me to say?"

Cap Ferrat. The view from the villa. "Say you are surprised it isn't finished!"

Nice. Eva Monley in café. "I always knew my fiftieth year would bring some great event."

Aloft. Otto advises Graham Cottle, "Be strict."

Paris. Margot Capelier and two of her "creatures for dreaming."

Otto and Denys Coop near an "Arabian village" in Israel.
"I want to *see* all this."

Israeli desert. "Here you believe a man feels he's safe."

Cannes. Palais rooftop
photo session. "Now
everyone will say I
have a chance for five
flops in one picture."

Georges Cravenne

Adrienne Corri *(Courtesy of Ben Jones)* . . .

. . . and Lalla Ward, in life . . .
(Courtesy of Keith Hamshere)

. . . and on film, as Lady Carter and her daughter. "Nothing's real.
We're doing Snow White." *(Courtesy of Keith Hamshere)*

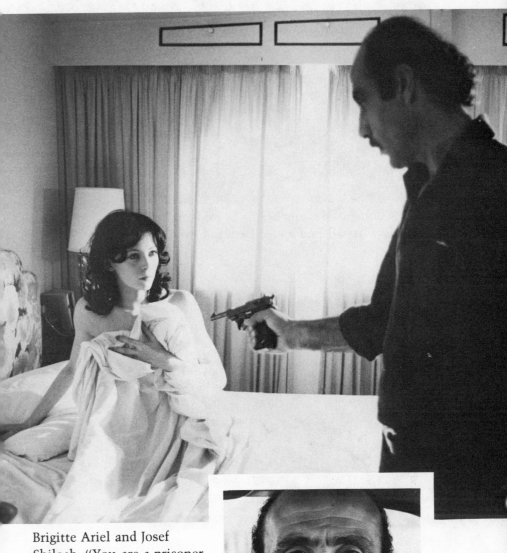

Brigitte Ariel and Josef Shiloah. "You are a prisoner of the PLO." *(Courtesy of Keith Hamshere)*

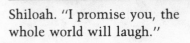

Shiloah. "I promise you, the whole world will laugh."

Juan. All-night shooting begins in mid-afternoon. Claude Dauphin and Kim Cattrall line up for Otto and Jimmy Devis.

Fantail. 5:00 P.M. rehearsal.

Georges Beller. 1:00 A.M. "Now we will roll without mercy."

4:00 A.M.

Nice. Preminger explains Amidou's killing weapon. "You will make him a charming killer . . ."

Amidou rehearses with his victim.

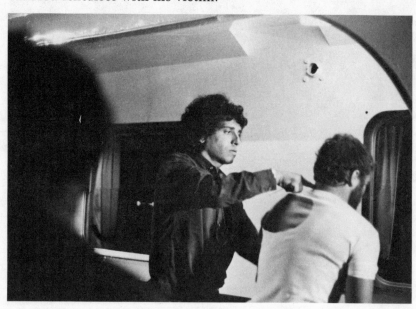

Facing page: Bastia Harbor. The longest day. *(Courtesy of Keith Hamshere)*

Bastia customshouse. Erik and Otto wait for the setup.

Mitchum and a young admirer also pass the time.

Holt and the flight simulator on the farm. "I don't want a set, I want a GAT!"

Isabelle Huppert. "When he shouts, I think I'm the stronger."

Cliff Richardson. "I'm always the optimist."

Angela Martelli. "This picture has had more than its share of troubles."

Mickey Murchan. "The best arm in the unit."

Ray Evans, a grip. "Have you written that we're all fucked?"

Penelope and Paul
Bonnecarrère on their boat
in Corsica watch the
filming. "It's sensational."

Wolfgang Glattes. Said
Preminger, "The best first
assistant I've ever had."

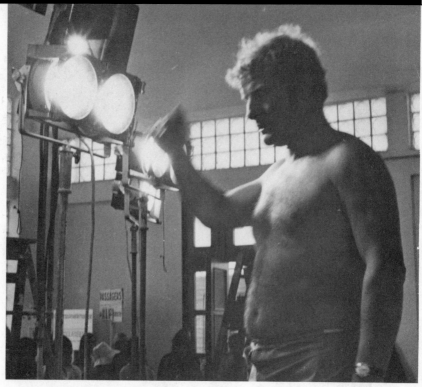

Ron Pearce, chief electrician. "We sweat our balls off."

Camera grip David Cadwallader ready to move the boom with operator Jimmy Devis. "Chained to the handles."

Author-plumber encouraged by Cliff Gorman and Peter O'Toole
(Courtesy of Keith Hamshere)

Cliff Gorman. "They're going for the popcorn."

Paris screening room with
John V. Lindsay. "You look
incredibly elegant." "But
which one is my
daughter?"

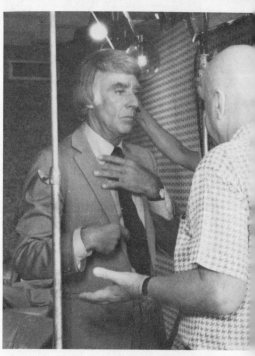

And with Peter Lawford.
"Make it like a simple
report."

Cliff Gorman. "All that time and money is spent, and the night before a big scene they hand you pages of new dialogue."

O'Toole waiting to work on his first day back from the hospital. "It's all so political . . ."

Otto and O'Toole in Paris. *(Courtesy of Keith Hamshere)*

Paris. Raf Vallone and Françoise Brion as Isabelle Huppert's parents. "It's not me on screen, it's someone else."

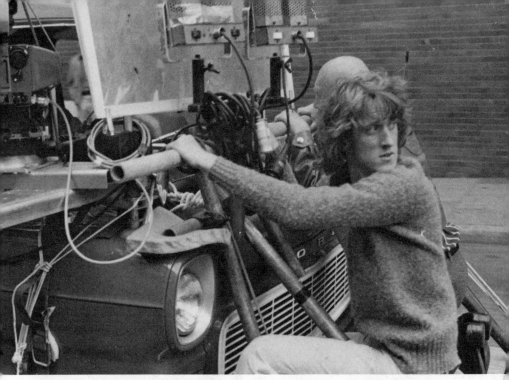

Hamburg. Dewi Humphries on camera platform, mounted on van.
He was nearly thrown when an actor at the wheel lost control
while adjusting his flapping toupee.

Street scene. "Half of *Berlin* is in my eyeline."

Israel. Sloat's cave.
The "cardboard" set.

And the crew waits
in the desert
for the parachutists.

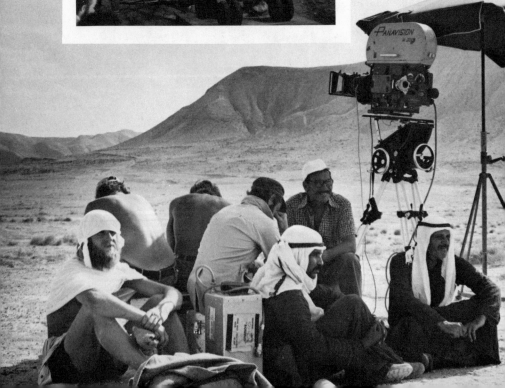

Richard Attenborough. "I'm
slightly lunatic myself . . .

. . . and he's one of the
greats."

Afterward. With Peter O'Toole's gift of a hat.

•TWO•
PRODUCTION

"A producer's care may be greatest after the irredeemable mistakes have been made."

—PAULINE KAEL

"Kinderspiel . . ."   —OTTO PREMINGER

OUTWARD BOUND

Drive, He Said

Now one felt Preminger's force. If troubles arose, if there were difficulties caused by others or by his own impatience, he simply overrode them, delegating authority, reversing himself, assuming things would work out, bulldozing ahead, regardless—imposing a tunnel vision on himself as if to earn the power to create any vision at all.

The only direction was forward.

If it rained, they would shoot in the Las Vegas. "It won't rain in the toilet."

If the boat next to the *Rosebud* wouldn't move away, "Spread the rumor I have cholera!"

If Brigitte was sick, "We'll go ahead anyway. . . . I tell you, she's indestructible. . . . I don't want advice, I just want to *do!*"

He began with a "preliminary day." Tuesday, May 28. One shot. Julian Pettifer's news show. After all the travels in search of "reality," they did the scene in the yacht saloon, pretending it was a TV newsroom, because the gaffers had already tied into the ship's generators to power the next day's work. Later, the newscast would be transferred to videotape and played on a TV set in another scene.

In front of a BBC poster, which masked the room, Pettifer sat in a suit, trying to ignore the boat's swaying and his own sweat.

Facing him were carpenter Vince Foley, head gaffer Ron Pearce, propman Tony Teiger, Preminger, focus puller Dewi Humphries, operator Jimmy Devis, Denys Coop with a contrast glass around his neck, camera grip David Cadwallader,

211

boom man Terry Sharratt, and, in the rear, Angela Martelli, Wolfgang Glattes, and Robin Gregory—a crowd becoming a crew.

Denys warned about Pettifer's sweat.

"Don't come to me with such nonsense," cried Otto.

"His hair looks a bit windswept—"

"His hair is the best part! It's beautiful! Let's roll!"

"Sound rolling," said Robin.

"Speed," called Jimmy Devis.

"Slate one, take one," said the clapperboy.

"Action!"

By take seven, Pettifer was glistening but Preminger roared, "Cut, fine, print it!" Like a shout of triumph. Months later we saw that the sweat would never show on the tiny TV image. Preminger had been lucky or right and it hardly mattered. What did matter was that with a whole afternoon for one shot, he had still driven forward.

Before leaving, Pettifer subtly stirred Preminger's doubts about Sloat. Having changed into a safari suit, the newsman stood on the afterdeck with the sun sparkling on his back like a shawl of metal and complained, so gently, with a tact coded in the genes, "It's a shame to see Sloat such a melodramatic figure." He suggested the examples of other Englishmen—even Lawrence—who had had a "romantic attachment to the Arab cause," and mentioned some reference books. As he left, Otto waved good-bye.

"Erik, start to think about it. . . . Don't write yet. We'll talk."

Erik sat on the terrace of his hotel room late that afternoon, in the humming heat, drained by Sloat.

Already, for me, the girls didn't work and the reactions of the world were muted. Now Sloat failed. The problem, said Erik, was that the character "is not *for* anything. It won't wash that he organizes this massive plot just to satisfy his anger about losing elections. But if he's *for* something, he can't betray himself at the end. Only creeps with something to hide can betray themselves."

Erik had logically pursued every idea to a dead end. Sloat had to be an idealist or an opportunist—and couldn't be either. Such logic was no help to a director whose best work had reached out to embrace contradictions of motive and behavior, had created moments like the end of *Laura,* when Clifton Webb dies proclaiming love for a woman he has tried to kill.

It takes more than logic to create sympathy for the devil.

That night everyone got a gift—a crimson *Rosebud* T-shirt with a thrusting-dagger logo on the chest. And everyone got a call sheet for the first full day. (See Appendix, pages 343–44.)

The Big Heat

An hour into the first day the T-shirts came off, as seventy people baked in anxiety, facing a trial in the sun.

Standing on deck, I returned a friendly wave to someone on the dock. Preminger saw it and launched into a tirade. "Gershuny, you used to be so quiet! What *happened* to you? Will someone please *throw Mr. Gershuny off the boat!*"

For a week the grips greeted me with Cockney-Viennese impressions: "Vil somevone please throw Meeeester Gerrrrshuuuuuuny off de boat!"

"Have a smoke, Tedward," said one. "Relax."

The focus of attention was on Thibaud and the young women.

They began with the galley scene.

Annalise worried about a pair of missing jeans.

"But he says it's okay to wear my blue pants—"

"Debbie, *please*! It's my business! When the jeans get here, *you wear them*!"

Inside the galley, there was more heat as five CSI lamps on the side deck poured in "sunshine." (Condensed source iodide lamps, developed for TV, were a substitute for brutes. They gave a good proportion of the same light, while weighing less, using less current, and being cooler—though you wouldn't have known it on that deck.)

Preminger had chosen the smaller of the ship's kitchens to shoot the girls falling over each other, Kim juggling rolls, Debbie "murdering" salad.

"It's more fun," he said.

Now Jimmy Devis, a big man in shorts and T-shirt, sweating under a padded harness, had to hold the camera steady during a two-and-a-half-minute scene. Above him a floodlight simmered. To one side, the oven kept a roast at four hundred degrees. To the other side was Otto. (A "Galley" diagram appears in the Appendix, page 346.)

On the rocks outside, a sullen, tiptoe silence had fallen.

From within we heard fragments of basso instruction. "Really *eat* the strawberries . . . work . . . *taste* the salad."

Actor Patrick Floershein, playing the treacherous *Rosebud* crewman, Frank Woods, lay on the rocks tanning and reading.

Seeing him, Annalise cried out, "Oh, my god, *him*! I've just sent the seamstress to the hotel for him!"

"Silence, s'il vous plâit . . ."

Everything had led to this moment from the announcement in December, from Preminger's dissatisfaction with the girls, to the quest for a yacht in the chill of February, the calls to Hochbaum, Onassis, brokers, and lawyers, the treks to London, Monte Carlo, and Cannes, the flights to Paris to see Margot's two hundred "creatures for dreaming" with their two hundred accents, the calls to writers, and the work, finally, with Marjorie and Erik. I thought of Eva Monley and the rehearsals in the Astoria, the anguished sessions working around Betty Berman, the discovery of Kim's nerves, Lalla's humor, Isabelle's grit—and the sweet scent of opportunity mixing now with sweat and diesel oil and heat. All of it would prove its value in the fragile balance of the next, uncertain hour.

"Silence, s'il vous plâit . . ."

214

"Kim, darling, you must wait till I say 'Action.' "

The punctuations of the silence outside were Chekhovian. A saw started and stopped. A boat passed. We heard directions.

"Why do you take these long pauses? . . . The lines must overlap."

On the dock, Vince Foley sauntered over with his hammer in the belt of his shorts.

"How's your book coming?"

"Oh, he's a tough man. . . . "

"Ooooo, you're right there. But that maybe makes your book, doesn't it?"

Suddenly, on take nine: "Cut and print!" The scene had tightened to a minute and forty seconds. Now came a burst of chatter. Jimmy Devis stepped out, soaked, as others dashed in to reset props and shoot stills. And Preminger roared over the mob, *"Will you please be quiet here!"*

Immediately he lined up the next shot—Thibaud's arrival—a web of movement: Yves Beneyton walking along the dock and up the gangplank, the real Captain appearing from the galley to meet him, Kim popping up in a window to flirt, and Patrick Floershein sidling over to eavesdrop.

As the dolly followed Beneyton, a crewman cried out, jamming his foot against a metal dock pole.

"Cut! We'll do this after lunch," said Preminger with a sigh.

It was like seeing the ghost of a movie through a veil of technology.

In the caterer's tent the tension went on.

For Kim Cattrall there was no break in a twenty-four-hour rite of passage from drama-school ingenue to movie actress. "I practiced juggling rolls and when one dropped I was so frightened he would shout at me. But he didn't. He called me 'darling.' It'll be perfect after lunch ... except he's cut three lines—" She dropped her fork with a clatter and apologized. "I'm just frightened I'll forget—" As she sprinkled pepper, the shaker came apart and poured over her plate.

After lunch, they struggled to master the scene. Yves flirted in English, and Kim battled with coy conceits about "kept men" and "the isles of Greece."

Every take had a problem. Jimmy Devis cut his leg on another dock pole, the sailor moved too much, Kim popped up too soon, Yves twisted lines, Kim forgot them, Yves was too solemn, Kim didn't look at him—it was an endless drain on time and energy in the suffocating heat, until they finally printed take twenty-two, however forced and false it seemed.

There was no time for regret. Lalla's arrival was next. They brought her on with her "mother" (Adrienne Corri), in her mother's open Rolls, driven by Klaus, her mother's handsome chauffeur, who in reality owned the car. Or did he?

A crewman whispered, "The car's not *his*. It belongs to his boyfriend."

"Oh," hissed another, "aren't we bitchy on this film!"

In rehearsal, Adrienne thought she was supposed to be hiding her own affairs.

"No, no," said Preminger. He wanted more companionship, more closeness. The two women were confidantes. "And don't stand so far away."

"I'm on Lalla's toes. And the English are reticent."

"Warmer, Lalla! A kiss at the end. A close embrace."

None of it helped. The limousine parked a hundred yards from the boat, the women played their bland good-byes standing on a barrier, Lalla kissed her mother and ran to the yacht.

"Very fast!" ordered Preminger.

Tottering on high heels, Adrienne repeatedly fluffed the same line about staying at the Hassler in Rome. Each time Lalla returned from her sprint to play the scene ever more breathlessly.

When it finally ended, the ladies were exhausted and ready for a drink.

"And Klaus too," Adrienne urged in a stage whisper. "He's marvelous. After no time at all he started telling me his life story!" Finishing the scene had liberated her. *Now* we saw a woman talking about life and love, writing her own performance.

"Klaus was in Amsterdam one night and wandered into a queer bar—he says it was his first time—and met a prince who became his lover and has the Rolls. And more Rollses! That's *his* crest on the car. They've been together sixteen years!"

"It was his first time in a gay bar?"

"He says so! Now, darling, that's what you call *beginner's luck*! Hahaha—"

Preminger heard her laughter and came over to embrace her.

"Oh, darling, I am so sorry about getting the Hassler so mucked up. Imagine! The Hashler!" As she spoke she tickled him. He wagged his finger and padded back to work.

"He needs a tickle now and then. I say it's good for him! Klaus, come with us, darling, for a drink. We all need cheering up."

"Well of course. Today we must have champagne!"

"Oh, he will cheer us up!"

Driving back in the Rolls, Adrienne explained her mood. "We've just mucked up a scene—"

Lalla, sotto voce: "Speak for yourself."

"—standing on a *wall*, trying to get the Hashler out of my teeth—they'd have spoken about the hotel in the car! And he hated it when I patted her hair. But I'm always doing that to my own daughter. . . . Nothing's real! We're doing Snow White."

Lalla laughed. "And I suppose we're the dwarfs. Sleepy, Dopey . . ."

At the Helios, the tension dissolved in champagne. The women acted like real friends, and there were flashes of what the film might have—the life it had been seeking. It was all there, in the most obvious place. I watched and celebrated that life, in a performance for an audience of one.

We toasted the movie in champagne and Klaus ordered more. "It'll be chilled when we're done with this bottle."

"Oh, Klaus," said Adrienne, "you *do* have style. You didn't *acquire* it. You were born with it."

"Well, I don't know . . ."

Tall and rangy, with reddish hair, clear blue eyes, and a musical Dutch accent, he slouched like a champion swimmer basking in unending sun.

"I just do what I want."

"Of course you do. Because you *know* what you want. . . . There's never any question. You should take over my life and manage it. Oh, why are most millionaries so beastly?" She ran her fingers through her hair. "You know what's needed."

"Caviar."

"Caviar! Oh, isn't he marvelous!"

I asked if Lalla liked caviar.

"I adore it."

"Oh, suddenly it's all bearable," exclaimed Adrienne. "I mean they are paying me so much just to come and get the Hashler hashed. But what do they expect? I was on my way out the door. They actually grabbed me. . . . I had my bikini on."

Klaus poured more champagne. "Now," said Adrienne, "I mustn't spill any on this dress. Oh, *wait* till they see the price."

Klaus smiled at the clover on Lalla's chest. "Lalla's dress is also very beautiful. She has good luck between her breasts."

"Oh, why doesn't the day *begin* like this!"

Lalla skipped dinner to get some sleep. "I have a seven o'clock call to do that wretched nude scene. . . . Please, just go have a good time."

So we drove on in Klaus's newly materialized Lamborghini, at Mach one.

"I don't know what Lalla's worried about," Adrienne chattered to Klaus and his friend, Jean Pierre, at dinner. "I was with Stanley for ten days being raped [in *A Clockwork Orange*]. He must have shot it from I don't know how many angles. And once I played on Broadway while three English nudies I did were on Forty-second Street. . . . People don't *care*! When I took my kids to Venice for the showing of *Clockwork*, they didn't worry about the nudity. "They only cared that I admitted how old they were!"

"I admit everything," said Klaus.

"That's why you're so happy! You don't have any hypocrisy."

"I am a homosexual." He touched his friend's arm affectionately. "Jean Pierre and I have no secrets. We live together five years."

The owner of the Rolls doesn't seem to mind.

"Oh, Klaus, you're so simple. So clean. All the rest of us are so wretched, but you know exactly what you want."

"I like to enjoy myself. To sit around the pool. And drink. And make love! All *ways*! I love going in from the back. And drive! Oh, cars are my love."

"Oh, Klaus, you cheer me up. That's your gift."

By nightfall every bit of cheer was helpful. The work of each day was summarized in a Unit Progress Report. (See Appendix, page 345.) For this first day Preminger had shot an extra scene, Lalla's arrival, plus the galley and Thibaud's entrance, for a total of three and three-quarter minutes of screen time. The report showed 4,840 feet of film exposed, 1,265 printed, 6 rolls of sound tape used, and 241 scenes left to do in 69 days.

But that wasn't the whole story. The report did not show how Preminger had edited the May 22 "final script" for the May 29 shooting. He had simplified Thibaud's scene by saving a walk to the fantail and pared down Lalla's arrival, moving it to the end of all the girls' entrances, so they climaxed as she ran along the breakwater toward the boat, with the sea glowing in the late afternoon sun. Then he would cut to the Las Vegas—to the noisy, neon café—for a nice contrast.

One more detail was missing: a call to Graham that night

telling of a traffic accident in which the film cans had been thrown into the street and run over.

Instead of being one scene ahead they might have to redo everything.

Body and Soul

On the second day, Preminger and the crew knew there was deep trouble. The actors felt it in their own thrashings. And the general sense of futility swelled as each further element went wrong; it would culminate that night in rushes.

First they would do a postcoital "love scene," then the big nude display with the hostages.

They began in the main bedroom of the yacht. Yves dozed on Brigitte's breasts after making love. She woke him tenderly and invited him to dinner that night with Fargeau. He refused, and she pulled him down with a kiss as if to persuade him. Then cut.

It looked so . . . simple.

Yet Yves and Brigitte, with their thin faces and narrow frames, seemed anti-erotic. The antidote to desire.

And everything was a distraction.

Mickey Murchan remembered last night. "I ended up wi' me trousers round me legs. Never did get me gear off."

Said a crewman, "Four A.M. the sparks came in. It won't change . . . In Singapore I saw them drink. God . . ."

And now the room filled with *things:* plywood sheets coming through the window for dollying, pin spots with blue filters to raise their color temperature to daylight, cables snaking through the doorway, Robin Gregory setting up his mixer in the marble bathroom while sitting with his headset on the toilet.

Wearing jockey shorts, Yves got into bed with indestructible Brigitte, who wore only panties.

Annalise brought in some bedclothes for a TV version of the scene.

"Don't interrupt me!" Preminger told her.

And Brigitte insisted she never wore anything in bed.

"Annalise, what about you?" asked Otto.

"Nothing."

"Not even a mask? . . . I apologize."

Against this blooming, buzzing background, Preminger turned to the actors to rehearse. "Okay, now be a little sexy."

But there was nothing, just two strangers in bed.

"Touch him. Grab him. You just made love. Four times!"

Outside, a mocking crewman grabbed his crotch.

When Brigitte kissed her lover, Preminger urged, "Make it longer. . . . *Hold* him like you want to kiss him again."

Yves responded with a bored peck, then leaned back. He was cast as an intense "radical," mostly from a film in which he made ransom demands. But the changes in Thibaud—to make him "a character"—had outstripped the casting and turned the cultural gap into a chasm. Now he was supposed to banter in bed, in a language he didn't fully understand, with a woman running a fever.

And thus are actors undone.

"Terrible," said a crewman.

"I've never seen anything like this," agreed another.

Knowing it was serious, Preminger tried to encourage the actors to use their imaginations.

"You must think, To hell with the other girls. Do what you want. Be free."

"Otto," said Denys, "she drops her head too low—"

"Don't think of camera! I can adjust positions later. Now they must have the freedom to develop it."

But they weren't free. They were lost. Imprisoned in physical reality.

"I saw his underpants that time," warned Angela Martelli.

Annalise produced some flesh-colored pants. "These are for girls but he can wear them the other way."

Finally, Preminger accepted take twenty-six and they started over for TV, taping the sheet up on Brigitte. By now, the psychic root-canal work, the heat, nudity, manhandling, and her illness had started to tell on her. Last night in the airport she had fainted and the rings had fallen off her fingers. Now she began to sob.

After seven tries, they got the TV version.

"Now we do one more nude! Rip the sheet off." He wanted to preserve her mood.

The next take was a print. "Good! She has become tender."

Or tenderized.

Having bared one small pair of breasts, the film moved on to bigger things: five nude hostages, to be photographed by the Arabs.

They would film at sea, under a steel-gray sky swollen with impending rain, perfect for "dawn." The Arabs came aboard in Juan, including Josef Shiloah (Hacam the leader), Amidou (Kirkbane the smiling killer), and two younger men.

There was a grim atmosphere on the ship, partly from the previous shooting, partly from the actresses' nerves. The French women accepted the nudity, but Lalla was tense and Kim had gone numb.

Preminger simply marched ahead. Hearing that yesterday's rushes had survived, he answered, "Well, we may redo them for other reasons."

Upstairs, he approved the stripped fantail, which created a sinister geometry of empty spaces: deck, water, and sky.

Soon they cast off. The diesels started with a rolling, deep shudder, the ship backed away from the breakwater, then moved forward with a thrilling, wasteful surge of power.

"It's another *Exodus*!" someone called.

The lighthouse slipped away on one side, and then only the churning, gray sea surrounded us.

On deck, in a bustle of preparation, Tony Teiger handed out weapons to the Arabs. The hand-held camera would start where a staircase opened out to the fantail. Amidou would lead the nude women up and out to five chairs facing the stern. We

222

would see the hostages only from behind, framed against the sudden view of the ominous sky. The shot ended with a close-up of Shiloah, demanding to know which girl was Hélène Nikolaos.

During a few (clothed) run-throughs, Preminger told the Arabs not to be harsh. "Mr. Shiloah, it's stronger if your gun is menacing, not you."

And the girls should be uncertain. "Brigitte, walk *slowly*. Not like a girl on the Lido!"

Then it was time.

Wolfgang herded the unnecessary peepers below.

On cue, at the foot of the stairs, the women stripped off their coats and started up. The crew's eyes glazed with professional detachment, trying not to stare, darting quickly over the naked torsos and back to the frightened faces. Shiloah followed the girls, holding his gun . . . and trying not to throw up.

"Preminger tell me to walk straight—like a leader—but *he* is holding on to a rail. . . . It's my first day, the whole ship is rocking, and *naturally I'm seasick!*"

After each take, Anna and her aides rushed up to cover the girls: then they all trooped below again. It was like backstage at the follies.

"Annalise, you still think these girls are badly made?" asked Otto.

"You twist my words—"

"You know, I must be old-fashioned. I still don't like to do this. It's more embarrassing to me than to them."

Yet, during the takes one forgot the seasickness and prudery. The simple reality of the shot took over, creating an erotic image of submission bathed in pearl-gray light. The scene was all movement, props, and bodies. If money could buy anything, this was it: the motors churning and the boat pitching in the open sea, the guns and flesh and clouds in all their physical reality. As the women appeared, looking so vulnerable, *Rosebud* became pure spectacle, beyond language barriers, as vivid as a nightmare acted out.

And Shiloah never did throw up.

They went on to a side angle as the girls sat down. Since no breasts showed, the actresses wore towels. Their shoulders were still bare and their faces pinched and cold.

"In some countries it might be funny to have so mild a view"—so Preminger repeated the action in a bolder version, shooting full-figure nudes head-on.

Next, Isabelle read the Arab demands. In the cold, with the wind whipping her hair and the Arab paper rattling in her hand, she sat naked, rigid, oddly composed, reminding me of the way she had faced Preminger's anger in the rehearsal room.

There was only one more shot to get—Shiloah giving the text to Isabelle—when the sun came out.

"Can't shoot," said Denys. "It won't match."

The girls bundled up in the saloon and the ship closed down to a three-knot idling speed, going slowly round in circles.

Preminger told stories in the saloon, summoning Darryl Zanuck and Tallulah Bankhead to pass the time.

On deck, groups of crewmen gathered, staring at the bright horizon. One of them spoke of a movie that had never been finished. It was *Man's Fate,* based on the Malraux novel, and its director was Fred Zinnemann. Preminger and Willy Holt had described him as quiet, closed, correct, and meticulous about detail. Now an assistant propman gave another view. His talk was, as much as any, part of the life of the film.

He had worked on the production in London at MGM, "just before Metro's closing in the U.K." The film was to be enormous, costing over $10 million. For the Chinese war scenes, thousands of guns and uniforms had been requisitioned. They were to shoot interiors in London, then go to Singapore, where a forty-man construction crew was already toiling. When the propman first read the script, he had had doubts, but seeing some rehearsals with Peter Finch, Max Von Sydow, Liv Ullmann, and David Niven, he knew it would be "a masterpiece."

Then new management took over the ailing studio and the film was canceled, a decision credited to James Aubrey, formerly the "smiling cobra" of CBS.

Zinnemann had invested three years and several million dollars in the project. When it was canceled, this "closed, correct" director came on a sound stage in London to tell the cast and crew.

Said the propman, "I could see that he was fighting not to cry."

A moment later Preminger announced, "The girls are finished for today. Let's go home. They can't match the shot."

That night we saw the first rushes. (Preminger let anyone watch them, but no one could see the editing. So everyone usually came to the screenings except grips and stars.) We gathered for this first session in a basement room where Robin Gregory had rigged a projector. On hardwood chairs, Preminger sat dead center with Coop on one side and editor Peter Thornton on the other. The rest were apart and behind, combining deference and protective distance.

Peter Thornton called out what was coming—"Three scenes, two takes each"—and Preminger ordered a start.

The door was locked.

Lights went down.

Ten seconds of leader appeared—the *Rosebud* logo—helping the boothman to focus.

Suddenly came the galley, with clapsticks near camera. They snapped. They were pulled away. Offscreen, Preminger called "Action!"

To read a film from one day's rushes is like imagining a marriage from one love letter. People can only know what they see, and will not easily imagine more. Possibly only the director can evaluate rushes. Yet everyone tries. And to me the galley was unbearable, two minutes of silly chatter. The single, unbroken angle only made it worse. Natural light seemed to pour in from the windows, but Lalla was thrust so close to the lens that any movement swelled her features in spherical distortion. It seemed as if all the falsity of the rehearsals was now magnified on the screen.

After that first shock, it was hard to judge the rest. Only when Lalla ran toward the boat, past the brilliant, silver sparkle of the harbor, was there any life. Otherwise, Preminger had gotten the opposite of what he sought. Instead of charming girls and a loving mother, they appeared like parasites. The promise of that long preparation looked broken. But then, I remembered Preminger saying on another occasion, "Look, you're speaking to an expert in broken promises." He had even laughed, as if, after so many pictures, no more surprises were possible.

Later, I asked a crewman what he thought of the work.

He looked at me vacantly and answered without emotion. "Teddy . . . what can you say?"

Juggernaut

There are times when it is an act of courage just to get up in the morning. Such days a director goes to work facing the indifference, even the contempt, of a crew. In the words of Chalky White, "It takes balls."

Otto began day three without speaking of the rushes. Maybe he already knew how little of them would be used. He surely knew that nothing in movies goes in a straight line. And there are hours when silence is the only strength.

Today the Arabs bribed the *Rosebud* crewman in the Las Vegas . . . and then crept into Brigitte's cabin. As Shiloah woke her at gunpoint, announcing she was a prisoner of the Palestine Liberation Organization, she covered herself with a sheet.

When the day's work ended, Amidou and Shiloah drank orange juice and poured out their feelings.

Amidou described the scene in which he promised to knock out the *Rosebud* crewman—to deflect suspicion from the man.

"Preminger want me to smile when I say 'Don't worry, you won't feel a thing.' Not just smile. Big smile." His toothpaste grin flashed against his dark complexion, then faded. "I say this is not an advertisement. The line must be gentle. Reassuring. Believable! It's false to smile!"

Meanwhile Shiloah brooded and sipped juice. "In Ma'alot the terrorists played with the children. . . . " He was trying to contain himself. "I only have the new script *one day* before we start. And English is very hard!" He glared bitterly. "I *promise* you—when I say 'You are a prisoner of the PLO' and she pull up the sheet, the whole world will laugh! A strange man with a gun is standing in her room! She would be paralyzed, not modest!

"I have spent sixteen years in cinema. . . . I know Hacam is tragic hero. There is nothing else he can do. He has climbed ropes, struggled, worked with a gun at night . . . his blood races!

"Preminger thinks so fast! And it *must* be his way! He tells me to be calm. Deliberate. That's all. . . . But I must be hard. So that later there can be a change. And the humanity can show. . . . I want to say to Preminger, 'Let me make him a tragic figure! He can be. Leave it to me.' But I can't talk to him. When this man say I will kill myself if forced to kill a hostage, should be tears. Passionate. Quiet. Pain . . . a martyr's pain. *I* am very moved by his idea . . . and his frustration."

Amidou wanted to be more sensitive and Shiloah more passionate. They both sought to be more like themselves. Along with Adrienne Corri they left their performances offscreen. Preminger hardly knew them. Perhaps that was a condition of bulling ahead. Perhaps, by now, all they had in common was the oncoming juggernaut.

June 1. Saturday morning. In the next twenty-four hours the frustration around the actors erupted. For background interest, there was also the arrival of a four-thousand-pound crane from London.

"I hate to think what the final bill will be," said Graham.

"Don't you *want* to use it?" asked OP. "Sometimes I feel like the youngest one here!"

The first crane shot would be on the sunny coast road near Antibes, as the Rolls came around a curve, on the way to the boat. The crane would drive along with the car for a wide angle, then glide down . . . down . . . to the open back seat where Lalla and Adrienne gossiped about boyfriends.

Unfortunately, the Rolls went much faster than the crane, so the crane had to be *carried* ahead of the car on a flatbed truck.

"Watch your legs, chaps!"

They heaved the beast onto the flatbed, clamping it to a nest of pipes. Others swarmed over the Rolls, stowing batteries in the trunk, running cables under the seats to two lights— Ianebeam "redheads" with fiberglass bodies that wouldn't singe the car's walnut paneling. The open sun and the quartz lamps made the car hellish for the actresses and worse for Robin Gregory, who squatted with his equipment under the dashboard, hidden by a heavy black cloth, baking.

Among other communications gear, Robin had a transmitter to send the actors' voices to OP's earphones on the crane. The crew also used eight walkie-talkies—for the vehicles, for the policemen at crossroads, and for the motorcycle cops ahead and behind the procession. Preminger himself would have a bullhorn.

"I think he'll like that," said a grip.

"Round about now," Denys guessed, "he's pacing the office asking 'Vy aren't they readdddy?' "

No, right about then he was firing Yves Beneyton.

It had begun a few days earlier, when Preminger wanted him to give up riding a potentially dangerous motorcycle until his part was done. Wolfgang relayed the request and Yves stormed away, saying, "I'm not going to change my life just to accommodate your fear of Otto Preminger."

Today, Preminger thought Yves hadn't learned his lines. "If you don't want to play this part, you don't have to—"

"Then I'll go—"

"This is the most unprofessional thing—"

"You think *that's* unprofessional? How about calling me at ten A.M. and asking if lines are learned? That's not the way movies are made in France."

"Then you can go on making movies in France!"

"In this country you don't wake actors at ten o'clock!"

Preminger was delighted. "He wanted to go. . . . I was unhappy with him anyway. He read like he was doing me a favor!"

Said Yves, "Preminger tells me my character is cold . . . reasonable. It's foolish if he *rages* at Fargeau. . . . After all, he is a professor."

The argument would never be resolved, and they would reshoot his scenes.

The grips laughed when they heard.

"Tedward, you writing about the blood, sweat, and tears?"

As for Preminger, he thrived on the crisis. He enjoyed calling "Golda" for a replacement. Once on the set, he liked hearing Raoul Baum joke to Lalla that she looked a little tired this morning. It was a grand excuse for a roar of indignation. "In the first place, she looks beautiful! In the second place, you never say such a thing to an actress! And in the third place, *you* would never look so beautiful if you slept a hundred years!"

Raoul could only sigh. "I would like to see a John Ford film now . . . or a Raoul Walsh!"

The caravan crept into the road for rehearsal. The intercoms crackled with Franco-American static. "Are we going? . . . Shooting now? . . . Are the lights on?"

Riding that open flatbed was sheer terror. Preminger was strapped into his crane seat, wearing a straw hat against the sun. The rest of us clung to stanchions, pipes—anything—as the truck rumbled off.

"Nobody knows wot's 'appening—"

229

The Rolls came around the curve supposedly followed by "background vehicles." But somehow they got in front.

"Wolfgang, the white car!"

Behind the caravan, real traffic piled up. After each take, the film vehicles pulled over while a line of angry tourists squeezed past, glaring at their obstructors.

There was no time to worry about the actresses who sat mutely in the car, only to erupt on cue in sudden laughter and dialogue.

"You should see Robin. He's in a bath of sweat . . ."

"We'll be in Juan an extra week . . ."

By take twelve they had a print. As they unstrapped Preminger, an aide whispered to him and he shouted, "We already have a new Thibaud!" Georges Beller was flying from Paris, and Preminger was delighted. It was almost like starting over.

Back in the production office, Preminger found Yves asking for expense money.

"Not one *cent*. You broke the contract."

"We have no contract." (Meaning nothing on paper.) "Let's say I came to see you. A kind of screen test."

"Nothing." It was cold and final, spoken from the heart.

Beneyton returned the chill. "So it's down to the bottom." He spun around and strode out, having finally played this one decent scene for Preminger, too late. Of the actors who left the film, Yves was the most puzzling—a talented man who could have brought something to his part but wouldn't. One would never know what chemistry bothered him in OP or in the film or in himself.

Graham watched his departure sadly. "I'm only in this for the money. Now even *that* doesn't look like so much."

The lone encouragement, and a modest one, was Claude Dauphin's TV confession that afternoon, set in the ship's saloon, like Pettifer's newscast.

Four takes. Four swift takes. Preminger sat on a chair

nearby, offering quiet suggestions. There were no malaprop-isms, no grammatical fractures.

A lean old man with a shock of white hair, Dauphin sug-gested iron will and craft. He told of illegally running guns to Hussein, accepted responsibility for the Black September massacre of Palestinian refugees, then removed his glasses, paused dramatically, looking red-eyed and uncertain, and ad-mitted he was also a Jew. One longed to see him work more on the speech, mining further defiance and shame. It needed all the credibility he could manage, since nothing in the film pre-pared us for these revelations or their confused implications.

But Preminger seemed grateful just to have him sustain an emotion through a take.

Saturday Night and Sunday Morning

Over the weekend everyone tried to forget the coming Monday. A big card game was held on Friday before payday, "so you can't be broke for the week." That left Saturday night for drinking, prowling the cafés, and wistfully remembering.

By now my own weekends had narrowed to Aristea. That was not her name or even close to it, but this story would be in-complete without her.

She was a bilingual beauty, English-French, whose connec-tion to the film left her evenings free. So we began to share din-ners, spending hours in the local Vietnamese restaurant and on the Juana terrace, over bottles of chilled wine, while the moon-light caressed her blonde hair and ivory shoulders.

Preminger noticed immediately.

"She adores you," he confided, in front of the whole crew. "Will you marry her?"

By slow degrees we did allow ourselves to care about each other, as if to fill the void of living in others' shadows. Our mu-tual distance from the film and all we saw of it gave us lots in common, until, this Saturday, it seemed natural that I should stay with her.

It would be pleasant to report a swell of rapture, but instead there was some gargle about . . . being patient. A chill theme. Aristea maintained that she was trying to love me, "But there is someone else at home. And the joke is he doesn't love me at all."

She lay beside me, her head turned away, her hair covering her face—looking like the soul of impacted lust—until I called her a "loathsome little creature." She was in fact a lissome delight and the ridiculousness of any waiting suddenly struck her as a wonderful joke.

Later she smiled across the pillow. "I'm so relaxed I even forget about *you.*"

We would go to Corsica in a week, then to Paris, then say good-bye. For now, she tempered the feeling of being a solitary witness to this lost cause of a movie, about which no one might finally care. She was the world beyond it.

Seconds

Monday morning Preminger started reshooting Beneyton's scenes. He also had to worry about losing the *Rosebud* before he had finished his work on it.

Said Graham, "We're really in the shit if he doesn't make it."

In this pressurized state, *Rosebud* welcomed Georges Beller, a tall, handsome, athletic young man, a genuine nice guy, and the embodiment of a Second Chance.

They began a retake of the "love scene" and some hearts sank as a familiar sound floated out over the rocks.

"If you don't want to do it, you can join Mr. Beneyton!"

"I try to do what you—"

"You will be good but you must concentrate! These few lines are not so difficult."

Preminger insisted on long, unbroken takes. He didn't want to make the performance in the editing room, but *get* it at once, on camera, as he had with Clifton Webb, Jimmy Stewart, Laurence Olivier, Paul Newman, and all the rest. But now he hoped to do so with actors who barely spoke English. And the observers who drilled the actors repeatedly only made the readings more mechanical.

For the retake of Thibaud's arrival, the dialogue was simplified. Kim's lines were less coy. There was no more talk of "kept men"—no more quoting of Lord Byron.

Preminger told Georges, "Remember, it's a beautiful day. Look around. . . . This is your first appearance. Be light!"

But having a new actor altered all the old rhythms, and mistakes were repeated. At last, the director accepted take seventeen, saying to Kim as she slumped dejectedly, "You run a close second to Kim Novak and Marilyn Monroe. Not in attractiveness but number of *takes!*"

And to Georges: "I want to point out that the Captain, who is *not* an actor, did the same line and the same moves every time! On the other hand, if I let *you* run the ship we go aground!"

Georges sat on the rocks later and mimed blowing out his brains. "It never happened to me before. He needs an American actor! Who can do the whole thing perfectly each time! I am afraid . . . I can't do it. And this way to work—it doesn't help!" He lit a smoke and sat, boiling.

Lunch was relatively tranquil except for the delegation of crew members who came to complain of the long hours and ask for overtime. Preminger answered by saying they had made "all-in" deals and if they didn't like it he would close the production for two days and hire *new* people.

There were bitter, whispered accusations of "damn lies" as the men returned to work.

In the next shot, Brigitte and all the other girls met Georges on deck, with kisses and banter and repeated exposition about the families' wealth.

It was easy, standing on the dock, to spot those repetitions. I

233

wasn't Georges Beller, going over those awkward phrases, choking on frustration. And I wasn't the director, sitting on a crane, racing to survive.

"*Kiss* her," he called to Georges. "It was good till then! Except for your speech, which was unintelligible."

Beller suddenly wheeled around and shouted up to Preminger, "Don't be on my back, Mister!"

Tools down. Silence. Seventy people in that mutinous atmosphere waited for a climax.

"*Really I try—*"

Preminger snapped back, "As I offered at lunch, you can go home!"

"I don't *want* to go home! *I try to be good!* You think I am bad on purpose! *Help me!*" It was a naked cry of pain. "I am here one day only! Since yesterday I get the script. . . . *I am French! I want to be good!*"

"That's why we rehearse! You can be good!"

The grips could take up their grievances in private. But this had to erupt publicly.

Beller strode off, seething, unable to say more, and paced along the deck, talking to himself, ready to hit out—had there been something to hit.

Said a crewman, "At least he got his balls back."

After five seconds, Preminger called another rehearsal. "Miss Huppert, you're a very talented woman and you know it. You can do this if you concentrate!"

The shouting was the same, the tension was the same, and to me the results looked the same.

Next day they heard that the retake of the love scene had been ruined because of faulty film stock. Once more Georges and Brigitte would have to go to bed.

"We do it over," said Preminger, "for the *acting*. It's almost habitual, this scene."

"It's getting better," Wolfgang felt later. "By the time we have to give back the boat, it should be ready."

234

Hurry Sundown

Against this futility, there are still good moments.

The actors begin to relax. Lalla says she loves being on the set. After a time, even Georges Beller agrees with her.

"The first day I would have left. . . . But now we get along fine. He tells me I'm the new Belmondo!" Georges smiles sheepishly. "I like to hear it."

And there are moments everyone shares, as when Fargeau's helicopter flies in on a sunbeam, beating dust in manic swirls over the rocks, landing with a shrill, metallic whine.

By now helicopter shots are as trite as car chases and slow-motion bullet wounds. But Preminger only uses the machine to show Fargeau's wealth. It will carry him away after dinner, into the night, while the music swells to announce the waiting Arabs. (See Appendix, "Helicopter Shot," page 346.)

They race to do the scene at the last dying light.

We will *just* see the flight on screen.

One rehearsal.

The Captain walks Dauphin to the chopper.

Helps him in.

"Mr. Dauphin, lead! Fast!"

Equipment is cleared off the rocks.

"Strike the ladder!'"

Preminger wants someone to guide the craft by radio. "If I control him, he will end up in La Guardia!"

Erik rides in the bird to relay instructions.

Takeoff.

Wind whips at the crew.

Everyone is riveted by the noise.

The composer wants music like the engines.

"Denys, if he takes off again right away, it looks the same—"

"No, Otto, it's getting darker all the time."

Up and away. Take four.

"They started without me!" says Preminger.

"It's cinema verité."

Otto laughs. "You mean directors are liars?"
"There's no director. It's improvised!"
Darkness.
They land.
Erik bounds out happily. "The whole three months were worth that!"

Another day, another shot, again racing the sunset.
Preminger lines up the introductions before dinner on the fantail. Three shots. *All* at sunset.
Each starts on an entrance.
First Brigitte drags out Georges to meet her grandfather.
"It's *funny*!" says OP. "*Take* him! Smile! Show this little girl has guts!"
And each shot ends on movement. One feels a rhythm, building to the sight of that glowing dinner table.
Hurry now.
Catch the light.
Tony Teiger produces wine, platters of beef, vegetables, strawberries.
Grips lay more track. Bring more quartz lamps.
A green sheet billows over the table to protect it.
Lamps are lit.
Quick!
The new assistant director, Richard Jenkins, hired to help Raoul Baum, summons the girls.
Denys takes meter readings. "Genny's gone down a bit. We've lost half a stop."
Ron Pearce rushes to check it.
The girls appear.
The green cloth is whisked away.
The actresses stare at the crystal, the china, the linen—with bovine wonder.
"*We* did this—?"
One girl stares, a scene starts, the bubble bursts—and the joy ends.

In each shot Preminger wrestles with the Intractable.

Often it is one line that an actor simply cannot do.

This shot ends as a girl brings on a tray, asking "Pâté, anybody?"

She looks like a teen goddess. Late sun gilds her hair in orange flame.

"But say the line I gave you? 'Pâté, anybody?' "

Take five. "You want some pâté?"

Take eight. "Say 'Pâté, anybody?' *as you walk*."

Take ten. "*Walk in!* Don't drift! And say 'Pâté, anybody?' "

Take eleven. "Don't *pause* before it."

Take twelve. The girl hits the wrong mark, blocking the others.

Finally they get something but Miss Pâté looks like a sleepwalker and thus, little by little, again and again, is the design of the piece chipped away, leaving only intractable reality.

The Racers

June 6 was D-Day on the calendar and desperate Thursday in the office.

Among other problems, they could not leave for Corsica on Saturday as scheduled; the best they could hope for was to fly out Monday after shooting a scene at the Nice airport.

Meanwhile Annalise was leaving, Willy Holt was close to quitting over the firing of one of his staff as an economy move, and even Graham had given a moment's thought to departing. "He really doesn't need me after Paris. . . . The French-speaking will be over then."

Into this gloom strode Preminger, freshly showered and crisp, asking why everyone looked so glum.

He quickly made some calls, including one to Jules Buck for a new wardrobe person, and then cut the scene at the Nice airport.

"Why are you so *sad*? I just saved you half a day!"

Watching him, I remembered how the French critic, Olivier Eyquem, admired his vitality. "Older directors are cynical or romantic. . . . Look at Billy Wilder's *Avanti*. So sad. But *this* man doesn't feel tired or old. In *his* late sixties he makes *Such Good Friends*—a comedy about death."

By evening, they had a new wardrobe man, a shorter script, and a director racing through a clash of generations and philosophies that should have been a high point. Ironically, after eight days, this was the first real "Preminger scene": the radical in blue jeans disrupting the end of a chic dinner party.

For this argument, one expected two-shots, shades of *Laura* and *Exodus*, Dauphin and Beller in a frame like a proscenium that established Preminger's own neutrality. His two-shot had become, as Andrew Sarris said in *The American Cinema*, "a stylistic expression of the right-wrong in all of us."

But tonight the only way to save time was to separate the actors. There was already too much garbled English in the picture to try anything else. ("He knows," said an aide sadly, "that he needs a month of dubbing.")

Preminger carefully developed Dauphin's anger, telling him to "be condescending" at first, when asking Beller's occupation. "You don't take him seriously. As if you asked ten minutes ago." On the next line, "You almost lose your temper." The character lived for Preminger, even down to details like his cheap cigarette lighter. "Your poor father gave it to you, before the fortune."

With Georges, Preminger simplified the lines. "And I'll pray you speak slowly."

The two actors were not in frame together except in a wide shot at the start and finish. The director split most of their dialogue into matching angles: each man between two women; each man alone. Neat and simple.

To connect the reverse angles, Preminger surrounded the men with movement. Thus Lalla left one three-shot and entered another to pour some wine—as the speaker changed. The frames would snap together like magnets.

Dauphin's shots went quickly. He seemed to give the first

performance in the film, patronizing the young man while loathing him. For Dauphin, the crew showed the ultimate respect. The clapsticks in front of him were not slapped shut but softly clicked.

Then they turned to Georges.

He surely had some of the hardest lines in the movie: all about "economic units" and their effect on "the political integrity of government." It was someone's idea of an intellectual's discourse.

Preminger divided the shots into smaller and smaller bits, struggling to keep his patience.

"*Mean* what you say," he ordered. "It's singsong. Make it an attack."

He hurried propman Tony Teiger, who bridled. "I'm emptying the glasses, Otto. Don't shout at me!"

There was an instant, breathless silence from the crew.

"Don't tell me what to do! I shout at everybody!"

"Don't shout at *me*!"

"You're right, now you can go." Preminger smiled but hard feelings remained. And they had to finish the scene.

"Now," he promised Georges, "we will roll without mercy."

Beller's painstaking English was no match for Dauphin. And the language struggles left no time to bring the Arabs closer to the scene. During the dinner, the yacht was never in the same shot with their raft, so they added no suspense, no edge of irony to the prattle about "revolution."

Months later, at the dubbing in London, Georges had a schedule conflict that forced Preminger to revoice him. Yet even an expert had to match the actor's lips. The pace was still deadly.

Only when the scene was accidentally run silently did its crisscross visual patterns build to Beller's departure. Then, for a moment, everyone could see what Preminger had intended.

The dubbing expert blurted out, with the appalling innocence of a newcomer, "It *looks* wonderful."

Dinner ended at four in the morning, and the crew went to
sea for a third try at finishing the nude scene.

The girls faced it grimly. "It's not how you start, it's how
you finish, I keep telling myself."

"Oh, shut up, for crissake! *You're* gonna finish drowned!"

An aide asked if they wanted to take off their clothes and
come up. Lalla shot back, "Of *course* I want to be on this
fucking boat at five in the morning with no clothes on!"

At 6:00 A.M. they docked and shuffled stiffly to waiting
buses and trucks, hoping to catch a few hours sleep before the
rushes that afternoon . . .

. . . where Preminger saw the love scene again.

"For *that* you made me get up?!"

In the production office, Amidou slouched in a chair. "How
can you *give*," he asked, "when you are afraid?"

Graham looked dazed. "What I don't understand is how
everything can go wrong?"

And Wolfgang stayed calm, knowing they had to finish that
night on the boat.

All that next night Preminger was cutting, compressing,
racing. He dropped the Arabs' talk about killing the crew. Now
they just *did* it. And he did the *Rosebud*'s casting off, half a
page of script, in one sweeping shot from Hacam on the bridge
down to the men on deck struggling with the ropes back to
Hacam starting the engines.

And still they didn't finish.

But Aristea and I left early, having seen enough. We walked
along the shore, past the casino, the *boule* park, and the cafés,
stopping only once to look back at the boat, ablaze with light
on the black water.

"It looks like a wedding cake, doesn't it?" she asked. "And
in a little while it will all be gone."

At a distance, the boat seemed only an ornament of that toy town, an image of luxury crafted in a world apart from movies, remote from the chance forces that shook a production and mocked anyone's pretensions to control.

Out of the Past

Somehow they arranged one more night on the boat, one last spasm, including another action ballet as the Arabs climbed out of their raft and scuttled over the rocks and up the gangplank, into the *Rosebud*, followed by the sweeping crane. (See Appendix, "Daily Continuity Report," page 347.)

By now an exhausted crew hardly gave a damn. Mickey Murchan lay on the rocks as the crane swung overhead and looked up at Preminger's soles. "Hey boys, Otto didn't wash his feet today."

There were a few tired laughs.

Then came the killing of the *Rosebud* crewman, Frank Woods.

All the filming on the boat ended with this surprising memory of past glory: a scene that was a director's signature, blending forties melodrama, seventies technology, and one man's enduring, impassive vision.

The moment evoked a world of *film noir*, movies like Wilder's *Double Indemnity*, Huston's *Asphalt Jungle*, Lang's *The Big Heat*, and Preminger's *Laura*. These melodramas, steeped in violence, mocking humor, and a pervasive sense of doom, were the underside of official Hollywood Good Cheer.

Within their exaggerated conventions, directors explored complexities of good-in-evil, hate-in-love, and "the right-wrong in all of us." Perversely, time has caught up with their vision to a degree. Today their images are seen as having a shadowy beauty, their views of humankind the sting of bitter truths.

As the filming on the yacht ended, Preminger reached back instinctively to this, the richest tradition in his work.

On the side deck, Amidou gave the crewman the rest of his

bribe and promised again to knock him out painlessly. Then, as the man counted his francs, Amidou killed him. The scene confounded an audience's moral expectations. The victim died of avarice. "Count the money," ordered Preminger, "and die as you greedily count it." And the killer was a charming idealist. Wherein lay the evil?

Probably Preminger was trying for the same ambivalence in Dauphin and Beller as they argued at dinner. But the text and the language barriers were too much there. He could only work with Dauphin to suggest the tough industrialist undone by his only decent feelings—for his granddaughter.

But here on deck the stark action and the darkly ambiguous morality worked together. When he was stabbed, the crewman collapsed like a balloon, dropping his money and cigarette. Amidou stepped into frame, pocketed the money, and flicked the butt into the water. It was an epitaph for a nobody, the punctuation of a neutral style that allowed, by its neutrality, a range of audience reactions. Preminger had mastered the style, had done as much as any director to invent it.

And no one that night either liked or understood what was happening, not the actors, nor the crew, nor I, uselessly remembering other movies. Amidou hated having to smile. "It says 'I kill people but I don't like it.' " As for the crew, they watched with suppressed laughter. But they had seen the blood tubes and the retractable weapon. They had been up two nights and were into a third.

Before the reviews had soured all reaction to the film, the killing—which looked so abrupt in Juan—became, to preview audiences, a terrifying surprise. They gasped in the dark. And in the darkness of an amoral underworld, the movie lived for a moment. Preminger was at home.

"All the Juan footage," said Erik, "will only be a speck on screen." It was an epitaph for ten days of shooting and four months of preparation, spoken amid rumors that Preminger had already made big cuts.

They trooped home in a gray Sunday dawn, too tired to care what was shot or cut. A public-address system blared music into the streets over tinny speakers. One exhausted grip stole across a plaza to snip the wires for a few hours of peace.

A New Leaf

On Monday they seemed to begin a whole different film. One had felt a Presence in Juan for a week. News photos showed the "Grand Cowboy" in white denims, the "regular guy" on the beach with his wife. Now, in the port, his face was reflected in the alien sunglasses of twenty newsmen. That huge head was recognizable at twenty paces—a monument of sags, pouches, and cracked-marble eyes, a billboard of ruggedness, living pop art. He wore a suit for the shooting, but his bulging gut and sauntering gait looked as if they could scarcely be contained by it. Especially in person, Robert Mitchum was a Presence.

At the start, he offered hope for controlling the shooting. Preminger was not so far behind, considering that he had fired two actors, redone most of a day, shot his love scene three times, and sailed out two extra times to finish the nude scene.

Now he could move quickly. Mitchum had worked for him before, they were friends, and the actor was a pro.

Lounging near a cabin cruiser, waiting for the first shot, he looked nerveless.

"He gave Angela the script," said Erik, "and said, 'I won't be needing this. What lines do we do today?' "

Meanwhile, newsmen fished for *their* lines.

How was Japan during *The Yacuza*?

"Strictly raw fish and rice."

How did shooting go?

"Left to right."

Complicated?

Mitchum shrugged. "You speak Japanese?"

No.

"That makes it complicated."

How did he like Juan?

"I'm just doing time. Anytime you're working, you're doing time. . . . This isn't bad. Compared to four months in Japan. And nine months in *Dingle!*"

He watched the crew wrestle the crane into place.

"Hauled one of *those* all over Ireland [on *Ryan's Daughter*]. Lean even wanted it for a phone-booth shot. Don't ask me why. Just looking at this one, I'd say we're in trouble."

An hour later the crane broke down.

Nature had made Mitchum a monument while giving Mark Burns the agreeable good looks that insured a long supporting career.

Playing a yacht broker, he traced the Arabs' cabin cruiser (which took the girls from the yacht to Corsica). The part was written without noticeable humor or color, so I asked him what Preminger wanted—besides agreeable good looks.

"I think he wants the lines remembered."

Mitchum had enough color for everyone. He sat in the cabin cruiser, waiting for his cue to walk out, nipping scotch eagerly proffered by the lady boat owner, and joking about night work.

"I don't mind it. . . . I just tell them I drink and they have to finish early."

The owner was enchanted, though she spoke no English.

"Action!" called Preminger from outside.

"I'm coming, action . . . I'm fuckin' coming."

He led the way, strolling out onto the gangplank as the others tried not to laugh.

Said Lalla, "It was all we could do not to fall in."

Seeing the work focus on him, one understood the natural craving of the cinema for faces. In most movies, faces are the major source of life and style. Even on the Côte d'Azur, Mitchum's eyes still peered across a shadowy no-man's land. He remained a quintessential *film noir* actor, a survivor of booze, insomnia, city alleys, dead ends, betrayal, failure, and the rest of life's little jokes. Simply casting him was an act of style.

Off camera or on, he seemed exactly the same. He had obliterated the boundary between himself and acting. Growling about "fuckin' action," it was as if he barked back all the demons of tension and freed himself to be himself. Action, cut, rehearse—even half sizzled on scotch—it didn't matter. He was big Bob, pure and simple, ambling along.

A French reporter asked about his rolling gait.

"Actually," replied Mitchum, "it's a desperate attempt to walk a straight line."

On a take, someone moved in the background. Mitchum drawled, "When we worked on westerns, they used to keep a guy with a fuckin' air rifle to clear the background."

Offscreen, the actor brought some life to the women of the film. Lalla became "Lallapalooza!" And Aristea enjoyed a few words with him.

Preminger came over, beaming about it. "Gershuny, you have lost out to Mitchum!"

I went back to my hotel to pack for Corsica. Aristea turned up an hour later with a bag of peaches and a sudden, urgent kiss. "Preminger said I was too hard on you, flirting with Mitchum. I told him that if *that* was being hard on you, you deserve to feel bad!"

That afternoon, as we all prepared to leave, Preminger had thirty to forty minutes of footage and a star who offered some cockeyed hope. And I had a wish to remember . . . moonlit suppers on the Juana terrace, a blaze of light on the hull of the *Rosebud*, Adrienne Corri's champagne laughter, a sudden death from an old *film noir*, the tarnished design of this new film. So many aspirations. . . .

The experience all came down to the footage, and with it the sense of opportunities missed, which haunts most films, most ragged departures.

A plaque on the side of the PVSR camera listed all the pictures that had used that particular instrument:

1969 TAM LIN
1969 THE MUSIC LOVER
1970 THE HORSEMEN
1970 THE DEVILS
1971 YOUNG WINSTON
1971 THE BOYFRIEND
1972 TRAVELS WITH MY AUNT
1972 FENGRIFFEN
1972 LITTLE MALCOLM & THE EUNUCHS
1973 ZARDOZ
1973 CARAVAN TO VACCARES
1974 JUGGERNAUT
1974 MURDER ON THE ORIENT EXPRESS
1974 ROSEBUD

They included unreleasable abortions, George Cukor's exquisite almost-valedictory, a single big hit, art films, ego trips, divine madnesses—everything. The run of the mill.

They had all probably evoked in their makers the same hope, pain, and silliness as this film. All those forgotten experiences only made these memories more important to me.

That afternoon, as the garden behind my room darkened in the disordered sunset, Aristea and I held each other close and made ourselves a few more memories.

CORSICA

The Longest Day

In Corsica the film began in confusion . . . moved to a brief moment of trust . . . then blew up so violently as to make everything that came before seem idyllic.

The confusion started with *getting* to the island. Supposedly everyone followed the instructions in the Movement Order (see Appendix, pages 348–49.)

"Please have your luggage ready in hotel lobbies by 10:30," read the plan. What it really came down to was people tossing *heaps* of bags into a truck, even as the hotels were invaded by new tourist hordes—Tartars, Vandals, Huns, and howling hunlets.

In Bastia, some bags were dumped in an airport parking lot. Others were just . . . gone.

"Even a crummy BBC show gives you stickers to put on!" The troupe sweated luggage to a bus and dropped into their seats—blasted by music from the driver's radio.

And *allons*! To La Marana—home for three unforgettable nights on the outskirts of Purgatory, only twenty minutes from Bastia.

It was, in fact, a camp.

"There's no transportation, no cars, no toothpaste in the store, and they don't do laundry!" said a crewman.

"Tennis in fifteen minutes!" boomed the loudspeakers.

"The dining room is filled with roaring Krauts! The English on holiday are bad enough, but the *Germans*!"

The unit was furious. Preminger had gone to another hotel (with the stars and key staff). Like deserted children, the others blamed him for everything.

"Those rushes are awful."

"And he's made it impossible for the rest of us to work."

"Christ, did you *see* those rushes?"

"His *son* writing the script! And, with all due respect, *you* as a plumber! It's not professional!"

Only to Lalla was he an angel. She returned from a dinner for the visiting press telling of his thoughtfulness to her—and to Wolfgang.

It seemed that Crystal had turned up.

"The black girl claimed Wolfgang was unkind to her—rude—and OP said, 'Not only is he the *best* first assistant I've ever had, he is the kindest man. He couldn't be rude.' "

Well, at least nobody disagreed about Mitchum. Lalla said, "He was roaring drunk and the journalists didn't know what hit them. 'I don't need you motherfuckin' journalists! . . . All you care about is your fuckin' advertisements!' "

Friday in Bastia would be the biggest day of the film, with the ferry, five hundred extras, and fifty reporters. There was a mass of planning on Thursday. And my debut.

Our band of Jewish commandos were disguised—shamelessly—as Boy Scouts, wearing shorts and gym socks, showing long, mortally pale shanks.

"If Aristea could see you now," exclaimed Otto, "she would ask for your hand!"

The others in the unit just laughed. Apparently we brought a little sunshine into their humdrum lives.

On cue, our two minibuses rolled out of an auto ferry with other traffic, stopped at customs, picked up our leader, Cliff Gorman, and drove off. Wolfgang called orders—mostly to hurry up—and we moved ever faster until they printed.

Immediately Otto summoned the flock to the parking lot to sort out the next day's work.

"Am I using the boat or not?!"

Indeed he was, and an industrial crane too.

248

That night at La Marana, a crisis was simmering.

Raoul Baum shouted because the extras had been summoned for 6:00 A.M.

"That is stupid! They will not be needed until eight! Who did that? Farrago?" Right. Farrago was handling everything.

6:00 A.M. Friday morning. I drive with the assistant directors, feeling their anger.

6:45. At the dock, in the blistering morning light, there is *no* Arab crowd to come off the ferry. No tourist throng. No industrial crane. *It is as if the recces never happened.*

There *are* sixty schoolkids in jeans. As "tourists" they carry three suitcases.

"I had a feeling!" Wolfgang seethes. "Thank God I came early. They must bring their grandmothers—"

"They must have luggage."

"Farrago's finally blown the whole thing."

"He says now *if* people come off the boat he'll keep them."

"The maximum off the boat is sixty."

7:00. The sun is higher over the bare dock.

"If we don't get this, we do it Sunday—"

"We're moving on! We *must* get it!"

7:30. "The boat arrives in fifteen minutes."

7:45. Preminger outlines shots. Suddenly the vessel appears between the twin lighthouses of the harbor—shimmering, white, enormous.

No one is ready.

"We're supposed to be shooting. Hurry up!"

Camera boxes are unloaded.

"Quick! The twenty-five—"

Wolfgang calls to the real crowd on the dock. "Look at the boat!"

It swings, catching the brilliant sun on its white hull.

Jimmy Devis is ready to shoot, bracing himself against a truck—when it drives out from under him . . .

They grabbed shots over the tops of heads. Finally the scene could have been anywhere. There was no great pan of the city, no visual rhetoric, yet there *were* six precious seconds to establish the docks, the ferry, and the gangplank. It was the bare minimum to start the movie—and close to the leanness of Preminger's best work.

They still had pages to shoot and the visiting newsmen to entertain and *no crowd* from Farrago.

"Mr. Baum," called Preminger, "get me *old* people!"

Raoul set off, accosting the elderly.

Farrago himself was busy playing the passport inspector. Lights were shoved close to him. The crowd, augmented by real passengers, came down the gangplank.

"Plus vite, plus vite—"

The camera tracked in.

"Down . . . left . . . zoom!"

—to the fabulous Captain, welcoming tourists to beautiful Corsica in a voice strangled with stagefright.

Watching were Paul Bonnecarrère, John Hemingway (son of Ernest and father of Joan), and some UA executives baby-sitting with the press. For nine takes they saw a tourist family come down the plank, with their bratty son telling us again that this was Corsica.

Well, if they got bored, they could always talk to Mitchum—and now to Cliff Gorman, fresh from New York.

Looking trim and puffing his cigar, Cliff asked, "What's there to see here?"

So far, there was mostly Mitchum.

Cliff laughed. "That cowboy act! It's perfect. Ah, he's got it down." Abruptly he *did* Mitchum: chin back, eyes locked into the middle distance, surveying the gentlemen of the press, speaking solemnly:

" ' . . . Fuuuuck 'em . . . ' "

By the time they made the best shot of the day, the press had mostly departed. It was mid-afternoon when Shiloah passed through customs in the bare, white room off the docks.

The complex setup commanded awe, like money talking.

Through an open door, behind the Arabs, one saw the dockside crowd, which tied this scene to the earlier ones. As Shiloah finished, they tracked out with him into the street, showing another crowd with traffic, then panned him into a bus and away. The frame included police, background vehicles, Arabs, tourists, guards, and a sudden *sprint* by the camera.

But on screen, Shiloah's movement would lead the eye effortlessly as he slipped, unnoticed, into this alien world.

That night I asked what had become of the "beautiful opening shot." People had theories but no single answer. And it finally didn't matter. Plans, recces, revisions, phantom crowds—none of it mattered. Of the last day in Juan-les-Pins and the long day in Bastia, almost nothing would be in the film: no passport inspection, no Farrago, no tourists, no one to inform us this was Corsica, not even a trace of Mitchum's scenes with the yacht broker.

Nothing moved in straight lines, and this confusion could even produce an astonishing success. Weeks later, in the editing, all the mistakes forced them to simplify the opening until it became a clean understatement, blessedly free of dialogue: a few frames of the boat . . . Shiloah coming down the gangplank and passing through customs . . . into the bus, with a glimpse of Bastia behind. Enter the unknown stranger, purposeful and mysterious.

That night, Aristea and I spent an hour in the throbbing disco of La Marana, watching the company pair off. Outside the motel rooms, in the coastal moonlight, there was a steady crunch of traffic on the gravel paths.

As I left Aristea at dawn, I met one woman coming out of a girl friend's room. The ghostly creature was naked under a black velvet wrap, while I wore only slacks. In the pale light, we passed with smiles of dismal complicity.

Next day, the company traveled to Île Rousse, shooting along the way on various roads and feeling very fragile.

One crewman told of his heroic efforts to pack the previous night. "Got up this morning after falling over in the sand. Thought, Well, at least I've *packed.* But what I'd done was to take everything *out* and put it in drawers."

At a location, Mickey Murchan stumbled out of his truck red-eyed. "We expected a hand-held shot on this . . . not a fuckin' track."

On the road again, Keith Hamshere, the dour, elfin stills man with three Nikons slung like millstones around his neck, regaled us with memories of *2001.* "I shot two thousand eight-by-ten color plates for backgrounds . . . seven weeks in South Africa . . . through the desert . . . hauling that bloody big camera around. . . . But it *was* the Dawn of Man." He spent two years on the film. "Couldn't get two days off to get married."

Keith's latest film had been *11 Harrowhouse.* "It's about the biggest diamond robbery since the last one."

The shooting ended at a cove where the five girls, hooded and roped together, were taken off a raft and dragged uphill in an image of cruelty and beauty, as the waning sun backlit the water brilliantly and several of the girls cried inside their suffocating hoods.

To outsiders like Paul Bonnecarrère, lounging on his sailboat in Île Rousse, this cavalcade of turmoil, this stumbling juggernaut, was haunting.

"The work yesterday, it's fabulous! . . . I would love to go to rushes! I would *love* to be part of it!"

"I would love to be part of it . . ."

By the end of the day that feeling had spread, fired by a revelation in the rushes.

We staggered into the Hotel Bonaparte in Île Rousse with barely time to unpack. The luxe hotel, a pink castle with crystalline views of the hills and the palmy shoreline, had opened especially for the film.

By eight, everyone had gathered in a meeting room downstairs to view the Boy Scout arrival. And it worked, without music or a context, perhaps *because* there was no context. The single piece of film was bathed in the cold light of an assassin's sky. As the vans appeared, the crane swooped down to them. The new, buff-colored vehicles emerging from the huge ferry, the four swarthy men in ranger uniforms, the speed of the vans, Gorman's determined way of joining them—the restrained urgency of it all—combined to make a one-shot étude, Preminger at his best. As the vans drove off, the crane rose for a view of the city. It was better than the original "opening shot."

We had trusted the director, and with these results. Erik rejoiced. "Everybody said the scouts wouldn't work, but they do!"

And Lalla exulted later. "The old shit is going to make a good film!"

I told her she was one of the few who thought so.

"Adrienne said it too. I adore him! And I want him to make a wonderful film!"

I asked about her own faith in him. How did she feel watching the galley scene?

"I don't know. . . . I can't see the whole film. I have to trust him. I have to do what he asks. . . . *I* haven't done thirty-five films. *I* don't know more than he does. And *I* don't know anyone who does!"

The Bad and the Beautiful

Monday, June 17. Back to reality.

They began shooting at the farm, twenty minutes from the hotel over barren hills or along a winding coast. The site lay surrounded by scrubby, yellow flatland, with burrs and thistles on every path and a summer buzz of flies in the torpid air. On the way to the compound, I passed the catering tent, with its massive lunches of veal, potatoes, vegetables, and salad, its plates of cheese, grapes, peaches, and pears. And no place to wash.

"These people must be unbelievably religious," Preminger mused. "They have a chapel and no toilet."

But portable toilets were set up. And a stone wall with a steel door, topped by barbed wire, had been erected to look as if it surrounded the compound.

"*Magnifique!*" Preminger told Willy Holt.

Once they started shooting, the problems were the same as ever. The material was still overstuffed. If a letter was to be delivered to the terrorists, we saw the mail van arrive, the postman put it in the box, and Amidou pick it up. And all of it—all those literal, connective shots—were finally cut.

Loose ends also haunted the story. Who exactly *were* the Tardetses? Why were there no guards around the farm?

And the biggest problem was still the accents. Preminger never mentioned them now. But he was in a straitjacket: the Arabs had lines that sounded like U.S. slang. Preminger had to drill the actors or cut the lines—never experiment, never improvise.

He repeated a line for one man. " 'Am I glad to see you.' "

"I'm glad to see you—"

"*No! Am—I—glad.*"

Another Arab had to declare he was "bored" in Corsica. Preminger stood in the dusty courtyard, reddening, emphasizing:

"*Bored.*"

"Bort."

"*Borrrred!*"

"Bordt!"

Critic Olivier Eyquem watched sadly. "That's not at all what he wanted." Later the actor dubbed himself. And was still "bordt."

The performers felt the frustration.

Josef Shiloah reflected grimly. "I can't breathe in the farm valley. In Juan I have a temperature. Three weeks I don't eat lunch. He tells me yesterday, 'You would be a better actor if you ate lunch.' Then he say, 'Why are you such a bad actor? You tell me you're a good actor.' And I say, 'No, I told you in Israel I only hope so.' Then he say, 'You used to speak perfect English. What happened?' But he never talked to me. He see me in hotel—'Shalom!'—he see the movie—'Good, I will be in touch!'—that's all."

Amid the verbal problems there was still great visual beauty, like the GAT flight simulator, sleek and surreal in the rude courtyard. Preminger had been absolutely right to insist on it and place it outside. Paul Bonnecarrère gasped at the sight. "*Formidable!*"

Filming became a war between Preminger's text and his visual sense, the verbal and the physical, the bad and the beautiful. They usually co-existed in the same scenes, as at the start of the film, when Shiloah and Amidou were reunited. While speaking about boredom in Corsica, they crossed the whole dusty compound. While discussing Mrs. Tardets, they descended three flights to the cellar. While reviewing the plans for the kidnapping, they toured the caves. (See Appendix, "Cave Plan," page 350.) There Coop created the ominous effect of single lamps dimly lighting each stone room by first hanging bare, working bulbs in the shot, then clustering his spotlights above them, out of sight, so their beams fell away in all directions. The glare of the hanging bulbs was softened by wrapping spun glass around them, which was invisible to the camera when the lights were on. The effect on screen was dramatic.

Until the actors spoke.

Watching the troubled work, one often thought of suggestions, but they would never be made. They were not wanted. At times, though, it was hard to keep silent. Thus, as Shiloah arrived at the farm, we first saw the compound. But there was a later, more dramatic view of it suggested by Coop. On a crane, the camera started from high inside the farm, looking over the barbed wire, out to the fields. The hooded, roped girls were led forward by Amidou. As he ran ahead, the crane came down, the wall loomed up, the Arab swung open the metal gate and brought in the girls. The camera followed them to reveal the compound.

But what if this were the first time we saw it?

It was a flash of possibly overheated insight: cut the whole opening in Corsica. Cut Shiloah's arrival, his reunion with Amidou, the gabble about Tardets's wife, the introduction of the caves and the plot. Start in Juan, with the girls arriving and the Arabs bribing the *Rosebud* crewman. The audience would know there was something up, but not *what*. After the yacht was found in Israel, we would see the girls taken off the Arab cabin cruiser and onto a mysterious shore. When they reached the compound, in Denys's crane shot, it would be a revelation, not a repetition. And perhaps we could see the girls brought into the caves. That seemed like a more dramatic introduction to the dungeon.

It was easy to second-guess. And for a few moments it seemed as if editor Peter Thornton had the same idea. He said,

"There is no title sequence. One way to start the picture is to begin in Antibes . . . crane down from the sea view to the Rolls. . ." But even as he approached the idea he veered from it. "Erik says the time scheme won't allow it."

For everyone the work now becomes an emotional rollercoaster. . .

Denys strides through the courtyard muttering, "Yesterday we had petrol with crap in it that hurt one generator. Today petrol with water that's hurt the other. If it's not one thing it's another!"

Willy Holt finds his job intolerable. "First they take the special-effects man—very unfair; then they take the buyer; then my assistant. There is no department *left*. I can't work this way. Graham ask me, for *him*, please stay. But it's not possible. . . . Preminger ask, 'You leave in the middle of a film?' I tell him, 'Yes, this one.' "

Others struggle on.

There is Angela Martelli with her watch from a 1956 movie. "[Director] Robert Parrish gave it to me at the *start*, not the end. A sign of faith."

And Wolfgang has his "producer's watch": five minutes fast in the morning, five minutes slow at night.

The work is ceaseless.

John Lake, the grip, mutters cheerfully, like a refrain, "It's not easy . . . it's not easy."

Ron Pearce, in cut-offs, like a heavyweight with a beer belly, sweats over the lighting.

Robin Gregory sets up a radio mast for talk with the hotel. "It takes *hours*. They think everything is done so fast. They see too many movies."

Laurent Petitgirard plays his score on a piano in the empty dining room, where Preminger feels a passage is too descriptive: "There is a car, there is movement—why make another movement?"

Cliff Richardson and his son John putter with their plumbing gear in the dust. "I don't like it," says Cliff, "but on *Lawrence* we lived in a perpetual sandstorm."

Tony Teiger, in shorts and sneakers, drags his donkey into a shot.

And, finally, Raoul Baum, at the simulator, fights the War of the Chickens.

The simulator is in the cobbled courtyard next to the house, surrounded by snaking cables and CSI lamps hung on ladders. *Formidable* it is, except to the chickens—a clucking, ravenous horde.

Preminger orders them out. If Isabelle hears one she'll know she isn't "flying."

Raoul is the man for the job.

"Mr. Baum, a chicken!"

"My fault, sir," says Richard Jenkins. He scatters seed to distract them. Four aides chase away the last birds. Almost.

"Mr. Baum, a chicken!"

Raoul, stripped to the waist, sweating and hairy, not laughing at all now, carries out the intruder.

And another. And another. Raoul chases each one through the maze of ladders and cables until he pounces on his prey.

The sun is straight down on the courtyard.

"Mr. Baum, your chickens are not quiet!"

"This is the day for my heart attack."

"Baum, don't you *hear* the chickens?!"

"I *know!* But there is many holes here! They come in!"

With a look of murder, Raoul dives through a stone arch, plunges his arm into a muddy hole, and drags out a screeching fowl. The unit roars with laughter and Preminger loves it.

"*You* are making them nervous, Baum."

Angela Martelli firmly tells her boss to stop teasing. "Baum's fed up. You wait till he directs his first picture and it's brilliant!"

At supper later, nothing will satisfy Raoul but chicken. "I want to *eat* one!"

Of all the troupe, Isabelle withstands the shocks best, even her arguments with Preminger.

"When he says to me, 'I don't believe you,' I know deeply he *does*. When he shouts, I think *he* is frustrated. *I'm* not. I'm the stronger." She alone deals with him on his terms. Because they are also hers.

The other actors try to "understand" him.

"Now," says Amidou, "I *feel* him more."

To Shiloah, Preminger is "an Austrian without a state, a Jew with an accent—and *he* tells *me* 'You must get used to the way Americans make movies!' As if he wants to *be* an American." Shiloah feels that Preminger only respects money and power. "I talk to Mitchum ten minutes—what a boring man—but I know Preminger never shouts at Mitchum. He is too rich and powerful!"

Maybe they understand Preminger too quickly.

Friday, June 21. The girls finished their ensemble work in the caves, which were filled with heat and dust.

Angela Martelli staggered out between takes. "Must breathe. I can just *hear* the dialogue. Can't see. . ."

And focus puller Dewi Humphries followed her, laughing. "It's *hell* in there."

Hell. There Preminger had tried to give the hostages humanity. Instead of taking Valium and waiting silently, they would envy and fight with and comfort one another. But none of it worked. They remained silly girls.

"When I think of how the time *could* be used!" exclaimed Lalla. "As it is, we might as well be sitting around in our Swiss finishing schools!"

Preminger had wanted everyone a character. Now, faced with these results, he had to cut back. Out with talk of escape. Out with "forgetting" they had no dynamite. Out with a "cultural hour."

Jimmy Devis chewed his cigar and watched a run-through, while the smoke and dust drifted up to the lights.

"Could I see it once more?" he asked.

"You will see it at least twenty-seven times more," said Otto. His family was on the way to the island that day. *"That interests me much more than this whole damn scene!"*

"Forty-seven pages so far . . . almost a third done." Angela sat outside, in the shaded garden, typing continuity reports. And Preminger studied more cuts.

"In Paris the girls are finished . . . here the Arabs are done. Now it will go faster." There was enough unsaid in that dappled garden to make me glad to get away.

A Plumber Prepares

My own acting ended in a Corsican ditch with everyone watching, even the donkeys. I was watching too, with a frozen, distant curiosity, wondering if I was going to make a fool of myself. That I could perform seemed irrelevant then. I had wanted to experience acting for Preminger (what a rationale!), then wanted to be involved in the production. At last, seeing what the role called for, I had no feelings but fear.

Cliff Richardson's plan for pumping sleeping gas into the farm was simpler than the original. But I still didn't understand the lines. It was typical: the French actors got English lines while I, with my English, got plumber-ese.

The Richardsons showed Otto a location they liked, near the farm, and produced two donkeys to carry four heavy canisters of "sleeping gas."

"I'm in your hands," Preminger told them. *"God help you!"*

We began rehearsing in a shed near the house. By now I had the same reaction to Corsica as Shiloah; it was a nice place to visit, but I wouldn't want to die there. Each dawn that vast pollen factory of an island brought desperate wheezing until Aristea roused me from our bed of pain.

There were pills and inhalers—for wheezes, sneezes, and

drying up the sinuses—but nothing for the fear that I would be doubled over in a hole in the ground, with some ghastly asthma spasm.

The scene started silently: fix a clasp around the waterpipe, then screw it tight.

Cliff and John, in the shed, did it effortlessly. *My* first time, the clasp fell off and the screw rolled between the floorboards. I tried not to look at their faces—and practiced.

Next was drilling a hole into the pipe until water squirted out, under pressure.

I could manage it in two minutes, leaning down with my weight against the drill. John Richardson, with forearms like cantaloupes, could do it in half a minute.

"With the same drill?"

"Sure." Only different forearms.

"John, Preminger is going to have a stroke waiting—"

"Practice."

"John, my asthma—"

"Just try it."

Right. Practice. I developed a very I-Thou relationship with the drill; my hands would be authentic once the calluses healed. And the time fell to a minute and a half.

"John, can you *see* him waiting that long? He'll have a fit."

"Practice."

Since there was no water in rehearsals, I had to imagine the geyser shooting up through the hole as I screwed a gauge over it, onto the clasp.

Later, at night, the gauge would show water flowing to the farm. I was then to cut the pipe—flooding the ditch—and hook the sleeping gas to flow into the empty pipeline and through an open ball-valve in the farm.

And I had to explain how it all worked.

In the dusty courtyard, Cliff Gorman saw me rehearsing.

"Remember, Ted, don't act. This is no way to have your big

moment. Stanley Flushman on The Mystery of Plumbing. And now—the *ball-valve!* Come on, where's the popcorn? They're leaving!"

It was like the old joke of John Wayne determined to play Hamlet. When he started 'To be or not to be,' the opening-night audience laughed. He waited for the titters to die down, then began again, to more laughter. Furious, he stepped to the footlights and announced, "Don't laugh at *me!* I didn't *write* this shit!"

Meanwhile, the darkest hour of the film drew near. In hindsight, many blamed Mitchum for the stresses. But he was preceded by the malevolent orneriness of things that, on this film, would not work.

After shooting the simulator, Preminger and Coop both felt it would look fine. But in rushes it didn't seem to move enough. So . . . retake.

There were also scratches in the film. So . . . fly in a Panaflex expert to check the cameras.

Retake, also, the Arabs in their rubber raft. The lighthouse beacon flickered. Redo it on black water, anywhere, at night.

And retake the hostages' TV speeches. Denys and the lab saw "fluctuations" of light. So ditch the CSI's. Get different lights.

Ironically, they did not have to redo Shiloah's dark warning that if he had to kill a girl, he would kill himself.

I met the actor later, staggering forlornly up the grand staircase of our hotel. Grateful for a friendly face, he smiled and took my hand like a lifeline. "He won't let me do the monologue the way I want. . . . 'No self-pity,' he tells me. 'Strong, direct, simple. Hard.' " It was the quintessential Preminger direction.

Suddenly Josef showed me *his* version—did it as if stifling his anger and pain, *trying* to be strong. At the end his eyes shone with anguish and determination, in a moment from an unmade movie.

By now people had no expectations beyond more of the same.

Editor Peter Thornton saw his work as only a routine splicing job: "joining heads and tails." After rushes, the crew dismissed the Arabs as "the Karl Marx brothers." Driving from location one day, Graham stopped for a brief swim, only to have his clothes and money stolen. And John Lake told how the grips' hotel had no water for three days and they washed with French mineral water. "Oh, I must go down to the sea again, the lonely sea and sky. I left my fuckin' socks there, I hope they're fuckin' dry."

Only Lalla and Cliff Gorman seemed to enjoy themselves. Cliff especially liked the town. "I thought it was going to be Sticksville, U.S.A. But they have everything. In the square, they're set up for Purim."

By Saturday everyone was ready for the comic relief. . .

For the scouts' raid, the script detailed elaborate preparations involving two Corsican contacts, Antoine and his cousin Locci.

Everything about the scenes seemed interminable. It wasn't just their length and irrelevance. It was the surrealism of the whole group. We weren't an ensemble of actors; we were a company of strangers summoned by a schedule.

Antoine was a swarthy, scheming type whose thick black eyebrows curled up like little tails in a parody of menace.

Locci looked like a sad sack with a walrus mustache.

Mitchum growled and belched. When I said good morning, he moved one hand as if vigorously masturbating.

Isabelle had returned to Corsica after being freed, to help find her friends—and now served sandwiches!

And Cliff Gorman was our Scoutmaster.

It began on a hilltop overlooking the Tardets farm, as Antoine explained, "Heen Corseekah we are hall cousins."

"*All* cousins," corrected Preminger.

"Hall cousins."

"*All* cousins."

"*Hall* cousins."

"What is a hall cousin!? Someone who lives in a hall!?"

Even the crew laughed—but, oh, the laughter to come.

Our band of raiders drove to a clearing, unloaded the four gas canisters, the gauges, metal detector, earphones, cutters, drills—all that clutter—carried it down a slope, and loaded two donkeys for the rest of the trip.

The animals were covered with a shining coat of blue-green flies, swarming around their eyes, mouths, and anuses.

I was, luckily, doped to the eyes.

Cliff Gorman picked up a cylinder and staggered at its weight. Then he took a tool and played as if it were a clarinet. "Artie Shaw. . . 'You're in the Army Now. . .' All right, you jarheads, get down and give me twenty-five!"

Rehearsal. Preminger waited impatiently with the camera, at the bottom of the hill.

"Gershuny, you move like a senile, eighty-year-old—"

"Boy Scout?"

"*Faster!*"

We stumbled downhill, loaded the stuff onto donkey packs, and pulled the beasts away, careful not to touch them. Our packs came slowly undone as we walked, and we heard, without daring to look back, the telltale clatter: thud, crash, thunk—pipes, guns, canisters falling in a trail.

"*Cut!*"

Mitchum and Gorman were laughing convulsively.

"Gershuny, you're a writer," called Preminger. "Why can't you load a donkey with three hundred pounds of equipment and lead it out any faster?"

By take three, there was a forest of nettles and burrs in our gym socks. A donkey refused to budge. Once we thought we had it . . . until a scout's belt fell off.

The unit roared. If this was a comedy, we were a smash.

Next came metal-detecting. While the troupe unloaded the donkeys in a clearing, I searched for waterpipe, wearing earphones and panning a detector over the ground, like a stereophonic vacuum cleaner.

When the spot was found, Cliff drove a pick into it to start clearing ground. It was a rite performed cleanly, despite the burrs and beasts and pollen and thistles.

But Gorman sidled up later and whispered, "We're out of luck. The mule stole the scene."

A Fire of Raw Rubber

Monday, after retakes on the simulator, the scouts drove to Locci's mill, where it soon became clear that the recent days were only a prelude. The crunch began here, in Locci's stone hut. Locci couldn't speak English, and Mitchum, drinking the local mason-jar liqueur, *eau de vie*, couldn't shut up. Meanwhile, Penelope Bonnecarrère, Paul's wife, was shooting stills of the star's drinking.

What a recipe for a frolic!

In the mill, which had lost none of its Antonioni-esque isolation since February, Mitchum watched Locci struggle with a map—and an accent.

His line was, "We're here, this is Tardets's boundary."

It came out, "Weeeurreeerr, zississ Tardets's boundareee."

He got more confused pointing out waterpipe: "Waaauderrr-pyeppe."

He got more confused pointing out waterpipe:

Preminger groaned. "He looks like Charles Laughton without the talent."

Outside, Mitchum had a few more snorts, while joking with the local kids and his pal Bob Simmons, who would stage the big fight between the star and Amidou.

By now Mitchum had chewed his cigar to a frazzle and rumpled his hair. He could barely connect with his glass, but the happy farmers leaned out of their windows to refill it. And Penelope Bonnecarrère kept shooting.

Mitchum was inviting people to Mexico.

"You have a place there?" I asked.

"I *own* the fuckin' country!"

Amidou wouldn't rehearse their fight. "It's dangerous," he said, making the sign of a drinker, thumb to mouth.

Inside again, nine of us lined up around a table for another look at the maps. Gorman called it the "Dutch Masters shot."

This time Locci couldn't say "mules." Somehow they became "murles."

"What is a murle?" thundered Preminger. "Can't you say *mules*?"

Mitchum, meanwhile, had reached another plane.

"We have this little problem," Wolfgang had said. And I began to understand about the press conference when Mitchum asked the journalists, "Suck *what*?" Or when he interrupted a rambling question about the Israelis: "—I don't care as long as it has *tits*!"

Now, he had to ask, "Okay, can anyone think of anything we've missed?"

"Okay . . . have we missed anyone? Anyone missing? Anyone thinking of anything? Who's thinking?"

We bit our tongues trying not to laugh.

(And I remembered Preminger's classic understatement: "After four he is a problem.")

"I would like to rehearse," called Mitchum.

"We did," said Preminger.

"Will the director please watch a rehearsal?"
Gorman laughed. "Stay loose, Bob."
"Bob," called Otto. "Let's go. Come on."
"What the fuck—hahaha—"
"Bob, please, there are ladies present."
"My apologies."
"Action!"
"I have two murles—uhh—" Locci peered at his map as if it could help his English.
Said Mitchum, "I should take out my dick and show him the map."
"Take out what?" asked OP.
"I should piss on his arm! Hahaha—"
"Bob, we are *rolling!*"
Glassy-eyed, he looked down at the murle-man. "I'd take out *your* dick. If I could find it."
Finally they got something, as we scouts choked back our laughter. After all, we didn't want to spoil the shot.

Now Preminger had to go to Île Rousse for an hour to be made an honorary citizen. Penelope had to go because Mitchum told her to. And we scouts had to depart in a shot—with Mitchum.
Before leaving, Preminger laid out the moves so that Wolfgang merely had to call "Action." But the director's absence clearly irritated the star. As a scout drove Mitchum away, he suggested they run over some pigs.
The scout tried not to hear.
"Kid, how many pictures have you done?"
Nervous laughter.
"Well, I've done a hundred and thirty-five and when I say run over those pigs, run over those pigs! They're gonna cut their throats. If I had a razor I'd cut your throat."
Shaking, the scout drove back. Mitchum then declared he wouldn't ride with this unsafe driver.

"No way!" he bellowed. "Put a shirt on Bobby Simmons!" In fact Simmons salvaged the remains of the afternoon by persuading Mitchum to go on.

Sort of.

"Action!" called Wolfgang.

"You know," said Mitchum thoughtfully, "Wolfgang has a green ass."

"What?"

"Wolfgang has a green ass. . . . He's all right . . . but you'd need a crowbar to get it open . . . an iron bar."

Through the embarrassed silence, the actor continued his ruminations. "Definitely a green ass. . . . I'm not kidding! *A green ass!*"

He stumbled to the van and was driven into the sunset.

The fight scene next morning loomed up with the charm of a tax audit.

Said Bob Simmons, "OP won't use doubles. That makes it harder. But it'll still be spectacular. Amidou sneaks up with his spike, Mitch whirls, knocks it from his hand, pulls his gun. Amidou kicks the gun from his hand, whirls, back-kicks into Mitchum's stomach. Now we've lost the gun—we can place it anywhere. Amidou picks up the gun and points it at Mitchum. That's *it!* It's the end for Mitchum!

"But no! He steps inside, deflects the gun arm, grabs Amidou's wrist, they struggle, Amidou's hand with the gun is pinned behind his own back—Amidou is held; his back is against Mitchum's chest. It's a double close-up: Mitchum over Amidou's shoulder. The gun goes off—Amidou dies. Mitchum lets him slump forward, face into the dust. We see his back covered with blood.

"It should take five shots."

June 25. Tuesday. 3:00 A.M.

In the silent, dark hotel there is no breakfast or heat. Crew

268

members mill about in the lobby, waiting for their rides, bundled in sweaters, too numb to speak.

The first shot has the agents breaking into the compound. The scouts cut the barbed wire atop the wall and Mitchum then jumps in.

It is ten feet to the dirt and the actor has been drinking steadily since yesterday.

Says Cliff Gorman, "My room is just below his. I hear Bob rocking all night. He never sleeps. So I never sleep. In the next room Otto is yelling on the phone, and upstairs Mitchum is rocking."

Graham strolls down to where the crew is laying dolly tracks. "You should've been in the catering tent," he tells me. "Mitchum actually had the center pole and was trying to shake it loose. I believe we'll see some more excitement."

Gorman has been there too. "The English crew is sitting. Polite. With the coffee and the eggs and bacon. 'How are you, mate? Morning.' And Mitchum is pulling down the tent. Nobody says a word. Like it's perfectly normal. . . . They're trying not to notice."

Mitchum appears, rolling down the road like a tank. He wears his costume—boots, jeans, denim jacket, and a T-shirt stretched over a bulging gut. One hand is clenched in a fist, the other hooked around his belt.

He roars at Preminger through the early stillness, "You wake me up at four in the morning to watch 'em lay a fuckin' dolly track!? Is that it?"

Everything stops, but not as it has for previous shots. This is a space without heartbeats. Half a dozen grips freeze with their tools in their hands, watching the two men.

Preminger is as quiet and firm as I have ever seen him. Being ten feet away, I can hear his words. Everyone hears Mitchum's.

"Bob, we cannot go on this way."

Mitchum's hand moves as if he is flinging away coins. "Yeah—right—can't—"

"You were drunk at four o'clock on the set yesterday—"

"Right, yeah. So what? Don't you like it?" He steps back, his open hand thrust toward Preminger, jabbing the air for emphasis.

Preminger continues, patiently. "It costs us time, it hurts the film."

Mitchum jabs with every word. "Yeah! Right! Say it to me! Shake hands!"

"Bob, I won't shake your hand. If I let you go, I'll have to sue you for every cent—"

"You want me to go, huh? Okay! I'm going! That's it!"

"I'm trying—"

"That's it! That's fine! Okay! Fuck it! Good-bye! *Bon voyage!*" He strides away, heading up the road toward his car. As he passes his blonde driver, he motions to her. "Let's go!"

She departs with him. Later, on the mountain road home, Mitchum tells her to stop, lays his head on her lap, and falls asleep.

A minute after the departure, Preminger radios the production office. "I want all the material—no, please, *listen* to me—I want all the contractual material with Mitchum and all the material on everyone else we thought about for the part. Everything. . . . Yes, I will be coming back."

With Denys and Wolfgang, he studies the production board in the dusty courtyard, deciding what can be shot without a leading man. Presently Preminger folds the board and speaks without rancor about losing his star. "I'm glad it wasn't later."

He gets into his car, to be driven back to the office.

And a costume man kicks a stone in the dust. "I don't understand. . . . Really . . . Mitchum was never like this before. Never."

For an hour or two, at the location, the company is in shock. They know that Preminger is stuck on an island with unreliable phones, a big payroll, and almost nothing to film.

They talk of pictures that have "done a Burton"—folded. They gossip. They sit in the sun. They drink coffee. And all the while they know that this picture is in mortal danger and there is nothing they can do to help.

Cliff Richardson reminds Angela Martelli of the film they did together in 1956, *Fire Down Below,* starring Robert Mitchum.

Does Angela remember his favorite line? "It is a fire of raw rubber, Monsieur. One does not extinguish such a fire. One keeps it under control. Infrequently."

In the office, Graham calls to have a "Corsican policeman" flown *that morning* from Paris, for afternoon shooting.

And Preminger gets on the phone to find a star.

At 7:00 A.M. in Corsica.

By noon, Mitchum reappears. Lalla informs him over lunch that he has been acting silly, which makes him lean across the table in the hotel and fix her with his menacing gaze.

"Heeeyyy. . ." he drawls.

"Yes?"

"You—want—me—to—kill—you?"

"Well, no, actually, I'd rather you didn't."

The press around the production (and there is always some) begins filing stories, which start "a flood of calls."

One aide tells an American paper, "I'm sorry, all I can say is what we tell everyone. Mitchum walked off the picture and has broken his contract."

Surrounded by crewmen in the bar, Mitchum takes a call from Beverly Hills.

"He says he's gonna sue me? We'll both be dead before *that's* settled. . . . I say he *canned* me! He's a prick!" The voice booms out across the lawns where yesterday Preminger had been made an honorary citizen.

"I say fuck him and the boat that brought him. It's called the *Exodus*. Hahaha!"

At twilight, Mitchum calls to a group of us in the hotel lobby. "You missed the big scene in the office. I go in and ask for my tickets. Four first-class round-trip tickets. It's in my contract, buddy. Four in the first cabin! . . . I'm standing right in front of the secretary. 'Where are the tickets?' " He mimes the woman at work, studiously ignoring him. "I say, 'I want my tickets. Get 'em up!' She keeps reading. I say, 'Let's go! Get 'em up!' Nothing. So I pick up the phone and drop it to get a little attention and Preminger says, 'Call the police.' "

Laughing, he flings his arms out as if to embrace the cops.

"Sure, call 'em. I've been in jail eleven times! What's the charge, officer? Dropping a phone!? Give 'im *life!*"

Other witnesses declared the director was calm, saying nothing. As Preminger walked out behind Mitchum, the actor called back, "Oh, no, Otto, not in the *ass!*"

That evening, Mitchum drinks in the bar, alternately thundering and brooding. By ten, he is deep in conversation with Josef Shiloah.

"He lean forward," says Josef, "and he hold my hand. He say, 'Kill me, brother. *Kill me!*' He is so sorry for what he do. And I tell him, 'If you are sorry, you must call Preminger because he is older.'

"He say to me, 'You Jew bastard, you stick with him.' And I say, 'No, if you are sorry, *you* must call Preminger because he is older man and this is right!' So he goes to desk and calls. But Preminger is not in."

Next day Mitchum leaves with his family, pursued across the airport grass by photographers. But they have missed the drama. Amidou has seen it, earlier. "I watch him leave. And I know he try to call Preminger and say 'I'm sorry' . . . but Preminger no hear. And I know is *not* a great star leaving. No! This is man with pain. He hurt to leave!"

Mitchum's side of the story was revised in a series of interviews over the succeeding years, until, in 1979, it appeared this way in a *Films Illustrated* story.

"[The] incident was all very sad and I regretted it later, as I'm sure Otto did. I only agreed to do the picture because of him, you know. I was one of the few people who understood him. One day the script had me looking beat-up and dishevelled, so I arrived on the set unshaven. *'You are drunk,'* roared Otto, *'and you cannot play this scene!'* I argued with Otto saying how could I possibly be drunk at 5:30 in the morning, and pointed out the instructions on the script, but he wouldn't listen. *'You are drunk and you are through!'* he shouted. So I turned and yelled *'Taxi!'* and that was that. It really did break my heart."

Ironically, by the time of this interview his career was going splendidly. *Rosebud* hadn't hurt him at all.

Heroes

On the afternoon of the blow-up, Preminger was his most jovial, waiting cheerfully for an actor who sped by car from the airport, half-awake and breathless, to play the half-awake, breathless *gendarme* who greeted Isabelle, after she was freed and walked into a police station (in a scene that was later cut because no matter how fast a movie travels it is never in straight lines).

People were rooting so hard for Preminger, hoping his movie would survive, that they temporarily forgot past woes.

"This picture has had more than its share of troubles," declared Angela.

Jimmy Devis added, "It may be better than anyone thinks. You never know. And happy pictures are never good ones." He sat outside, sipping beer, puffing a cigar, radiating good humor.

But this was an hour in the lifeboats and at times a darker feeling showed. He told of failing in the lights-rental business and now being "chained to the handles" as an operator.

"My ship," he added wistfully, "is always about to come in."

Flash. The top choices for a leading man were a French ladykiller who dripped Vitalis, a mature American with a "liberal" image, and Peter O'Toole. But the American was a bit old and the Frenchman a bit . . . French. They were close to a deal with O'Toole, despite problems of UA putting up more money and worries about the actor's reputation.

Said a unit historian, "He hits people, you know, when he's drunk. He's much worse than Mitchum that way."

By now, one ignored such stories. With so much movie work created by and focused upon a few actors and directors, it was inevitable that those figures be explained. Thus, to simplify reality, people fashioned myths. Enter "Peter O'Toole" and "Richard Burton," "John Huston" and "Otto Preminger"—and all those others with epic contradictions to justify so much success and failure.

But *Rosebud* would have to deal with the truth.

Jules Buck, O'Toole's partner, arrived in Corsica, intensifying the pressure on Preminger, who tried to structure a deal while knowing that every foot of Mitchum's work would have to be reshot, that each "idle" hour on the phone dragged him further behind, and—for good measure—that the simulator retakes, like the first scenes, were scratched. There could be no more tries; they would have to edit around the scratches.

While Preminger worked, the great optimist among the crew was Cliff Richardson.

Since beginning as a studio tea-boy in 1924, he had known that movies were for him. From 1932, he had spent fifteen years

at Ealing developing the art of miniatures—like a tropical
bridge washed out in a tabletop flood.

"Freddy Young shot it. I asked some people later, 'How was
the model shot?' 'What model shot?' they asked. That's good
enough for me!"

For him the work had become its own end, beyond any film.
On *The Day of the Jackal*, Zinnemann said of the crutch that
turned into an assassin's rifle, "I hope my picture is as successful as your gun."

For the demolition of a train in *Lawrence*, Cliff trucked
rolling stock into the desert, laid rails over the sand, and set
boiler plates under the dunes so the overturned railcars would
slide. And still the shot was almost obscured by smoke.

"You can't *learn* special effects," said Cliff. "The only way
is to try. . . . I'm always the optimist."

Suddenly Preminger had O'Toole. There was hardly time to
savor the coup as the company moved into the desert at night
for the freeing of Isabelle.

Preminger wanted tears as she struggled with her ropes.
"Think of *me* and cry."

For further stimulus, she could consider the actor who left
her in the desert, telling her to rub her rope on the rocks. He had
been magnificent in *The Battle of Algiers*, had appeared in the
world premiere of *Waiting for Godot*—and in English he *still*
sounded like Elmer Fudd.

"Wub the wope on the wok," he told Isabelle.

Wub the wope on the wok!?

Preminger stormed at an observer, "I have to dub practically the whole picture. Up till now, no one has known his
lines!"

When the ropes gave way, Isabelle was directed to raise her
arms in triumph, which looked a bit theatrical for such a down-
to-earth actress.

Regardless, Preminger pressed into the dawn. The crane

faced the first light as it appeared over purple rock whorls and burgundy water. Dim striations of blue and gray in the sky created a chill splendor around Isabelle as she awoke and set off on the lonely road. The crane moved up and back with her to reveal the surrounding desolation. And one thought that surely the scene would live in this setting.

As the exhausted crew ate a cold breakfast in a nearby stone hut, one man asked, "Have you written in your book that we're all fucked?"

The dawn was already giving way to heat and worry.

Besides O'Toole, his stand-in was coming, plus a writer to touch up his dialogue (making it more "English"), plus a makeup man who knew O'Toole's allergies, plus a new art director (who had been an assistant on *Blow-Up*) and *his* assistant. I wanted to meet them all and it was also Lalla's birthday, which Preminger celebrated with a small dinner of lobster and Dom Perignon.

But I could hardly concentrate, as my plumbing aria loomed up. To begin the lines—"Whenever this needle drops—" set off the whole scene compulsively. I was in the grip of words, a Manchurian Candidate. In dreams I moved the drill and woke, startled, my arm jerking.

On a day of rest, everyone waited for the new arrivals and marveled at Preminger's finding a star in forty-eight hours. It was as breathtaking as Cliff Richardson's exploding trains. And, like Cliff, Preminger had been preparing for decades.

"This script came totally out of the blue," said Jules Buck. Except that he and Otto had been friends for thirty years, and that Jules had once asked Otto to finish a picture he produced, to which Otto had answered, "I don't want the script. Give me the *pages.*"

It was out of the blue. Except that Jules called Otto "the most generous man I've ever met," that Otto called Jules for help ("Do this for me as if it were your own picture"), and that Jules claimed tactfully that O'Toole would have played Lord Carter "if only there had been a *little* more."

An associate producer of *Brute Force, Naked City,* and *The Killers,* Jules had later produced at Fox, then created Keep Films with O'Toole to make the actor's pictures.

In effect, O'Toole had become Jules's career. "Because this film is a loan-out," he explained, "I keep out of the creative side. . . . The script is good. . . . Peter will have his own ideas. I have great respect for Otto. It's only bad directors who have to tell actors how to act."

Round and sleek in his chinos, blue sports shirt, and matching blue loafers, Jules was a veteran who knew all the rules. Despite his friendship with OP, he had negotiated a contract for O'Toole that was tougher than Mitchum's.

Graham sent three cars to meet O'Toole's plane.

"Mr. Buck is so nervous, you'd think it was Nixon coming."

While waiting, Preminger rearranged and cut some connecting scenes, like the scouts loading the donkeys, thank God. He also considered giving the fight scene to Gorman instead of O'Toole.

"I hate to start a new actor this way. It's panic acting."

Suddenly Graham called, "The plane's arrived!"

He had burst across movie screens unforgettably, striding in a white caftan, his followers chanting, "Aw-rence! Aw-rence!" At twenty-nine, with only three small parts in prior films to his credit, he was at the pinnacle. He had everything. Yet today, there was a feeling of lavish gifts squandered, credits that ran downhill, a whiff of Barrymore and perdition.

After *Lawrence* (1962), the roles were inevitably lesser: a gallery of eccentrics, deluded and obsessed, specialists in large losses: a king who slew his loyal adviser in *Becket* (1964), a general betrayed by his twisted sexuality in *The Night of the Generals* (1966), another king who connived against his children in *The Lion in Winter* (1968). Not one was truly sympathetic. As a loser he was too lofty—not our kind of loser.

In *The Ruling Class* (1971) he appeared to turn on his own aristocratic image, mocking the whole notion of aristocracy. By 1972 he played Don Quixote (in *Man of La Mancha*) as a natural devolution. Lawrence the idealist was reduced to an old "gentleman" dreaming of impossible triumphs.

Then came two years without a film, until *Rosebud.*

The personal rumors spread quickly over the years: drinking; hell raising; failing health; talent burning out in mediocre movies as if talent were so much Sterno.

Even history hurt him. In his class at the Royal Academy of Dramatic Art had been Albert Finney, Richard Harris, and Alan Bates. Once the whole group might have been bankable. Not today. "English" films had disappeared, replaced by international productions for world markets. And action was more exportable than poetry.

There was danger in O'Toole's screen presence, an edge of challenge as sharp as Brando's or Hoffman's. But O'Toole was mostly dangerous to himself, facing cowardice in *Lord Jim* (1965), madness in many films, and compulsion in virtually all.

To an age that worshiped self-confidence, O'Toole offered chasms of self-doubt, wry humor, mocking absurdity. In the public eye, he was a has-been. Perhaps a failure.

The man who came to Corsica was something else again.

He appeared at night in a town square that resembled a Fellini set after the clowns had packed up. A breeze swayed the tiny pin lights in the trees as he called across the empty plaza to Robin Gregory, "Robin, hel-*lo!*"

Lawrence had hovered like a numinous presence on the edge of the film since Eva Monley summoned it in February. Now, that single, overriding image blew away all gossip and stories. "Peter hates talking about it," said Jules Buck. But one saw and heard Lawrence.

O'Toole's voice was a gift, projecting weariness, delight, and the frayed nerves of a long journey in four syllables. It reminded one immediately of his "otherness." American moviegoers would never hear themselves in that voice, with its richness and theatricality.

His splendid physical gifts emphasized his difference. Stepping into the light around our café table, he was taller, louder, thinner than the rest of us—a flayed, gangling root of a man hung puppetwise from wide, bony shoulders, with narrow ankles sticking up from low boots, narrow wrists poking out of his jacket, a profile sharp and scooped as a garden spade, and those blue eyes veiled in politesse.

Even the rumors of his entourage increased his aura of royalty. Yet he tried to be friendly. He ordered a soft drink, fitted a cigarette into a holder—a small gesture done with deliberation, as if he was accustomed to being on display. Nothing much was said beyond the usual pleasantries. Like a man giving an audience, it was enough that he had shown up.

"Whenever that needle drops..."
I couldn't stay with Aristea that night. Too nervous. At her door she kissed me good night and said she loved me.
Didn't she love her boyfriend at home?
No, he was too much in love with himself. Try to sleep. I put in a call for 5:00 A.M.

"Whenever that needle drops..."
I awoke before the call, tense as a guy wire, waiting for the first light. The call sheet on the dresser said we would leave the hotel at 7:45 A.M. It was O'Toole's first day.

The room was still cold at 5:30 when I unfolded the scout costume, shook out the donkey hairs and red dirt, and dressed. For a time, leaning on the windowsill, I watched the sun rising over the yellow hills.

"Whenever that needle drops. . ."

I measured out more hay-fever pills and tucked them in a shirt pocket, with an asthma inhaler.

"Whenever that needle drops. . ."

The view fell away with those words and I was in the ditch, explaining to the group that this wild idea of pumping sleeping gas through an open valve would work. "The commando" was winded and sweaty, with his shirt off after all the digging, speaking deliberately to reassure the others, trying to control his own nerves.

It was an easy mood to sustain, for I knew what this day meant. I would earn the right to watch the others, even to write about them and criticize them, by facing the same trial they did. This day was an initiation and a license to go on working.

I ride to the location with Denys and Jimmy Devis, saying nothing, yearning for coffee.

At the oil mill, a healthy shout is under way.

Preminger doesn't like some revisions. "This nonsense must stop!"

O'Toole walks away with a calming, "Come *on* now."

Jules Buck and the writer make conciliatory sounds.

And the push is on. At first, each shot is one or two takes. This time Martin has no lines around the map. Everything is streamlined.

Except the "murles."

I try to watch O'Toole, try to connect to the shooting, but my mind is in the ditch.

Eating lunch is impossible. I hurry to the location, where Cliff and John are working, climb in, and arrange the tools on the ground in a pattern, practicing the precise way each is gripped and set down.

280

I put a bottle of mineral water at my feet, out of camera range. Shoes and socks come off. And sweat starts, a light coating of fear. Stoked to the eyes on hay-fever pills, I settle into a high, private silence.

"Whenever that needle drops . . ." triggers everything: the flow of props, their weight in the hand, a set of reflexes tuned to a moment's use.

Gorman and O'Toole meanwhile play a funny scene, digging the ditch and wondering if it's the wrong place. The crew even laughs. I barely watch.

Preminger calls me over as they set up for my scene. "Gershuny, do you know your lines?"

"Yes."

"So? Let's hear them."

Angela checks the script as I read.

"Good," he says. "Fine." He goes off to see Denys.

The next twenty minutes are endless. I climb into the ditch because it is out of everyone's way . . . again check the tool layout . . . drink from the water bottle and spit out the water . . . rub dirt on my hands . . . wipe them across my chest.

Cliff Richardson wishes me good luck. And John says they have put a new bit in the drill so it might go faster.

Wolfgang calls rehearsal. I look up to see two cameras, one wide, the other, on a platform, shooting tight angles. Seventy faces mill around, gradually focusing on the action. Denys calls minor adjustments as I mime the moves. Then the other actors are placed offscreen to feed lines. O'Toole. Gorman. Isabelle. Locci. The other three scouts. Squatting, they all look down at the surgery.

Lights are fired up. Scattered on the slope are art directors, drivers, caterers—even Aristea. Of course. This is the special effect, the show Cliff and John have been planning for a month. Now they start a pump offscreen to circulate water through the pipe. For a second the motor seems to throb, then I forget that too.

"Gershy, are you ready?"

"Yes."

"Cliff?"

"All set."

Then Cliff turns to me. "Ted, we only have five sections of pipe . . . enough for five takes. Best to get it soon if you can."

I feel my breath tighten, try to use that fear, brush some sweat from my eyes, take another swig of water, dry my hands on my shorts like a safecracker, look over the silent hillside and feel the crew's energy flow down.

"All right, let's go," says Otto.

And still, today, I remember the claps.

"Scene one-forty-four A and B. Take one." Snap!

"Action."

Silence. I am alone. Concentrated. Start now. Carefully . . . carefully I sandpaper a narrow section of pipe . . . brush it clean with my hand . . . screw the clamp around it. My fingers know each turn of the screw. The sound fills the silence as metal touches metal. I take an oil can and let three drops fall into the clamp hole. Then the drill . . . set it in the hole, lean over it— you little fucker, *cut*—and the bright, new bit *eats* into the pipe. It won't take a minute—they handicapped me before! Water bubbles up around the bit. Push in. A freshet shoots up, then a stream.

Carefully . . . so deliberately—put down the drill, take the gauge, join it to the clamp, screw it tight—the water is choked off. Dying. Finished.

Now, speak.

I had feared that after the long preparation there would be a frog in my throat, a clot of fear.

But the words come—a little breathless but there. I am wet, water on my chest, dirt on my hands—but all right. All right.

Explain the gauge. "Whenever that needle drops, water is flowing into a storage tank at the top of the house. There! Someone in the house must be using water." Pause. This is the key. Make sure they understand. Explain the ball-float valve that opens when water flows in.

O'Toole asks how I know what system they have. He really asks, How can I be sure?

"They're the same all over the world." I tell how we'll cut the water supply after dinner, while they're washing, to make sure the valve is open.

Isabelle asks why not cut it now?

I can't help a smile. "If we cut the supply, and they run out of water, they'll suspect something."

I see in their faces: they believe. They know it will work. The smile is frozen on my lips. There is no more to say. The silence hangs for one interminable moment. I feel my breath—a heartbeat across the hills . . .

"Cut!"

There is a pause. Then, from the hill, comes applause. The smile thaws, becomes a grin of surprise, and over this wave of support and delight comes Preminger's voice.

"Gershuny, you are a great actor! You should play King Lear. A *Jewish* King Lear! At last I know what Aristea sees in you!"

O'Toole comes over afterward with a compliment, asking if I've acted before.

I might say a few words about directing and understanding the work—but instead mumble something unmemorable. And he goes on. "When you were down there, we were all *willing* you to do it. Cliff's fingers were working along with yours!"

I know. I felt it then—and now, as I write this.

And it makes *Rosebud* worthwhile, whatever else happens.

Once More, With Feeling

As hope sprung up around Mitchum, it did so again around O'Toole. Immediately he brought the film a certain brisk authority; we saw it as he told his stand-in, "Roy, I want something hot with sugar," and Roy served tea in a paper cup, on a tray.

Monday morning, July 1. With O'Toole to help, Preminger raced. In the stark geometry of the courtyard, with the sun casting hard shadows across the dusty-yellow walls, the fight became more ragged, less rehearsed.

"I'm glad it is not so perfect," said Preminger.

"Well," replied O'Toole with a teasing look, "you're not going to get it anyway."

But he did, surging ahead. "Amidou," he called, "you die too slow? Like old melodrama!"

The scouts heard the shot and jumped in. "Fast, fast! You walk like on Fifth Avenue, looking for girls."

In the rush, it was every actor for himself. Cliff Gorman turned an ankle jumping down the wall and Amidou wrenched a shoulder in the fight. Only O'Toole carefully lowered himself down and carefully dodged Amidou's karate kicks.

"The sun, the fight—it's sensational!" exclaimed Paul Bonnecarrère. Indeed, the struggle had a big, hot, dusty feeling but also the crisp choreography of a movie fight. Preminger had wanted reality. What he got was a spectacle, a movie death.

One phase of the filming ended as the newly freed girls ambled into the sunny courtyard. In a nice touch, Brigitte saw Amidou's body and covered it with her shawl. But the hostages didn't even seem groggy as they entered the sunshine.

Aristea marveled at them. "When you've just been in *bed* for a week, you can't walk steadily. . . . They don't *think*!"

Preminger dropped the scene later, inevitably. It could only have worked if the hostages had been "characters," if the acting had lived—if we had cared. But movies don't go in straight lines, even as they near the end of the line.

At twilight, Lalla and O'Toole sat almost alone in the hotel bar. The actor slumped forward with a soft drink, looking light-years from the hell-raiser one had heard about. His pants were dusty and baggy. Beside him, on the bar, was his tweed Irish hat. His eyes, once veiled in politeness, now were dim and watery. Now, even the common touch was work.

As Lalla told of her own work and how she felt everyone was on her side, he tried to listen politely. "Oh . . . we all want *so* to be popular."

Complimented about his fight, he simply shrugged. "One approaches a karate champion . . . with a bit of caution."

"Everyone's rather bruised," said Lalla, "but you took that wall quite well."

He slipped a cigarette into his holder, lit up, exhaled—all in slow motion. "I'm too . . . *old* . . . for derring-do." He picked himself up and eased off the barstool. "I shall go slide into a steamy tub." He started out, then turned back with a dead-tired expression. "It's all so *political*. Keep the director happy. Keep the unit happy. Keep them working well. Because in the end it's *you* up there on screen."

And he shuffled out.

We started a long good-bye in Corsica.

At dawn, after a night of sleeping-gas drill, Cliff Gorman fumbled with his gear exhaustedly, then gave up, laughing. "The gás is odorless, colorless, and to order just call Judson 6–5000 where operators are standing by . . ."

We staggered home to rushes, to say good-bye to a few hopes.

In the desert, Isabelle's awakening looked flat, regardless of the splendid scenery.

Brigitte's TV speeches had a grating inflection: "I can't stand it" became "Eye kyant styand it."

As for my plumbing, the water pump made so much noise the whole scene would have to be dubbed and I couldn't see past my overhanging stomach. What a wound in the self-esteem!

About the star, it was hard to say. Finding the girls in the cave, he seemed awed by his victory, and amused. But often he looked overly made-up and sounded overly snide. His writer was replacing flat Americanisms with lines to bite into, claiming O'Toole wanted to take the part seriously and not be flippant. Yet the actor's tone was aloof and superior from the start. A reference to an Arab was changed from "that little guy" to "that little brute."

"He's playing the Scarlet Pimpernel," said a grip.

Another hissed, "The Mauve Pimpernel."

But he had just had the script a few days.

And of all his films only two or three "sort of knew where they were going from the start." *The Lion in Winter* was one of the charmed few.

"I talked Kate into coming out of retirement for it," said O'Toole. "I knew it needed someone who could really stand up and punch me back and, believe me, I can go a few! So I sent it to her. She was in grief over Spencer. She'd helped me as a boy. Spencer had helped too. . . . And she called back and said, 'Let's do it before I die, Pig.' What a tough dame she is. Always called me Pig."

As we all boarded buses and cars to the airport, it was time to say good-bye to an island we would likely never see again. And to three *Rosebud* debs.

"I am secretly in love with one," said Preminger.

With her acting?

"With her departure."

We left on an $18,000 chartered jet flight to Paris because no commercial space was free.

The plane was only half full and all through the short flight the stewards poured champagne, as if there were something to celebrate.

In Paris most of us took a bus to another new hotel, where our rooms overlooked mansard roofs and silent streets. From our windows, the Right Bank of the city seemed deserted on that summer weekend, its emptiness reflecting our own dislocation and solitude.

PARIS

Creatus Interruptus

They seemed safe at last in the bosom of routine: they had O'Toole, they were in a city, most of the girls and the Arabs were done—now they were beyond the forces of chance.

Tuesday, July 9. They began filming at a big commercial airstrip outside Paris. Mike Seymour, the new art director, had suggested it because of "OP's predilection for pizzazz and production value." In one day on the film, he had understood.

The crew milled about under a gunmetal sky, worrying the safe, comfortable worries of normal filming: possible rain, Lalla's fear of flying, O'Toole's irritation with the hotel.

"It's so *Germanic*! You press a button for Perrier and get whiskey. So I cleverly pressed whiskey and got—orange juice!"

They would shoot in the air, where O'Toole realized that the Arab flights were false because the girls' ears never popped.

Once aloft, the little plane dived and dipped with Lalla shrieking, *"Father's* jet is pressurized!" When they landed, she bounced out happily. "Father can *stuff* his pressurized jet. I want one of *these*. It's totally different from your fucking great commercial planes!"

O'Toole was done for the day. At lunch, he seemed edgy, peering around the noisy airport room, then down to his bit of boiled egg on a lettuce leaf. "Roy, why are we still here? We could be having a real lunch." He summoned his car.

That night we heard it was more than a bad mood. Someone mentioned an ulcer. A somber notice went around:

SHOOTING IS CANCELLED FOR TOMORROW—WEDNESDAY 10 JULY—
THEREFORE, WILL ALL MEMBERS OF THE UNIT REPORT TO THE

PRODUCTION OFFICE AT 8 A.M. FOR INSTRUCTIONS FROM HEADS OF DEPARTMENTS.

A harried Jules Buck flew in. "This is the first time in all the years we've been together that he hasn't worked. . . . He really fought to work."

One heard rumors.

The insurance men were coming from London.

The insurance doctor examined O'Toole and left without a word.

The editor and the English writer, disputing whether O'Toole's character was still in the CIA, were cut off by Graham: "He may not be in the CIA, but he'll be in the American Hospital soon."

O'Toole's wife called during the worst of his illness, and the hotel told him to come down and take it in the lobby!

On Wednesday, July 10, he left for the hospital.

Suddenly, incredibly, they were again without a star.

Uncertain and foundering, they tried to carry on with useful work. Their only choice, without O'Toole, was to do the scene where Beller provoked the police and was beaten up.

It was an interlude of contemporary screen brutality, arranged by the head of the French stuntmen's union, Claude Carliez. In contrast to the Corsican fight, this was no James Bond spectacle. *This* hurt.

Carliez snapped out orders while rehearsing in the basement of a disused prefecture. His plan was clear. Beller got aggressive, two cops grabbed his arms and held him while a detective punched his face and neck, Beller sank to the floor, and the detective kicked him repeatedly.

The swarthy heavy-hitter was Jack LeNoir (nicknamed "Black Jack" by John Wayne), who got the role by chasing OP's taxi outside the Plaza. Two cameras covered the fight. Blows were aimed to their blind sides and the kicks "landed" below frame. With sound effects, they would be jolting. As Beller was hit, he even spat out a "tooth." The rushes projectionist said it looked "terrific!"

It was the first, maybe the only, scene in *Rosebud* with that kind of punch.

Offscreen the blows went on. Preminger dismissed a location manager because lunch was late.

"By this time we could have had lunch at Maxim's! These people work hard. They must eat!"

"A director with a stomach," mused Robin Gregory.

Someone called out, "Stand by, we're trimming the arcs."

"Arcs? Bruuuuutes? We're back in the nineteenth century!"

Later the grips called me over to see a sign in their truck: WHO WILL BE NUMBER 19? They actually had odds posted beside those likely to be fired next.

By the end of the day a notice came.

THERE WILL BE NO SHOOTING TOMORROW FRIDAY 12 JULY—ALL UNIT MEMBERS TO CHECK WITH THE PRODUCTION OFFICE AT NOON.

Without O'Toole they could not go on.

Aristea and I used the time to see *Emmanuelle,* lured by the poster of an actress slouching half-nude, simmering in a wicker chair. We lasted forty minutes. "So *bad,*" Aristea said. "So stupid! You want to *hug* Preminger, Denys, everyone!"

Back at the hotel people sat morosely.

They saw O'Toole's aide rush through the lobby with some grisly specimen, on his way to the hospital.

They heard Jules Buck's reassurances. "There was a small polyp . . . internal bleeding . . . lost two pints . . . through the bowel . . . had every test there is . . . today he's much better . . . swearing at the doctors."

Finally came the facts. O'Toole would be out at least ten days.

The key man on the film became the avuncular English claims adjuster who represented the insurance company. Jim Guild dealt with the same film people repeatedly. The picture business was small. And unlike normal businesses, where there might be one catastrophe in a lifetime, movies *generated* them.

"The real problem," said Guild, "is to assist the production." He maintained that insurers always pushed for completion, as when Tyrone Power died during *Solomon and Sheba* and Yul Brynner was brought in. The insurer's job, after all, was keeping movies alive.

Thus Guild had suggested they do the police brutality scene for morale: "to avoid the fear of abandonment."

Beyond that, he explained that all the losses from O'Toole's illness would be treated as a single, individual claim—which would surely exceed the deductible exemption.

Those losses included the cost of now putting everyone on standby with full pay. Of course, if they went home, they paid their own fares.

There was an immediate stampede to leave, regardless of cost, especially since Preminger and his department heads were going to Israel.

"Creatus interruptus," Cliff Gorman called it. Then, with mock surprise: "Heeeyyy, that's good for the book!"

Even O'Toole's entourage moved to a better hotel. "Where you see a bit of Paris," explained one. "And in each doorway there's a lady waiting to meet you. Costs a bit, but that's love."

Preminger himself left in glory, as *The New York Times* carried a front-page story about John Lindsay doing the film. "It will be tremendous," the director had predicted. For a ten-line part it was almost surreal. Particularly since some of the press was after blood.

In Germany, *Bild Am Sonntag* had a double-page spread of

Mitchum drunk at the Corsican oil mill. The photos, by Penny Bonnecarrère, had been sent to her agency, Sygma, with orders to hold, then released routinely, without anyone from the film knowing about it. More depressing was the English satire magazine, *Private Eye,* flirting with libel:

Otto "We haf ways of making you talk" Preminger thrives on adversity like President Nixon. But even Otto may get more than he likes on his latest film. . . . Robert Mitchum . . . was dropped by Otto in Corsica and replaced by Peter O'Toole. According to reports, Herr Otto decided that Mitchum was getting too tired and emotional to carry on. However, according to latest reports, Herr Otto is discovering that O'Toole can get very tired and emotional too. . . . Meantime, Herr Otto is complaining loudly that *Rosebud* is . . . as one of his aides put it, "out of the bottle and into the vat."

The truth: when O'Toole saw the Paris airplane scene, months later, on a London dubbing stage, he gasped.
"That was the day I *died!*"

With the company dispersed, a grave silence descended, as if *Rosebud* had evaporated in pain. The few who remained now had time for their own feelings.

Graham mourned his movie. *Good Morning Midnight* was to have started filming that very week in Paris, but his backing had collapsed again and now he had "more or less abandoned the project."

Ron Pearce complained of his electrical gear, sending it all back to London for checking.

And Paul Bonnecarrère looked beyond *Rosebud* to a new book with Martin and Hamlekh, which would be ready when the movie was in release. Meanwhile, *Emmanuelle* came up in his conversation, as it did everywhere in Paris that summer.

Paul knew that the man who wrote the book was "very clever," but dismissed the film as "incredibly stupid. The wonderful scene where she makes love in the plane and she knows people are watching her—it's so *bad* in the movie. No people watching! No sense of the dark plane. No real lovemaking!" Paul could see every flaw in an adaptation of someone else's novel. After all, he had no stake in it.

Grand Illusion

In a basement of the Paris hotel, editor Peter Thornton and his assistant, Russ Woolnough, followed the director's explicit orders, seeking to give the movie its last chance. Here Preminger had the most control. And here there was hope.

Russ had seen in Corsica that the film was long, but added, "It's coming together much better than we thought. It works for me."

Peter first assembled scenes in the few cases where there was coverage from different angles. For the German girl landing the jet, there were three views: one from behind the actors looking out the cockpit and one favoring each actor. Alas, the daughter's flat drawl colored every shot.

Peter said, "One schools oneself to accept totally what is given. Otherwise one would be demented, thinking, Oh, that's awful."

He started from behind the actors "because you know immediately you're in a plane. . . . We cut to Papa as he says she's not qualified to land. . . . When he says, 'Not at all, Gertrude,' I'll cut to her so we learn in the strongest way *she's* Gertrude." And so on. Back and forth. "Like playing tennis."

Meanwhile, Russ marked and stored every trim, which had to be catalogued for customs.

"A huge, boring job."

Much more time was spent streamlining the film, where the creative possibilities were greater. *Rosebud* was a multilayered story in which Brigitte made love in her cabin while her friends cooked in the galley and the Arabs bribed a seaman in the Las Vegas. By intercutting these scenes, Preminger could shorten and accent them.

He had no illusions about the footage and no qualms about axing it. That work became the final, most successful try by a man who tried everything. Watch now, if you would see him sacrificing the efforts of months to save the remainder . . .

Peter reads Preminger's notes. Lots of notes.

"Sometimes they fall thick as snow."

Reel two starts as Georges Beller goes up the gangplank to meet Kim. Cut when he tells Kim he doesn't want to know Fargeau.

Thus they end after one page of a two-and-a-half-page scene.

Then go to Brigitte and Isabelle bringing up the groceries along the dock. Cut the opening talk about overtipping the cab. Cut the end talk about cooking. Just use a piece of their walk.

Then go back to a short Georges-Kim piece that shows the crewman eyeing them. It's two lines. Most of the scene is dropped. Beller's angry outburst, Kim's struggles for lightness—all for nothing. Out.

Next the grocery girls come on board.

And Lalla arrives with mother, talks of *Rosebud,* runs to the yacht.

Cut to the Las Vegas—pinball noise, bribing the sailor to betray the boat that night.

Stop before Amidou's talk of knocking out the sailor, his assurance that it won't hurt, his toothpaste smile. End on the money changing hands.

Cut to the galley. Isabelle orders them to make salad. It's a page into the scene. We lose the gabble about Kim's bike trip, her "dynamite hash." All those rehearsals flash by: "Either the hash is important and you say it or it's not and we cut it." End as Lalla says what "pills" they are.

Cut to the love scene. Start after Georges wakes up. Brigitte says he's coming to dinner. End as he says no. Before they kiss.

Return to the galley, a page later than where they left it. No more chatter about boyfriends. "It brings the galley down fifty percent," says Peter. Use three lines. Cut as Isabelle opens the smoking oven.

Go to Fargeau at sunset on the fantail. Introductions are made. Cut just before Miss Pâté.

By now *pages* have been dropped.

Two months later, in London, the same work goes on. It is a gray September in Soho, amid film offices and strip shows, opposite a house where Karl Marx once lived. Two editors, Peter Thornton and Thom Noble, now supervise ten reels each. Preminger sits for hours every day, viewing and cutting their assemblies. He has begun dropping Corsican elements.

The scouts at the wall don't wait for Amidou to die before jumping in. At the gunshot, cut to them leaping down. Cut to Amidou crumpling. Cut to the scouts running up. Save fifteen seconds of *sprinting.*

The simulator is pared. All the arguing and searching and retakes result in this: Isabelle is led to the courtyard. Cut to a close-up of Amidou "flying." It looks real for an instant until we zoom back to see . . . the simulator with Isabelle inside. No more is needed. We've been fooled. Along with Isabelle.

Finally Preminger cuts what he most wants—knowing it eludes him. He drops the German girl in the plane.

"It gets better and better," he says fretfully, "but it gets better slower and slower!"

In the editing, a design begins to emerge: high and low life contrasting. They go from the Arab preparations in the cellar to the Rolls on the highway.

"Very impressive," says Peter. "Whatever one thinks of the film, his pictures always have a very professional, 'finished' look. When it's cut tightly, it will really *move!*"

I often disagree with the production of the movie, but every

294

cut seems right. The picture changes dramatically as so much dull material falls away. One is inured to the rest by seeing it so often. Having come so far, it is once more possible to sustain a brief illusion of hope.

Much later, as the film opens, the view is clearer. All the editing has simply made the picture . . . releasable.

The Rage of Paris

Saturday, July 20. O'Toole was ready to work on Monday, and all department heads were back from Israel, relishing the story of how Preminger had fired two drivers. But he had stayed an extra day and now might be delayed. A war in Cyprus had disrupted air travel.

If he didn't get back, the fathers' big scenes would be directed by Erik.

"I'm prepared. Though there are lots of scenes I'd rather start with than five characters in search of an emotion. Anyway I'm scared but ready."

Unfortunately, he asked for advice on the technically complicated scenes. Perhaps the staff had been stifled too long, but within minutes a recce to the screening room erupted in "creativity," the crackle of those "private conversations" Preminger hated. "Take out the seats . . . put them in . . . close the curtains . . . open them . . ."

Round and round.

Said an aide later, "It'll be a joke. . . . The biggest scene in the picture."

"Gershy, you should have come to Israel! *This* would have been something for your book!"

Monday morning he strides into the screening room, jokes about John Lindsay's coming press conference, and briskly stages the scenes.

"Let's put the fathers on curved seats . . . there's *war* in Cyprus . . . strike the magazines, people remember dates. Here sit Fargeau, Donovan, Carter, Fryer, O'Toole. Denys, shall we start with the wide shot?"

"Fine, Otto."

They are a crew again.

But not an ensemble. Outside, the actors have mostly never met one another. They dress in separate hotel rooms, preparing to do tough shots in a cramped space that is hot enough to grow orchids.

The press waits in the street, lusting after Lindsay.

And the crew, dashing in through a narrow foyer with equipment, includes a new prop assistant and a new second assistant director, Nigel Wooll.

It is July 22. They are supposed to be in Hamburg. In three weeks they are due in Israel for Sloat's scenes. And they don't even have Sloat yet.

"Otto, I *knew* you would make it!" Claude Dauphin shakes Preminger's hand with an ironic smile.

Nigel Wooll, florid and grinning, ushers in Lindsay.

"How do you feel, John?" asks Preminger.

"Marvelous. Relaxed."

"Bring in the press!"

"Drop that dimmer," calls Denys, "while we beat back the invaders."

As the crew tries to exit, the press jams in like rush hour on the Tokyo subway. The crush at the door becomes a lumpy, churning outline in dim worklight: shoulders, heads, camera gear held aloft amid the dancing dust.

Preminger introduces the actors and fields questions.

To their credit, the reporters ask how big Lindsay's part is. To his credit, Preminger distracts them.

"Mr. Lindsay was an actor . . . even wrote his own lines."

Shutters snap. They love it.

"He was a congressman, mayor of New York—"

"Eight long years." Lindsay's weariness seems overrehearsed, but he looks like any director's Top Wasp. Over six feet, with curly, sandy-gray hair, he is Yale *jeunesse doree* at fifty, handsome but not macho, an inheritor obliged (by what Puritan background?) to do good, to be good, and now—by the ethic of the media—to look good.

"Mr. Preminger, will this help his political career?"

"I can't tell you how uninterested I am in his political career. He is now an artist."

More strangers arrive. Lindsay sees Cliff Gorman and asks, "You're with the production, aren't you?"

"Well, yeah—"

"No, I mean—"

"An actor. I'm an actor."

"Playing Hamlekh. Riiight!"

And Hans Verner, the German father, who missed the press conference, asks Lindsay about his career.

"I'm on a sabbatical."

"But you're an actor?"

"I was the mayor of New York."

"No—!"

"Yes."

"*You?* The *Burgermeister?*"

Lindsay turns to an observer. "*Tell* him. I was the mayor."

"Yeah. He was the mayor."

The room grows hotter as the lights come on.

"Nobody listens!" Preminger exclaims. "I want a zoom at the end."

From the shadows, O'Toole sings sweetly. "Why does my heart go zooooooom?"

The first shots are easy, as the actors simply watch the Arab movies.

Lindsay has a silent close-up, reacting. Preminger tries to relax him. "You look incredibly elegant, John. Are you going back to the Republicans?"

"Afraid they won't have me. Afraid I don't wish to. . . . I'll give you all kinds of reactions. You can pick and choose."

"Rolling."

"Now," says Preminger, "look higher—"

("Why me, God?")

"—show your blue eyes—"

("Haven't I always been a good sport?")

"Cut? Print? Beautiful?"

Then they have to speak. First comes Peter Lawford's big scene. Lindsay actually begins by saying he'll pay any ransom—an unfortunate line for an ex-mayor accused of selling out to municipal unions. Stung by Lindsay's fear, Lawford responds with a tough "no-compromise" speech.

As the "stuffy" Lord Carter, Lawford looks aggressively hip in a Beverly Hills haircut. It sits like a helmet over his bewildered gaze as he gropes for lines.

After lunch, the words are still elusive.

"*Act* as though you know them," suggests Otto. "By now even I know them."

But Lawford's words are slow and slurred.

Angela Martelli says, "I've never *seen* such a thing."

"Make it like a simple report," urges Preminger. "Make up the lines if you want."

Again: "Peter, you can't have difficulty with a small speech."

"But I am . . ."

Before a take, he looks miserable.

"Let's go, Peter. You're more senile than I am—"

"I *know* the lines."

"Just make them up."

The room becomes a pit of embarrassment, stinking of heat and fear. For whatever reasons, Lawford is desperate.

Preminger's only course is to encourage him. Take three. "Very good . . ."

Again: "Come on, Peter, don't get flustered. It happens to the best. . . . Jack Barrymore was much worse."

On take nine, O'Toole fluffs—one of his few. "I can't think of a fucking *word* to say!" The actor's hand trembles slightly.

"You have the right to one mistake," says Preminger.

How long will this go on?

As they reload after take fourteen, someone complains that the room is getting hot.

"Getting hot!? That is the understatement of the day. At times like these, only humor helps."

Finally on take fifteen they get something printable and we useless observers are promptly banished.

That night, John Lindsay displayed his feelings over a beer in the hotel lobby, mostly to Lalla, who displayed her tan shoulders in a little summer dress.

"I told Peter O'Toole there's only one thing wrong with this script. And that's that the CIA is not that good. . . . O'Toole lifts the film for me. The difference between O'Toole and Mitchum is huge—at least in New York."

He seemed like a character in Cheever or Updike: a modest, earnest suburban pilgrim.

"Somebody asked if the Senator I played was modeled on someone real. I said he was a slightly pompous figure, so there were plenty to choose from.

"At first I though he was unsympathetic, but the man's feeling for his daughter is important. I think of my own daughter as we're running the film."

He laughed about the call sheet specifying "tears for Donovan."

"All I have to do to cry is think of eight years as mayor of New York. . . . I'm well out of it."

Did he worry about his acting?

"No, I've done so many political commercials. And I'll be going back to New York to work on CBS, then ABC."

He was more concerned about writing. "I got a big advance [on a book] but wasn't happy with it. A lousy book. I'm always deathly afraid to take money and then maybe turn in a lousy book. I don't have that much confidence in my writing. The editor was someone I've known since I was nine years old. He wanted so much to publish it. Maybe too much. I've written for magazines, but it's always heavy. It's really a trick to communicate."

Next morning they returned to the steamy Salle. I stayed only long enough to see Preminger give a line to Cliff Gorman. The German father's anti-Semitism now "rang an ancient bell" in Gorman's head—and set the record for mangled clichés.

"I knew it was coming," said Cliff. "I'm surprised I'm not doing it in an accent." He mimicked an assistant director. "You have your star for this scene? You know, yellow? The six-pointed decal? Paste it on. Be the first on your block to suffer persecution."

It hardly mattered when we watchers were kicked out again. Laurent Petitgirard said sadly, "Preminger work very hard to put the film better but he have not the material."

He had viewed the latest assembly. "You wait for something to arrive but it doesn't. . . . I don't see Preminger for two days, I say, 'Hello, sir,' and he say, 'Make the music and shut up.' There is here a film with half a heart."

Bonjour Tristesse

They worked to salvage and survive.

In the splendid Nikolaos apartment and in Fargeau's ba-

300

roque office, people described offscreen action, chewing at length on great bites of indigestible verbiage. "My part," said Raf Vallone, "is all exposition."

Preminger and his unit struggled to bring life to this Plaster of Paris. One admired their sheer doggedness, converting apartments and marble reception halls into sound stages, lavishing energy on every setup.

At Fargeau's, grips rigged battens around the crystal chandelier (for lights) and marbleized support poles to blend with the walls. Outside they erected towers to pump arc light through the second-floor windows. (They were back to brutes again.) Standing by, the crew had a video recorder to show Pettifer's newscast and a pulse generator to keep it in sync with the Panaflex.

One saw money and care in every detail. If this was folly, it was the folly of experts. (See Appendix, "Fargeau Office," page 351.)

The supporting actors passed through a revolving door.

"I don't go to films much," said Vallone. "It's not me on screen . . . it's someone else."

Françoise Brion, the cool French beauty who finally played his wife—with a copper rinse to match Isabelle's hair—was not the type to break down, but that was her whole part.

And the press pursued Lindsay to the end. His wife laughed about a headline, LINDSAY WATCHES NUDE FILM. "We're long used to that. John already has a list of topless beaches for Copenhagen."

They left, smiling, taking home more money than most Americans earn in a year. As did Peter Lawford, who insisted he had known his lines when he started for Paris.

They came and went, leaving the regulars to get on with work.

Cliff Gorman converted his anger and frustration into laughter.

"Otto asked me if I had any reservations about jumping

down a rope ladder from a helicopter to a moving boat. So I said, no, I had no reservations, I just wouldn't do it."

"Cliff was lovely and graceful," said Graham, "and you *have* to ask an actor that."

At least Cliff and his wife were seeing Paris. "Went to Pigalle. Compared to New York, it's a nursery. Went into a sex shop and saw one tiny dildo—in the back—on special reserve. Like at the public library."

As we became friendly, he spoke of his career. "Luck comes on a silver platter. They called me to offer *Boys in the Band.* For nothing. For a month in the Village. . . . Before that, who knew?"

Waiting near the set, he remembered things he hadn't done—like Norman Jewison's (unproduced) film of *Last Exit to Brooklyn.* "I'd be in bed with a guy and start to tongue his ear. Strong stuff. But no way I'd do it after *Boys.* People would say *two* times? Un-*huh.*"

And there was always TV. "Shouldn't be doing TV. It's all one, two takes. Nothing of me."

Cliff began cleaning his desert boots with an emery cloth. "A bit of *haricot vert* from Île Rousse, a gumball from the Duomo. The whole trip is on my shoes."

Eventually I asked his feelings about this film.

"Feelings?" he snapped back. "I take it out in the hotel room! I don't want problems. 'Did you see what happened between Otto and Cliff Gorman? Oh, *boy!*' Don't want that. As a kid, you think you're special at home. Always have to do things your way. That's what acting is about. I was known as a bad kid but had none of a fuck-up's fun! Got thrown out of UCLA. Worked as a busboy's helper. You don't *know* as a kid what to do with your rage. It's internalized. . . . I was an only child. Got all the pressure. Thought I had to spend my life in a jacket and tie—like for Assembly in school. Oh, boy!"

As for O'Toole, he never went to rushes and never uttered a negative word. But he knew. Of course he knew.

With the crew he always tried to be friendly. Arriving one day, he announced, "Whoever invented early morning should be fucked by a jack donkey with a septic prick."

"I haven't been to bed," growled a grip.

O'Toole seemed to melt with nostalgia. "Ah, them was days, Joxer . . . them was days."

He even tried to keep Preminger smiling, drawing him aside during one furious exchange in the Chambre de Commerce. "Don't go *on*," Peter soothed. "It's not the end of the fuckin' world. . . . Look at the perspective on that tapestry."

Of all the actors, O'Toole alone managed complexity, ambiguity, a performance you could hold up to the light. He wore his own eccentric suit (narrow lapels, stovepipe pants) with the extra, lordly touches of a cigarette holder clamped in his mouth at a jaunty angle and the Irish tweed hat, which he kept in every scene. "It gives me comfort. . . . It's my whole performance!" He looked less like an agent than a don wrenched from his classes or a country squire down for a weekend.

Soon his character was clear. Playing almost the only rational figure in a world of zealots and victims, O'Toole *used* his lofty tone. As a mother broke down in tears, he lit up and smoked. As a hostage cried, he studied her clinically, like a modern Sherlock Holmes, all logic and icy lucidity. The performer was at a peak here, as a hero shorn of sentiment, whom you might respect but wouldn't love—unless you loved reason, manners, the precise functions of mind.

People actually wondered what was behind that composure. What did the character—or the actor—really feel?

We found out in Martin's Paris apartment. The actor was handed an envelope addressed "to the alleged Irishman Peter O'Toole."

A note inside criticized the film, saying that O'Toole brought shame to the IRA and that a bomb would go off at noon.

O'Toole was shaken. "If this is a joke, fair enough—"

"It's no joke," said a crewman.

"Then fuck off out of here!"

A grip ran shouting into the bedroom to clear it.

Everyone hurried downstairs into the street.

Except Angela, who walked. "This is not the spirit that won the war."

Outside, someone called the Manchester *Guardian*, as the note instructed. (The IRA supposedly informed that paper of its operations.) The Paris bomb squad was summoned. And elsewhere in the building the Tour D'Argent was evacuated.

O'Toole, meanwhile, had gone white, as the violence one read of on the inside pages of *The New York Times* was now a reality, in this street, targeted at him.

Back in his hotel room, Cliff Gorman heard the news as he tasted some undrinkable coffee. Immediately he thought of a conspiracy. "I saved the poisoned coffee grounds for ballistics."

On location, he watched the police ambling from their "Tonka Toy trucks" into the building. "Well, I'm not working *today,* I'll tell you."

The Manchester *Guardian* had no notice of a bomb.

Had a unit member done it, as a joke?

Said O'Toole softly, "It's done by a diseased prick."

A café near the apartment soon jammed with crew people, including a man in his mid-forties who had been on the picture a week—a gentle, self-effacing Englishman now drinking brandy at eleven o'clock with tears rolling down his cheeks, who would say only that he was leaving the film.

A co-worker explained that the man's child had been maimed in a London bombing.

Finally, the real tenant of the apartment, Thomas Quinn Curtis, an arts reporter for the Paris *Herald-Tribune,* caught up with Preminger and O'Toole on the sidewalk. Curtis explained about a party at his place the night before . . . too much to drink . . . the note being suggested as a joke. The English critic, Kenneth Tynan, was mentioned.

A grip shouted, "It's a fucking 'orrible thing to do and I'd like to punch 'im in the mouth!"

Otto agreed. "To a man who is halfway intelligent, it's not a joke!"

"Well," called Mickey Murchan, "has he left a bomb or not?"

No. Curtis had realized that a joke was being played and tried to call Preminger, but had been unable to get through to the hotel.

That was good enough for Otto, but the crew wouldn't go back before noon.

"Then I'll get another crew!"

Hearing that, the new worker, trembling at the bar, put down his brandy and strode up to the director, shouting tearfully, "All you think about is your fuckin' film! A poxy couple of thousand people'll watch your film for ten minutes and that's it!"

It was the shout of the movie.

Preminger said, "I'll do anything the majority wants. And I don't blame anyone for being scared."

As they broke for lunch, in a swirl of cops, cooks, actors, and busboys, someone asked O'Toole if he really was an IRA man.

"No, I have enough trouble worrying about my career." He went off alone.

Cliff Gorman, meanwhile, shrugged. "This is no longer creatus interruptus, it's creatus dissolvus. They'll get to my scene eleven minutes before the plane leaves."

Peter returned with two crewmen during lunch, turning aside all questions. "All over . . . don't worry."

They had visited Tynan. One of them confirmed, "It's a hoax. He's left Paris. And he won't be writing any more letters."

O'Toole's knuckles were scraped raw.

The director soon got a nine-page letter from Tynan, telling how O'Toole and the other two had beaten him up. Later, in the London *Daily Mail*, Tynan was quoted: "I was even kicked in the groin."

For now, the publicity office was told it knew nothing of a beating. And I thought how *Rosebud* hoped to use the facts and emotions of terrorism. Yet this one morning was as close as it came—and then by accident, by a bad joke.

A worker was moved to tears.

And we saw the anger behind O'Toole's composure. But it never showed on screen. Perhaps the part didn't call for it. Perhaps he didn't want to spend his feelings on this material. In any case, he resumed playing the civilized, rational hero, at once amused and appalled by the emotions around him. In some ways it was an ideal vision of himself. With his emotions controlled, after all, the agent and the actor who played him both had a better chance of survival.

That afternoon Preminger shot seven long setups, the story of how Sloat stole a fortune and became a terrorist, as told by Cliff Gorman.

" . . . All that time and money is spent on travel and locations, and the night before a big scene they hand you three pages of new dialogue. I'm supposed to sit there like an ass and say, 'Now folks, there's five million in a numbered Swiss bank account because Turhan Bey, who in reality is the Sheik's cousin by marriage, is in effect plotting the overthrow of the republic with Cesar Romero and his desert henchmen. . . . All over the world people will be saying '*What?*' . . . In my contract it says they can cut but not add substantially . . . so now it's cut down again."

Nevertheless, the cynicism of the scene as it had been written in the novel was smothered by talk of German couriers, Lebanese comic books, et cetera. Cliff ran through it nervously, and O'Toole looked bleached with worry.

Said Cliff, "I come into Martin's apartment and see Isabelle. . . . The whole world is looking for this girl. I wanted a *moment* there—a reaction. But Otto didn't. He likes everything to move."

So we began our farewells. Raoul Baum said good-bye over dinner, guessing that he would next work on a French porno.

And Aristea said good-bye until Israel, where Preminger would let her visit. "The old shyster will probably say he saved the romance, but he was wonderful. I love the old man. And I love you." We spent a final day—a last hour—in the Jeu de Paume looking at some Renoirs so bright with life one had to remember they were just paint on canvas.

As our bus to the airport drew away from the hotel, the whole French staff, all those who had survived and were now done, gathered on the sidewalk: Raoul Baum, two young Arab actors, a French soundman, two location managers, and more, many more, cheering, waving, swept away and disappearing in the back window.

GERMANY How They Lost the War

Hamburg. With the juggernaut. August 1. By now the company was facing the consequences of decisions made long ago, and fighting a final, rear-guard action against reality.

Events rushed together in bursts, starting with the loss of four hundred kilos of baggage, as the troupe arrived at the Atlantic Hotel. Who had a toothbrush? Who had no clothes? Angela Martelli was fascinated. "I must say it has more suspense than anything in the picture."

The sumptuous production offices, with chandeliers, carpets, and names on the doors, made people wonder how the Germans had lost the war.

And the revels at night, at Madame Pompadour's off the Reeperbahn, were a revelation. "There were naked birds all around," said one man. "The curtain opens and there's this girl playing with herself. . . . And she comes right to our table, right over us, and she takes a whiskey bottle and pours it over her—all over—and gives it to ——. He doesn't know what to do, so she says, 'Put it inside.' And right away those naked birds are all over us. Costs eighty-five marks to take a girl."

Work, however, was the same old "catering to reality," which didn't return the favor.

In the museum scene, O'Toole and Klaus Lowitsch, the German agent, had a big entrance. A long tracking shot showed off the gallery of primitive art and the surveillance equipment, ending as an aide called out that a suspect had just appeared across the street.

Unfortunately the local actor froze on the line. It was "Pâté, anybody?" all over again. For seven takes O'Toole and Lowitsch raced upstairs through the artifacts, breathlessly discussing the stakeout, only to have the shot killed by a bit player. He was one of Hamburg's best actors, hired at a fat fee to make *sure* of a good performance, but as Preminger thundered that this was scandalous, the poor man looked like he would cry.

Months later the line was dubbed.

After the museum, the city held four days of car shots. Once the autobahn scenes were cut, the agents simply followed the courier from his studio and saw him switch taxis and arrive at the airport. It was as thrilling as a mail delivery. But there was no time for more. And Preminger didn't seem to mind.

"Cars," he said, "are the most boring thing in the world to direct."

A general feeling of unreality only grew as they pursued a star to play Sloat. Making him English, the film had gone over the brink. I asked Erik how he justified having the part non-Arab.

"Basically it's a work of fiction. By using a figure like Sloat, you save the negative things otherwise said about Palestinians."

In other words, it didn't offend.

Erik went on. "I tried to use an Arab . . . but Otto talked to Bonnecarrère, who's convinced the Baader-Meinhof gang is in charge."

They had originally spoken of ascetic, menacing types for the part. But now came fleeting rumors about Orson Welles and Alfred Hitchcock! The idea of Israeli commandos raiding Sloat's headquarters in the desert and finding Alfred Hitchcock there in a sheet raving about a Holy War went beyond absurdity into Cloud Cuckooland.

Of course there were other possibilities for the role.

As Richard Nixon resigned, Cliff Gorman saw at once: *"That's* Sloat. Can you see him? 'I want to make one thing perfectly clear. This is no ordinary war. This is a Holy War . . .' "

The speed of shooting magnified all the tensions. Survivors all together, we shared the bile of the passing days, Joxer.

"I've noticed around four o'clock Preminger has to take it out on someone," said an assistant.

Outside Hamburg airport, it was me. I had quietly answered a crewman's question when OP let loose what the English called a fierce "bollicking."

"I've told you ten times not to talk to technical people. If you don't stop, I'll throw you out!"

(This was in front of crew *and* crowd.)

"I don't want you asking questions!"

(Now he's telling me. After eight months.)

"I don't give a shit about your book!"

(The coup de grace.)

"You can go home! Why are you grinning?"

"I'm not. I'm sad."

"Why do you *take* it?" Robin Gregory asked later.

The truth was, I was addicted to the movie. I couldn't leave—not this close to the end.

At sunrise one morning, as they prepared to fly to Berlin, the office resembled the headquarters of an evacuating army. Under crystal chandeliers, papers and folders spilled from open suitcases.

"You ask the Germans for a ball of twine," said Graham, "and you get *this*!" Six of them.

The crew gathered in the lobby, looking sour and worried.

"Scenes here could've been done anywhere. You never know it's Hamburg."

They worried about the equipment trucks passing through East Germany.

And they worried about their hangovers. "You look awful," they told one man. "For a minute we thought you had your glasses on."

Borne along by the juggernaut, flying to Berlin, they swapped a few more myths. From *Our Man in Havana*, Denys remembered the confrontation of fussy, mechanically perfect, take-after-take Alec Guinness with Ernie Kovacs. "Ernie was joking right up to the last second, calling Guinness 'Gwines' [as in "swines"] and asking if a peerage was for life or if you had to renew it every year like a driver's license?"

And Robin Gregory added to the Kubrick lore, evoking *Barry Lyndon*. "What Otto did in one night at the airport, Kubrick would have done in a week. He'll shoot a scene over and over. Change artists. Change weather. Every scene he shoots is an experiment. He lights by setting lamps at random and taking Polaroids. Spent fifty-two thousand pounds on Polaroids."

In Berlin, some of us spent a precious rest day touring the Eastern sector in a gloomy rain. As complete outsiders, we drifted by a shopping center and a radio tower, drank wine in a hotel, studied the grit-gray desolation of empty avenues, the pitted Wall, the People's Guards, the theaters and monuments along Unter den Linden, the eternal flame within a stone mausoleum, burning in a crystal coffer for the memory of dead soldiers.

History spoke here, demanding a response. Thus Wolfgang told of his father, a U-boat captain who spent the war interned in Canada.

O'Toole remembered urging Jules Buck to see some Yiddish theater in East Berlin, only to find that the building and photos advertising it were just tourist propaganda. There *was* no Yiddish theater.

Preminger of course was as sentimental as ever. "In Vienna

today you click your heels and salute and seventy-five percent will follow!"

Computerized Filming

As if recoiling from this reality, the shooting narrowed to the efficiency of the Kempinski, the green Studio Hamburg vans lined up at the locations, and Preminger's black impatience at dawn on the empty, gray, rain-spattered K'damm. A crowd began gathering as the candy store was transformed into a photo shop; someone wandered in to buy a camera, someone else tried to post a letter in a fake mailbox, another man sought to board a rented bus full of extras—and still they kept coming, until Angela Martelli asked O'Toole if she was in his eyeline and he answered, "Half of *Germany* is in my eyeline."

Preminger plunged ahead, shooting almost what he had wanted to on the recces (for a change), giving the material a spare elegance.

And all day the tumult on the streets grew. By afternoon the crazies were on hand. Preminger threatened one young tough with calling the police; heard a fat psychopath from the subway's bowels laughing like Woody Woodpecker through a take ("Hahahahaaaaa haaaaaaaaaaaa!"); angrily singled me out of a thousand people to declare, "If you stand here with a camera you only *add* to the confusion"; and had the assistant directors shouting through bullhorns to little or no effect ("mesmerized by their own verbosity," said O'Toole's makeup man).

It was Sunday, August 11. They were leaving for Haifa on the fifteenth. And still there was no Sloat for the Israeli shooting. Preminger continued to hold out for a star.

But his search was narrowing.

"What about Richard Attenborough?" he asked Angela Martelli.

She answered without hesitation, emphatically. "*Good* idea."

Shortly afterward, Attenborough was signed.

312

For the next three days in Berlin, Preminger made up for lost time at a pace Angela called "unbelievable."

Klaus Lowitsch, who wanted to play thoughtfully, said, "He tells me to speak English faster than I speak German."

Would Klaus do it all over again?

He laughed, with a big grin. "Sure, why not?"

Robin Gregory called Preminger's speed the closest thing to "computerized filming." But computers don't make films, appearances often to the contrary. The work is done by the fallible and the brave.

Thus they came to a handsome, turn-of-the-century café for the TV showing of the Arab film.

Brigitte had read the Arab text, calling for a contest to help the Palestinians. Then Lalla reread it for clearer English. There were howls from Brigitte's agent, but Preminger had the right to make such changes. Now, in the café, O'Toole and Lowitsch would see the speech.

It was another extravaganza. Journalists played extras, plates of sausage and noodles steamed on the tables, and a German announcer was ready to introduce the film. There was endless checking of the black-and-white TV set and the pulse generator that tied the Panavision shutter to the TV scanning to kill any black "phase bar" across the tube. But when Preminger called "Action" . . . the bar was there. It stayed for an hour, while technicians fiddled and the café became a crucible.

In rushes, the TV set reflected lights, which Preminger hated. Thus Brigitte's speech and Lalla's retake and the recces to find the special café *and* the whole electronic salad would have to be augmented by an expensive matte job.

But that never happened either. The Arab demand was a key step in the book, but on film it slowed the story. So Preminger cut it—cut the whole café scene.

To a man who called himself an expert in broken promises,

this was just one more, like the actors who seemed not to think ("You just saw your daughter nude. Remember? You *love* your daughter. Remember?"); like the actress playing a secretary who couldn't type; like the airline that lost a pulse generator to replace the first one that didn't work; like the old Panaflex with snags, replaced by a new one with new snags; like the Arab movies that had to be matted into the screening room, despite all the costly projection gear; like the art assistant who lost a vital sign . . .

"We have three art directors," said Preminger in amazement, "and it was never done!"

"I apologize, Mr. Preminger—"

"That does no good!"

There is no filmmaking by computer. The trick in Berlin was to finish. And so they did, almost to the day Preminger had predicted three months earlier.

Good-bye in Germany came almost before hello. O'Toole made his farewell on a TV news documentary, saying with laughter and awe about Preminger, "He's a *monster!*"

Thursday, August 15. We gathered at five in the morning in the Kempinski lobby, to fly to Israel. Preminger joked that he could have finished sooner, but "I didn't want to embarrass Cottle. . . . These people make so much of traveling. And what is it? Nothing."

No, not quite nothing.

In Jerusalem, the papers had carried stories of the filming "so all the bombers know we're coming," as Wolfgang said.

Angela Martelli remembered a prior attack. "I believe that a young German actress lost a leg."

In a dramatic meeting, Preminger dismissed the worries. "I can't promise no war. We had the same situation in *Exodus.* . . . I understand if you don't want to go. I can't take the responsibility to tell you to go. I bought two million dollars' worth of 'war insurance' "—he looked at one crewman—"but if some bomb shaves your little beard, you won't get anything."

His speech, said Olivier Eyquem, the French critic, "was straight out of *Red River.*"

For the "nothing" trip itself, four thousand kilos of freight were shipped to Frankfurt, where massive pressure was applied to avoid a twenty-four-hour security delay.

Meanwhile, the company flew to Zurich for a connecting flight. There, we charged through five hundred people stranded because of Cyprus, all clamoring to get on El Al, the only airline then flying to Israel. In Zurich, El Al security men fine-combed our baggage for two hours, digging through every sack and pouch. In Zurich, Graham handed out tickets from a fat stack and everyone followed him down a marble corridor until they realized he was only going to the men's room. And in Zurich, Mickey Murchan drank from a champagne bottle in the waiting room. "You've never had the pleasure of my company before, but you'll sure have it today! Look what the guv'nor of the hotel gave us. Said it's full of Coca-Cola, but I don't think so— ah, Gershuny, vot is de matter? You are not *singing*! Onward, Christian Soldiers . . ."

On to the Holy Land.

ISRAEL Tatters

The juggernaut was racing, faster and faster, like the demented carousel at the end of *Strangers on a Train*, in a spinning whirl of travel, baggage, bewilderment, booze, and urgency. Emotions hung out like torn pennants as people gathered for the shooting in Haifa.

"I've been in the business since I was fifteen and it's terrible . . ."

"All you are is a prostitute . . ."

"I've seen the world . . ."

"But you give up your self-respect . . ."

They hated themselves for their complicity in folly and seemed to hate all directors. H. had $20 million and only made movies to have people to shout at. L. had the seats of his dune buggy taken out on a scorching location so he could ride to lunch alone and "concentrate." F. was "a whining little rat who fires people behind their backs." W. was "a crude, ill-mannered bastard who crawl-asses to the artists and makes life unpleasant for technicians." X. ate "like a gorilla without ears." And R. screamed at a fine actor who came through the wrong door in a shot, " 'Yew khunt! Yewww've just rue-end a shot!' The actor let him have it with a goblet."

There were a few kind words, however. Karel Reisz was "a lovely director"—and Cliff Richardson, returning to the film, had a fresh perspective on Preminger. "I like the way he listens to technicians. And one of the nicest things I saw was the way his kids kissed him. The man's human."

In their raddled mood, the unit braced for Israel and most of the film's action: the *Rosebud* almost going aground, the Israeli raid on Sloat, his capture and humiliation. There was even

316

a possible new ending, a plane hijacking to free Hacam and the other Arabs captured in Corsica.

With so much to do, Preminger hurried more than ever. The juggernaut was relentless.

The Israelis deplored his "industrial approach," while awed by the resources that approach had marshaled. "This is going to be a hit," declared one man. "Peter O'Toole, Lindsay, Attenborough, Preminger, four million dollars, politics, Israel—such films have to be a success."

Yoram Ben Ami, the location manager, agreed. "He is a *great* producer. If he throws me away, I'll still say it."

The English crew saw the industrial approach differently. "It seems," said one, "that he'll do whatever takes the least time, more and more, as we get near the end."

As usual, the truth was in between.

To speed the work, he made cuts before shooting. A scene in Sloat's cave as the Israelis gunned down the praying Arabs was dropped because it might start a rockslide. And because the Israelis objected. "*They* are animals. *We* would not behave like animals."

Also cut were the observation posts that spotted the *Rosebud*, those same posts Preminger had liked on the first recce, so long ago. Now the yacht was tracked by radar and an observation plane—which still produced *reels* of rushes.

Once shooting began, the industrial approach came to this: Preminger tried things once. If a problem arose, he had enough to cut around it . . . or he dropped the scene. There was no other choice.

Thus, the *Rosebud* was supposed to sever a net between two fishing boats and the deckhands were to be pulled into the water. Instead, they seemed to *jump* in, waving. At rushes, people laughed. The scene never made it to the rough cut.

During the raid on Sloat, Israelis were lowered on ropes through holes atop the caves. The praying Arabs were turned away and supposedly heard nothing—but they had to work to ignore the shower of dirt and stones on their heads. There was no time to put the Arabs further back and relight. In editing, Preminger tried to use mostly single shots of the Israelis to isolate them from the men below.

Capturing Sloat in his white caftan, the commandos trussed him up in a harness and hauled him out through the roof. He looked hilarious, like a Christmas angel ascending in a high school play. During the editing, Preminger cut away as soon as Sloat started up.

In the next scene, Sloat was dragged to a waiting Israeli helicopter while his troops charged across a field, shooting in vain. But the Arab soldiers were more interested in sleeping under the trucks and fighting over cold Cokes and dope. During the takes they loped along, firing playfully at each other.

The local casting aides had failed badly and cost Preminger a powerful cut from the Arabs shooting in the air to the stillness of Israeli HQ as Sloat is led in.

There was no time for anger or regret. Said Preminger, "If this is the Arab army . . . I think we leave out the whole charge." Which he did.

Thus whole chunks of days perished, irredeemably. The laughing soldiers, the dirt-spattered Arabs, Sloat as a Christmas angel—all the sudden surprises of intractable reality— were ignored as the juggernaut rolled on. The time spent in Juan-les-Pins took its toll here. Preminger, after all, had struck a bargain with reality; the world had given its share of traffic, sunrises, and faces to the film. Now, when the enterprise was most vulnerable, the world took back more than it had given.

Israel became a blur as they worked under a scalding sun in a river of sweat.

Fade in: Slow agony in an Arab village as some locals surround O'Toole's car, while others look down from rooftops, through windows, and behind ropes, where Israeli assistants shout and kick them into line.

Children mimic the clapsticks, flies swarm over an open drain, Preminger yells at the Arabs—*"Will you stop this!"*—dust blows up from the road, a woman throws down a bowl of dishwater, tiles clatter, a flowerpot falls, goats and donkeys wander past, more rocks crash down, the sun hovers over the throngs on the roofs so that we expect bodies to start toppling, and the children and old women—in a scene out of *Emmanuelle*—gather around Aristea to stroke her blonde hair in wonder.

"This," she exclaims, "is the scene we walked out on!"

Jump cut: Akko, all gold and green minarets, a Turhan Bey city (Universal, circa 1950). Heat shimmers off the docks while the *Rosebud* sails back and forth. Israeli pilots wait under a Coca-Cola umbrella, listening to the crackling walkie-talkies, as the boat calls for seasick pills.

The sea work is horrible and nauseating, made harder by every swell. An Israeli patrol boat slams into the *Rosebud*, Preminger chases some journalists off the yacht because someone moves before a shot, and camera assistant Dewi Humphries calls it his "worst day" in films—worse than almost being killed on the camera platform of a car in Hamburg, when an actor who was driving lost control while adjusting his flapping wig.

Jump cut: After the sea comes harder work in Sloat's cave, thirty miles southwest of Jerusalem, a site chosen by Preminger on his last recce. In the midst of a desert, one climbs three stories up a rock pile to the cave mouth, then down again into a series of huge chambers, with those roof holes admitting cones of faint sunlight. Here is Sloat's "headquarters" with a printing press and cots for his men and a private area lined with Oriental rugs.

It feels like a series of underground aircraft hangars with immense, sand-colored, sloping walls.

"It's three thousand years old," says an Israeli. "Dug by hand. Slaves lived here." And work here now. Equipment is carried up to the cave mouth and down again, inside. Or it is lowered in on ropes, through the holes. Grips run up and out of those caves and back in again, ten times an hour, because the production has reached a spot on the globe where only sweat can make it go. Sweat and money.

A scaffold is assembled in one cave, hammered into place with thunderous mallet blows, and topped by brutes, which are hauled up by ropes. Towers and brutes are both dwarfed within the caves. And up on ground level, CSI lamps pour in more "sunshine" through the holes.

It is a once-in-a-lifetime set, except that Preminger suddenly hears that *Jesus Christ Superstar* has already used it. He is furious with the Israelis, but there is no turning back. The towers are up. The mallets are singing. And context is everything. After all the money and work expended, one *Rosebud* critic calls the location "a cave made out of cardboard, a set even Buster Crabbe would have rejected." (See Appendix, "Desert Caves," page 352.)

Jump cut: The nadir is the desert work during the parachute drop, near the Jordanian border. Since December, the movie has been pointing here—to this baked flatland bordered by purple ridges in the distance, inhabited by Gila monsters, clouds of angry flies, and a few scattered sheep herds.

The crew packs up in the caves one night, rises before dawn to an Israeli hotel breakfast featuring runny eggs, herring, and soggy cornflakes in chafing dishes—then moves out—to a total breakdown in communications.

An old Hercules transport flies over the drop zone. Slowly people realize the unthinkable. They have *no radio contact* with the plane.

Where would the men jump?

"One place we can't cover is straight up," says Denys.

On each pass of the Hercules, they shoot footage while Robin Gregory tries to reach the plane through the airport.

"They're coming! Be ready!"

The transport flies low overhead.

"Everyone, thumbs up! Give them the sign!"

"Maybe," says Preminger, "we should lay down and give a signal. In Hebrew."

"Move back—"

"Move the cameras back!"

Signal flares are lit.

The jumpers are in the plane door.

"Surely," says Angela, "they are not without radio contact. This is absolutely ridiculous."

Then they are spilling out. Cameras are snatched up again and hauled back wildly.

When it ends, Jimmy Devis leans back in the shade of a truck and shakes with joyless laughter. "It's the biggest fuckup since the relief of Mafeking."

Later that day they surpass themselves. Doubts arise about whether to have an afternoon jump. An Israeli is sent to the airport to find a relief crew for the Hercules. The jumpers follow by truck to board the plane. Suddenly a car is sent to cancel the jump and bring the troops back for a ground shot. Then another car speeds off to cancel the cancellation . . . while Preminger rests. It is the only time I have seen him sit down during a filming session.

Despite all those vehicles strung across the desert in confusion, three cameras shoot some real parachute drops that day and get more than enough coverage, including the soldiers freefalling against a vast, pitted rockscape that looks like a moonface.

It is a victory of money as limited as most industrial victories, for money can only buy vehicles and vistas, not suspense.

As they finished, one tried in the usual way to salvage a few decent memories.

Working on the assembly, editor Peter Thornton still believed. He felt the film began when O'Toole appeared. "From reel four it *crackles* on!" Then he added thoughtfully, "I worked on *The Agony and the Ecstasy* and *The Cardinal* and loved both of *them*, too. I've never been right."

Yet some moments had clearly worked. There was the ritual suicide of a Sloat follower, rigged by Cliff Richardson with a blank bullet, a bit of oil for smoke, and an electrical charge to trigger a blood spurt. It needed only one stunning take.

"Did you see the fear in his eyes?" Otto asked Jimmy Devis afterward.

"I did. When you shouted at him."

"Well, it's no good my shouting at you. You have no fear."

There was Preminger's surprising feel for extras, at the outskirts of his frame, as when he told the guards around the suicide victim to have no guns because "there must be no feeling of force."

And finally there was pure spectacle (laden with emotion only if you believe that a camera move can express, at times, the ineffable). Such spectacle reached its zenith with the Mobius, a state-of-the-art aerial camera taken from London to Israel.

By then the hope of the film was in visual display, with scenes like the *Rosebud* racing toward the coast on a crash course.

An Israeli helicopter flew over the boat to lower two agents on a cable. As Cliff Gorman dropped thirty feet to the fantail, the airborne camera would tilt down, then follow while he ran along the deck to the bridge. We would be with him . . . dropping and running.

A conventional gyroscopic-mounted camera might have vibrated too much. The Mobius offered a remote-controlled alternative. The movie camera and its gyro-stabilizer were enclosed in a black, four-foot, fiberglass ball with a narrow window. A cable led back to the operator's console. He panned and tilted the ball by squeezing a joystick with one hand, and dialed zooms with the other.

In effect, he *thought* his shot and manipulated his console accordingly, while watching a TV monitor that showed what the camera saw. Total development costs of the unit, according to Tom Wadden, president of Mobius Wescam Ltd., had been $7 million.

Preminger had seen the ball months before, hanging in a truck in an English industrial suburb. Three burly men shook that truck hard. The ball jiggled nervously, but the image on the TV monitor was rock steady. Otto was convinced.

And when Cliff Gorman stepped out of a helicopter over the water—without a stand-in, after all—another chopper flew nearby with a black ball hanging from it. Below were the yacht and a flatboat with Preminger. Voices cried over nine radios: "Action. Go! Rolling. Gorman's coming now . . . here he comes . . . *where is he*????"

As Cliff told it, the problem was the other actor in the scene:

"This guy, man, is too much. I mean we're waiting at the airport in Haifa—for the helicopter—the seven-oh-five to— uh?—Akko? And there's one cot. That's it. No chairs. One cot. He says his back is bad and right away lays down. For two hours. While I'm waiting there in tennis shorts. Leaning against a wall. How could he *lay* on it? There were bloodstains . . . it must have been used in three wars. But later was the worst. We're in this helicopter, and he's supposed to go first. Only he has trouble with his gun. I don't know what—but he gives it to me all of a sudden. And he takes *mine*! I don't have time to argue. He's out. . . . Then I put on my harness and tuck his gun in my belt . . . and it falls apart. An Israeli gun! The thing falls apart in my hand. I have a flash I'm gonna come down on the boat and pull my gun out and it's in pieces. . . . Otto is gonna go berserk. 'Vot is diss, Mr. Gorrrrman!? Your gun is broken!' Just before I went out, the *pilot* put it together. Lucky!"

In the rushes the scene had such grace and speed that someone called it a hundred-thousand-dollar shot.

Later, during a sneak preview at the Criterion in New York,

I sat behind a couple who gasped audibly at the shot as the whole theater seemed to be racing over the water for a moment.

But that was only a moment.

At a critics' screening, some friends didn't remember the shot.

And when the film opened, one reviewer called the cinematography generally "murky." No miracles of levitation—no spectacle—could overcome the context of the movie.

By the end of Israel, all the work seemed like so much sleepwalking. One night, near the Lebanese border, on a barren road where the genny throbbed in the dark and the truck headlamps cast long shadows on the earth, a hundred people milled around, plus twenty-five soldiers carrying Uzis, sent by the army for security. Far ahead, we could see tracer bullets fired regularly across the border to intimidate Palestinian terrorists.

The unit had been up all day and night. Now a single brute lit a desolate crossroad where O'Toole would drive by, on the way to Sloat. But the passing car caught reflections on its side. So the whole unit, a hundred and twenty-five people, squatted motionless in a ditch at four in the morning, until the shot was done.

"What am I doing here in the middle of the night?" wondered Mike Seymour.

Up on the road, O'Toole sang, "I'm only a strolling vagabond, so good night, pretty ladies, good night. . . . Will someone get me a beer, in the name of Jesus?"

"I shall go home," whispered Angela, "have a neat whiskey, and throw myself off the balcony."

"*Kinderspiel,*" muttered OP. Child's play.

Israel ended with a convulsive spasm as local aides besieged Graham in the halls, waving vouchers, while he tried to clear out. It was a mob scene akin to the closing of the banks in Shanghai.

"Anything goes," Graham said. "They think they can throw in aaaaanything! It's like a printing press out there!"

Chalky White was appalled. "We've actually run out of vouchers!"

And an Israeli shouted at Graham, "Don't complain about how this film is organized. Don't *pay*! Just don't *pay*!"

They were off to Juan-les-Pins for a last day, to reshoot the yacht broker scenes with O'Toole.

An Israeli was coming as a guest of the production. "That guy!" exclaimed a grip. "We sweat our balls off and can't even get any overtime? It's a bloody crime!"

The departure was chaos.

At six in the morning, the bus driver wouldn't leave the hotel unless he got cash. "Look," he shouted, "dees ess 'uman medhouse! Deh buhhs kumm, evvvyvun runn avay!"

"Good heavens," said Angela, "we're respectable people!"

Wolfgang paid him, and the bus started up . . . leaving the wardrobe man locked in his hotel room, dead drunk amid the costumes needed for Juan-les-Pins.

"That fat idiot!" Preminger stormed on the plane. "That drunken bum!"

"He won't have the courage to turn up!" said a crewman.

"They'll find him on the floor," said another, "wearing O'Toole's hat and Lalla's dress."

Exeunt

As we left, I thought about the four men who had dominated the Israeli shooting.

Richard Attenborough had learned one script and was pulling out of the driveway on his way to the airport when the postman delivered a "totally different" one. He spent twelve hours traveling and then shot immediately.

"Even five words" changed in those circumstances was a problem, he said. But Attenborough, at fifty, could cope. His acting career had begun in 1942, with *In Which We Serve*, going on to *Brighton Rock, I'm All Right, Jack, The Angry Silence* (co-produced by Bryan Forbes), *The League of Gentlemen, The Great Escape, The Flight of the Phoenix, Seance on a Wet Afternoon, 10 Rillington Place*, and *Brannigan*, among others. He had produced *Whistle Down the Wind* and *The L-Shaped Room* and lately emerged as a director with *Oh, What a Lovely War!* and *Young Winston*.

Like OP, Attenborough had a thirst to *do*, to be in and open to the world, playing parts, making films, being chairman of a soccer team, running a radio network. Outgoing and cheerful, he dwelt on the possibilities of life.

As actors, O'Toole and Attenborough could not have been more opposite. Oddly, they had both played sex murderers, in *The Night of the Generals* and *10 Rillington Place*, respectively. O'Toole's Nazi general was a psychopath whose anger erupted publicly, while Attenborough's shriveled behind a mealy-mouthed propriety.

Connections surely existed between their styles, their looks, and their careers. Attenborough, the avatar of the average, must have struggled to be noticed. "I died in *The Great Escape*. That's the one thing everybody remembers. . . . Obviously it was a relief to the audience."

But his work *had* been noticed, and now he trusted his future.

O'Toole, in contrast, might have been handicapped by the lavishness of his gifts, as if they let him glimpse the furthest limits of what the future could hold and it somehow wasn't enough.

At fifty, Attenborough was full of projects and hopes. At forty, Peter was a darker figure, with a taste for ironies and good-byes. They could have almost switched parts.

"I play a lunatic," said Dickie (for so everyone called him), "and I'm slightly lunatic myself." Accent "slightly." His first words on screen were to his Arab follower who was about to commit suicide. Speaking with quiet compassion, Attenborough established himself as a muted Messiah.

Another time, he used his stature. Facing O'Toole and Gorman as a captive, he drew himself up to his full (medium) height, bracing for a blow, determined not to flinch. It was vulnerable and oddly sympathetic.

In dealing with Preminger, Dickie was relaxed. "OP's wonderful if you just send him up a bit and don't take everything seriously."

On the set, Preminger got miffed when the actor put down a heavy prop between takes. "So I picked it back up and said, 'Oh, Master, I always carry *all* my props with me.' Well, he had a good laugh and everything was fine."

Attenborough's only real problem came in the scene with his captors, where he "betrays" himself. He told of it with his tired, red eyes shining over a stubble beard.

"He's had a go at me today. . . . I was being pretty florid. But you can't say those lines—'I seek the restoration of the holy state of Islam'—like you're ordering a cup of coffee. He even said the reading should be dramatic. Then when they turned round to do my close-up, 'Dickie, why are you so dramatic? It's like you're doing Shakespeare.' Well, I told him to leave me alone at that point or I'd blow. It's too late to change all the rhythms and accents just then. And the lines *should* be dramatic . . . but then he said later I was wonderful. Shouting or not, it's an extraordinary experience! I look back at playing with John Wayne and James Stewart—and working with this man—and I have to say it's a thrill. He's one of the greats!"

Attenborough gave the role intelligence and care, but one felt it was heaped on a straw figure designed to beguile our sense of history while finally insulting it.

One night in Jerusalem, he turned away completely from

the movie. It was his birthday, and he invited several of us to supper in the hotel.

I asked if he'd eaten there before.

"Oh, I know!" He laughed. "It's hell!"

At a big, round table overlooking the hills and a purple sky, at Grossinger's-by-Jordan, amid a clatter of cutlery in a mess hall with tablecloths, the actor told us about his plan to film the life of Ghandi. Like Judd Bernard and Graham Cottle, like all the second assistant directors and location managers, like Erik and Otto Preminger, Attenborough had his dream project.

An Indian had brought him a biography of Ghandi years ago. "He told me, 'People in the British film industry keep mentioning your name.' He hadn't the clearances, the permissions, he hadn't a script or money, he hadn't *anything* except the biography. Well, I read it and I said yes. I'll mortgage my house, sell my art, but I'll do it. And it's brought me to the brink of bankruptcy. We were set to go on January first and the financing fell through again. I had thirty-five people on the crew and I was paying nine of them myself."

Earlier he had visited Nehru. "We sat in his office for hours . . . talking about Ghandi. At the end he ran out to my car as I was leaving and called after me. There was one thing he wanted to say. 'Whatever you do, *don't deify him.* He was too much a man. Too great a man.'

"Ghandi was walking in South Africa with another Moslem. Two whites came the opposite way and there was no question Ghandi and his friend had to step into the gutter. Afterward he said it's amazing that human beings should derive pleasure from humiliating their own kind." Attenborough was moved; his eyes shone with wonder and a loving awe. "Imagine! He was *twenty-one* when he said that. To have said something so profound at that age."

The script had finally been done by Robert Bolt. "Robert went to India for three months, and he's written a *wonderful* script!"

Currently Attenborough would direct one of three projects he'd been offered. "It's important for me to get the experience for the Ghandi film. . . . I must keep working. You're not a director unless you direct."

As the sun set, we toasted his birthday in Jerusalem and his dream.

And then he was gone.

Done.

It was all finishing. Cliff Gorman had one last preachy scene. His fellow "agent"—the other man in the helicopter—also wanted to be in it.

Cliff laughed. "That pushy bastard. Wanted me to speak to Preminger. Jerk! I *should* have. Let *him* say those lines!"

While waiting, Cliff told of his dinner at the U.S. Embassy, when he suggested to one woman that America should invade South Africa to keep in practice.

"She didn't crack a smile. Like a Disney dummy. Kept on cutting food."

They called him then. He dashed out—and returned suddenly for his glasses. "I don't want to lose my character."

He waved, for the last time. "So long. Good to work together. Hope to do it again."

And was finished.

They were all going.

O'Toole slumped in the lobby of the resort hotel, a solitary figure on a plain of marble, itself an extension of all those terminals and lobbies along the way. The Muzak was stilled, a barman cleaned glasses, and darkness crept over the Judean hills in the windows.

Chalky White turned up, bulging and jolly in a yellow jumpsuit, and Cliff Richardson.

"Cliff! Go home!" cried O'Toole. "Every time I see this man, I think he's going to blow me up."

Rumpled and dusty, O'Toole still seemed supernaturally elegant in a checked sport shirt, worn outside his trousers, and gold-rimmed aviator glasses. He fiddled with his cigarette holder, sipped cold beer.

Clearly he was in a mood to perform. Whatever was lacking on screen, he wrote his own lines here, created his own "Peter O'Toole."

"I was climbing Masada—the south face—it's a long, steady climb, and when I got up there I was *nackered!*"

The voice vibrated. At this range there was no tuning out.

"I got to the top . . . and there was a man who looked at me strangely and said 'Don't I know you?' And I said 'I know you.' Chalky, he was the man who managed the Dead Sea Hotel! Do you remember?"

"Oh, do I remember!" The jumpsuit shook with laughter.

It was a hotel in Amman where the toilets flushed boiling water and the showers coughed out spiders.

"Sam Spiegel was going to come and we were to welcome him. They had this lone waiter—One-Eyed Ali."

"Aoh, Gawd!" Chalky roared.

"One-Eyed Ali always made this great production of handing you what looked like a menu. But it was a wine list. There was *no* menu, because they always served the same thing. Ali would rattle it off. Beans, chicken, and lamb. Always!"

"Aoh, Gawd!"

"Then he would slide up and whisper out of the side of his mouth, 'You wanna buy some American cigarettes?' Well, Spiegel was coming to this hotel—I don't know how they got him into the country—and we were going to greet him: John Box, Robert Bolt, and I were there. And there was *dinner* . . ."

He paused to let it sink in.

"Dinner . . . in the *Dead Sea Hotel.* They brought Spiegel the wine list—all there was—and I remember One-Eyed Ali standing there and taking it all down very seriously. And Spiegel very *care*fully saying, 'It doesn't have to be *vintage!*'"

There was a chorus of laughter.

"He asked about the food. And Ali said, 'Beans, chicken, and lamb.' Then he came up beside Spiegel and out of the corner of his mouth he said, 'You wanna buy some American cigarettes?' "

The story seemed hilarious. For those were days, Joxer, and the days were ending and laughter was precious. If the textures of these lives were only barely suggested on screen, at least one saw them now, to be preserved in memory, long after the troupe departed.

Wrap

It ended in Juan, with Preminger sitting in the shade, deathly pale, nursing an upset stomach. Sick, exhausted, struggling to finish, he tried one last gesture, which told everything about his movie.

An Arab hijacker was to appear on an airliner, threatening to kill everyone with a grenade unless Hacam and the other Arabs captured in Corsica were released from jail. In Juan, O'Toole would then take a call from his CIA masters and refuse to get involved in the new hijacking.

The phone call was the last shot to be made, the end slate, and Preminger's final chance to show a human reaction to terrorism.

The orange sun flared off a glass phone booth as O'Toole sipped a cold drink nearby, waiting for the setup.

The costume man had returned, contrite and sober, and now O'Toole cooed sweetly to his hat, "You don't like traveling, do you, my lovely? But a sauna, a drop of champagne, and a massage and it'll be all right." He looked up and addressed the crew in a casual tone that still overrode the traffic noise. "Suppose . . . just *suppose—*"

We waited, as we had waited to hear of his career, his hat, his One-Eyed Ali.

"Suppose this is the *first* day . . ."

Smiling perversely, O'Toole goaded us as if to affirm that risk was his element.

"Suppose all the film remains to be shot? We're starting to redo it all over again . . ."

A drink. A silence.

"*Would* you?"

Finally an American observer called out, "Yes, *I'd* do it! Definitely!"

Otherwise no one spoke.

Peter mused, "Heavy silence . . ."

On "Action" he entered and leaned on the phone booth, eyeing a parking attendant, and waiting. Preminger had earlier speculated that the actor hadn't done a film like this in a while and was enjoying it. Now Otto cued "phone" and let him work.

He answered, listened, then interrupted. "No . . . no . . . give it to Nick." (The crew joked that Nick was Mitchum.) As O'Toole hung up and shambled off, a fat woman shouted from the curb, "That's Peter O'Toole . . ."

Everyone was moved from his sightline.

On the second take he was more polite, masking his distaste. "No . . . no . . . no. Get Nick."

Preminger took him aside, explaining that he would use this as the end scene, "If we can make something of it."

"All right, let me show you some more versh-yuns."

Take three. The "no's" were softer. He hung up as gently as a hangover victim trying to preserve his equilibrium, and shuffled off toward the port. It was starting to be interesting. One could hear music swelling under that walk.

Take four. He entered from the other side (better for camera), showing the splayed walk and the eccentric clothes that by now made up his image, along with his amused, slightly contemptuous look. Hearing the news, he gaped so that his cigarette fell from his mouth.

He repeated his "no's" numbly, hung up, doffed his hat to the parking attendant, and shuffled into the orange light as if leaving a whole career behind.

Take five had no falling cigarette. And Nick himself was on the line. "What you must do is follow your instincts . . . quite simple . . . believe me." As he walked away, one could visualize the end credits.

He had reached the exhaustion of a civilized man before the ceaseless irrationality of the world. Take seven was wordless. "No" formed on his lips without sounding. He hung up softly, tipped his hat to the parking attendant, and strolled off.

Cut, print!

"That's a wrap."

Suddenly the camera crew danced down the road, following O'Toole. He and Preminger embraced, both looking ravaged. The orange had bled from the sky, leaving a misty, purple veil. And, a month later, in London, the scene was cut.

Once more the inevitable choice was dictated by the subject: end with the hijackers on the plane, making their demands. They were stronger than any civilized recoil by O'Toole. As good as he was, the sudden yawning danger in the plane was stronger, bringing us as close to terror as this picture ever would.

I packed for the flight back to London, thinking how I had wanted to show where movies came from but had seen only the source of this film.

I had watched a director driven by a producer's need to hurry, to finish with economy—to avoid the least taint of creative self-indulgence.

He was a man doing a suspense film in which the premise itself was the "star"—yet his every instinct led him to stop the film repeatedly to dwell on character.

He had pursued reality until it led him to a fog of impenetrable accents and then ignored reality at its critical point, avoiding offense by making Sloat English. It was the act of a reputed tyrant with a fatal . . . tact?

He had exercised total control where there was no such

thing—any more than one might have total control over one-self. In this case, control was an illusion, a giddy freedom that let a man reproduce the best and worst of himself, as he might in a child.

And he paid the price of his freedom. Later, when the shooting ended, through the looping and editing and printing, through the premiere and failure of the film, after all the company had departed for other movies, he was left alone with his.

I remember now an hour in London when O'Toole had come to loop a few lines, clowning with Otto and crowning his bald head with the gift of an Irish hat.

There is a photo of Preminger mugging in a street with that hat. Seeing the picture, remembering the contradictions in the man, I think of the one constant in his life. You have seen and known it from the start of these pages. I mean, of course, his laughter, which accepted and dismissed all contradictions. It was the laughter of a man who took seriously everything and nothing, hating only to be bored. It was a magician's laughter, at the instant after his disappearance, the last trace left of him on an empty stage.

There is a gasp, a hush—

Then, with a fanfare, he reappears, bowing. Having survived.

EPILOGUE

Though the filming ended in Juan-les-Pins, for me the experience really came to a conclusion years later in New York.

And this is what happened during those years.

Professionally, most people carried on.

Among the writers, Marjorie Kellogg finished a screenplay of *The Bell Jar*, and various TV scripts. She still seeks backing to direct a script of her own.

Erik Preminger sold a script and pursues new projects in California.

Paul Bonnecarrère died of a heart attack in 1977 without completing a new book.

On the production staff, Graham and Anna Cottle sold *Good Morning Midnight* after being unable to finance it. In Los Angeles, Graham tries to launch new films while Anna is an associate producer at Warner Brothers TV.

Rudolph Hertzog, the German location manager, continues to work in production, with emphasis on German tax shelters.

Cliff Richardson is semiretired. His son, John, did the special effects on *A Bridge Too Far*, after recovering from a catastrophic car accident in which his girl friend was killed.

Peter Thornton found no work for a year after *Rosebud* and emigrated to Africa.

Margot Capelier still casts many international films made in Europe, like *French Connection II* and *Julia*.

Wolfgang Glattes has joined the Directors Guild of America as a first assistant. He might direct on German TV, but the pay as an assistant here is better.

Willy Holt soon forgot the *Rosebud* experience. He was art director on Woody Allen's *Love and Death* and a co–art director on *Julia*, for which Annalise Nascalli-Rocca did costumes.

Denys Coop photographed a low-budget feature, *Inserts*, helping its young director lay out shots, then photographed much of the flying material for *Superman*.

"I look back," said Denys, "and, you know, I find myself *defending* Otto. I mean, he's absolutely unique and you have to like him. No matter what you've gone through."

Of the actors, Kim Cattrall, the American deb, is under contract to Universal Pictures.

Lalla Ward played young Queen Bess in a film, while continuing an active career in English TV.

Betty Berman left Paris for unemployment in New York.

Debra Berger lives in Rome with her child by a local prince.

Amidou, "the smiling killer," landed a major role as a fugitive terrorist in William Friedkin's *Sorcerer*, which ultimately proved a bigger flop than *Rosebud*.

John Lindsay is a TV reporter.

Claude Dauphin died in Paris.

Cliff Gorman returned to Broadway in a major hit, Neil Simon's *Chapter Two*.

Richard Attenborough became Sir Richard and directed *A Bridge Too Far* and *Magic* for Joe Levine. There is even talk of reviving his Ghandi film.

Robert Mitchum's career entered a new phase when he played the seedy, middle-aged private eye, Philip Marlowe, in *Farewell, My Lovely* and *The Big Sleep*.

Peter O'Toole and Jules Buck ended their partnership. O'Toole continues to look for the right film, after *Foxtrot* and *Caligula*, both long delayed in their release. A recent interview describes "The Wreck of Peter O'Toole." Classical actors, it is said, are less in demand, his wife has left him, and a bad pancreas threatens his health. His ideal is "to do crap, get paid a lot of money for it, then never have to suffer the embarrassment of having it shown." Bitterly he adds, "The good scripts never get made. Because the hacks . . . don't make anything unless they recognize the cliché."

Otto Preminger announced several films which did not go into production. Undoubtedly the failure of *Rosebud* has hurt him. Yet, as I write, he is finishing the shooting of Graham Greene's *The Human Factor* with a screenplay by Tom Stoppard, starring Nicol Williamson and Richard Attenborough. This time he has chosen a book where everyone is, indeed, a character and where the ultimate mysteries reside in the hearts of those characters.

In some ways *Rosebud* preceded history.

Marcel Dassault, the model for Fargeau, is to cede control of his aircraft company, lately rocked by tax-evasion scandals, to the French government.

The raid on Sloat's cave partially foreshadowed the Entebbe raid.

And the Israelis reiterate that Baader-Meinhof remnants help direct Palestinian terrorists.

In Paris, Anatole Litvak, Preminger's long-time friend, died.

So did actor Jean Gabin.

In London, the Dorchester Hotel, which Preminger often said was like no other in the world, was sold to Arab interests.

In New York and Los Angeles, the executives of United Artists who financed and distributed *Rosebud*, and who had a long-term relationship with Preminger, left the company after a dispute with the conglomerate that controls it, and formed Orion Pictures. The surviving entity called United Artists is virtually a different organization from the one that made *Rosebud*.

Finally, the picture that everyone disliked in that summer

of 1974, *Emmanuelle*, is still playing in a first-run Paris house after five years.

On a personal level, I got a letter with Aristea's good-bye a week after returning to the United States. A year later, my wife and I were finally divorced. She married an agent and spends most of her time painting in Beverly Hills.

Among the whole *Rosebud* company, the one who scored a career breakthrough was Isabelle Huppert, in her film *The Lacemaker*. She was hailed by American critics for "one of the best performances in years." Also praised was her co-star, Yves Beneyton—the same actor who played Patrice Thibaud until he was fired.

During her press conference at the 1977 New York Film Festival, as she met the critics, I remembered the plump, taciturn girl Preminger had first auditioned.

Now Isabelle was a slender, beautiful young woman and a successful actress.

She would soon begin *Violette* for Claude Chabrol and play one of the Brontë sisters in another picture.

And Preminger alone had seen what she might become.

In his office, three years after *Rosebud*, they talked for an hour. That's when the production ended for me, at the white marble desk where it had begun.

As they spoke casually of Paris, family, and movies, it seemed that if *Rosebud* meant anything beyond its own demise it was as a crossroads for their two careers. There was surely a moment in Isabelle's growth when she needed the discipline of trying to keep her identity on a big, impersonal film. There would be other situations like *Rosebud* later, but she had been alone on that one, at twenty, and had survived with a sense of her own strength. After all the anguish, I could not see that the film had produced more.

Indeed, most films don't accomplish that much.

After her meeting, Isabelle was delighted and surprised. She had earlier visited another older U.S. director. "But what a difference. [The first man] works in a little room all day trying to write—and you feel that he is angry and bitter. . . . But Preminger! He is wonderful! I love it when he talks about his children. You feel *no* bitterness. He's a happy man."

There are two final footnotes, both, in a way, about survival.

Outside a screening room where a new print of *Julia* would be shown, I met a man whose name had been often mentioned on *Rosebud*: Fred Zinnemann was quiet, with a chilly, careful, Anglo-Viennese accent. It was especially careful as he said he wouldn't have let me write a similar book about him.

"I don't mind if people watch who must be on the set, but to have anyone there who is not supposed to be . . . makes me nervous."

And, yes, the cancellation of *Man's Fate* had hurt. "But the pain came later. We actually did not believe at first the film would be canceled. I must say, everybody behaved beautifully. They went on rehearsing. And there was a party later. But it was like a miscarriage."

About directing he was reserved, preferring to put his emotions on screen. Thus he knew the troubles of *Rosebud* and was sorry about them.

Without a pause, as if he had accepted it for years, he added, "Sometimes Otto's personality makes trouble for him. But he is a great director."

The second footnote is about Eva Monley. She was there at the beginning, in London, and was still a friend, long after the end. True to her prophecy, she had done better by leaving the project, subsequently supervising seven location films for a Warner Brothers unit. Now she was about to co-produce a huge picture in the Far East.

Her style was as tart as ever when I saw her in New York.

While visiting Coppola's Philippine sets for *Apocalypse Now*, she had questioned the building of a "Vietnamese" village so close to a river. They told her the water levels had been carefully researched.

"Well!" She laughed. "After the flood, the insurance claim was the biggest in the history of filming."

She talked as always in a staccato hailfire of names and places, telling how her London apartment had a still from each film she had done, a wall of famous faces . . . how she had bought an island home off Kenya with her bonus for bringing in a picture under budget . . . how Joe Strick (director of *Ulysses*) had his terrible heart attack alone on a plane and thought, "No, there's too much to live for, this can't be it" . . . how she was hoping to see Lean and Huston in Los Angeles . . . how her place there filled with friends in a few minutes, all talking about Africa, London, and New York . . . how Paul Newman recognized her in Picadilly Circus after all these years . . . and how, finally, that's what it's all about. Making friends and keeping them over the years.

"And not worrying about making mediocre movies because so few good ones get made. That's the business."

Thus she had survived.

And that is the business.

Appendix

Index

OTING PRODUCTIONS S.A.

CALL SHEET   NO ..1..

PRODUCTION: "ROSEBUD"   DATE: WEDNESDAY 29 MAY 1974.

LOCATIONS: 1) PORT GALLICE - ROSEBUD   UNIT CALL: Leave hotel 8.25 a.m.
                                                        1st location 8.30 a.m.
              2) PORT GALLICE - ROSEBUD   (except as otherwise
                                                        arranged)
              3) LAS VEGAS BAR (COVER SET)
                  18 Av. G. de Maupassant
                  Tel. 61 05 56

SETS: 1) Int. Galley of Rosebud   SC. NOS: 27 DAY.

              2) Ext. Port Gallice &   18, 19 DAY.
                  Rosebud & Fantail

              3) COVER SET - Int. Bar   25, 26 DAY.
                  & Penny Arcade

ARTISTES	CHARACTERS	M.U./WARD.	LV. HOTEL	ON SET
YOSEF SHILOA	HACAM	S/BY for Wardrobe from 9 a.m.		
AMIDOU	KIRKBANE	S/BY for Wardrobe from 9 a.m.		
YVES BENEYTON	PATRICE	S/BY at hotel		
ISABELLE HUPPERT	HELENE	7.00	8.50	9.00
BRIGITTE ARIEL	SABINE	S/BY for rehearsal & Wardrobe 9.00		
LALLA WARD	MARGARET	7.00	8.50	9.00
KIM CATTRALL	JOYCE	7.30	8.50	9.00
DEBBIE BERGER	GERTRUDE	7.30	8.50	9.00
MOURAD MANSOURI	(CHEIKH	S/BY for Wardrobe from 9 a.m.		
SAID BOUSSOUAR	(KATEB	S/BY for Wardrobe from 9 a.m.		
GARY BUNCE	JOSHMAN	To be notified		
PATRICK FLOERSHEIN	FRANK WOODS	ON ARRIVAL to s/by for Wardrobe then TO BE NOTIFIED		
ROSEBUD CREW		To be notified		

ACTION PROPS: "ROSEBUD" as arranged.

PROPS: As per script to include Patrice's Bag, Sun Lotion,
                     Towels, Bag with Organic nuts. All necessary utensils
                     for preparation of dinner:- roast beef, vegetables,
                     potatoes, bread, pate, strawberries, rolls, bottle salad
                     dressing, basket vegetables. Saucer, wastebin, salad,
                     oven glove, Helene's watch.

PRODUCTION: 2 Guards from Port.

MAKEUP/HAIRDRESSING: Suite 602 in Hotel Astoria.

CATERING: 10 a.m. morning break, lunch and 4 p.m. break.

ARTISTE AND UNIT   As attached list.
TRANSPORT:
        NOTES: Once again we request that every care is taken on the
                     boat.
                     NO SMOKING WHATSOEVER ON THE BOAT AND SOFT SOLED SHOES
                     AT ALL TIMES.
                     ONLY THE PERSONNEL ACTUALLY INVOLVED IN SHOOTING ARE
                     ALLOWED ON THE BOAT.
                                         Wolfgang Glattes
                                         ASSISTANT DIRECTOR

APPENDIX

TRANSPORT LIST - WEDNESDAY 29 MAY

NOTE: ALL CAR KEYS MUST BE RETURNED TO THE FRENCH PRODUCTION
OFFICE AFTER USE - UNLESS APPROPRIATE PERMISSION HAS BEEN
GIVEN TO DO OTHERWISE.

1.   CAR 1.   (J. SOKER) to be at the Hotel Helios from 8 a.m. to
pick up Mr. Otto Preminger, Erik Preminger, Wolfgang
Glattes and take to the Rosebud at the port.

2.   CAR 3.   (AMI AMIR) to be at the Hotel Helios from 7.50 a.m.
to pick up Mr. Denys Coop, then go to the Astoria
Hotel and pick up Mr. J. Devis, Mr. D. Humphreys and
take to the Rosebud.

                       Then return to the Hotel Astoria at 8.30 a.m. and pick
up Paul Rabiger, Colin Jamison and Keith Hamshere and
take to Rosebud.

3.   CAR 5.   (H. NONN) Pick up Angela Martelli from the Hotel Astoria
at 8.15 a.m. and take to location.

4.   MINIBUS 7 For Ron Pearce, Ron Taberer, Ray Evans, Alan Grayley,
David Cadwallader, Mick Murchan and Vince Foley to
leave the Hotel Passy at 7.50 a.m. for the location
at the harbour.

5.   CAR 8.   (BIRGIT WINSLOW) to pick up Isabelle Huppert, Lalla Ward,
Kim Cattrall, Debbie Berger at the Hotel Astoria at 8.40 a.m.
and take to the port by 9 a.m.

6.   MINIBUS Tony Teiger and Charles Tarbot.
       PROPS

7.   SOUND VAN For Robin Gregory, Terry Sharratt, Michel Naud and Peter
Downey at the Hotel Astoria to be on location by 8.30 a.m.

8.   CAMERA For John Lake, Colin Davidson at the Hotel Passy to be
       CAR   on location at 8.30 a.m.

9.   CAR 2.   To pick up Patrick Floershein from airport and take to
Astoria Hotel. The car then to be at the disposal of
the Production Office.

BREAKFAST: PLEASE INFORM YOUR HOTEL TONIGHT WHAT YOU WOULD LIKE
FOR BREAKFAST AND AT WHAT TIME.

CATERING: THE LUNCH WILL BE SERVED ON THE QUAI OF THE PORT DE
CROUTONS - THE SAME TRANSPORT WILL TAKE YOU THERE.

344

OTING PRODUCTIONS S.A.

....1st..... UNIT PROGRESS REPORT No.   PROD. No.   DATE .WEDNESDAY 29 MAY ... 1974...
(DAY OF WEEK)

TITLE .... "ROSEBUD" ....   DIRECTOR .... OTTO PREMINGER...............

PICTURE FOOTAGE				
STAFF CALL ..on..loc.... 8.30		Exposed	Waste	Colour	Print (B. & W.)

		Exposed	Waste	Colour	Print (B. & W.)
STAFF CALL ..on..loc.. 8.30					
SHOOTING STARTED 10.00					
SHOOTING FINISHED 6.30					
TIME DISMISSED.......... "	PREVIOUS ... 2,000	810	1190	-
MEAL PERIOD .. 1.10 - 2.10	TODAY'S ... 4,840	220	1265	-
OVERTIME	TOTAL ... 6,840	1030	2455	

		SOUND FOOTAGE			SCREEN TIME	
TOTAL SCENES 245		Exposed	Print	PREVIOUS 55	
PREVIOUSLY TAKEN ... -				TODAY'S 3.45	
TODAY'S SCENES 4	PREVIOUS ... -		TOTAL 4.40	
TOTAL TAKEN...... 4	TODAY'S ... 6 rolls		DAILY AVERAGE ... 4.40	
BALANCE 241	TOTAL ... 6 rolls			

SETS WORKED IN TODAY	COMPLETED OR NOT	SCENE NUMBERS SHOT TODAY	SCHEDULE STATUS	
Ext. Breakwater	NOT	27. 18. 19. 24a.	TOTAL SCHEDULE 70	
Ext/Int Rosebud	"	- - - - - - - - - - -	DAYS TO DATE...... 1	
		Scene part shot	BALANCE 69	
Port Gallice	NOT	Tues. 28 May:-	CORRECTION	
		83 part.	DAYS TO FINISH	

SETS TOMORROW........ "ROSEBUD" .... STAGE No. Port Gallice - The Brave Goose

CAST CONTRACT AND DAY PLAYERS	Time Called	Time Arrived	Time out For Meals	Time Dismissed	S ...... W ...... H ...... R ...... F	EXTRAS USED	
						Number	Total Rate
DEBBIE BERGER	9.00	8.55	1 hr.	11.30	1 W	2	Members of
ISABELLE HUPPERT	"	"	"	11.30	1 W		Brave Goose
LALLA WARD	"	"	"	17.15	1 W		crew used.
KIM CATTRALL	"	"	"	18.15	1 W		
ADRIENNE CORRI	1.30	1.30	"	18.15	1 W		
PATRICK FLOERSHEIN	9.30	9.30	"	17.15	1 W		
HANS VERVER	1.30	1.30	"	18.15	1 W		
CAPTAIN GARY BUNCE							

REMARKS:

ACTION PROPS:

"Brave Goose" boat.
Rolls Royce.

Tuesday 28 May
Unit shot scene with TV Announcer, Julian Pettifer (83 pt) and
scene 27 was rehearsed and lined up.

Footages above: 'Previous' are tests shot in U.K. and France but
only those shot on our stock. Today's footages include yesterday's
shooting.

Stock delivered:

55 x 1000 ft.)
20 x 400 ft.) This includes 2 rolls sent to U.K. for tests.
20 x 200 ft.)

Special Equipment:

Delivered, but held by Paris Office:

29 x 1000 ft.
10 x 400 ft.
10 x 200 ft.

S. = STARTED CONTRACT
W. = WORKED
H. = HELD
R. = REHEARSED
F. = FINISHED CONTRACT

PRODUCTION SUPERVISOR

345

APPENDIX

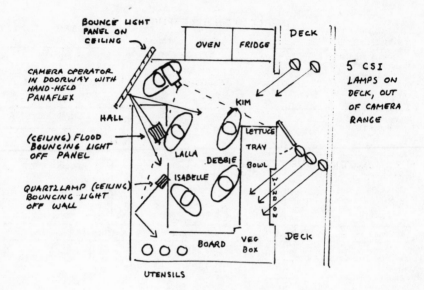

Galley

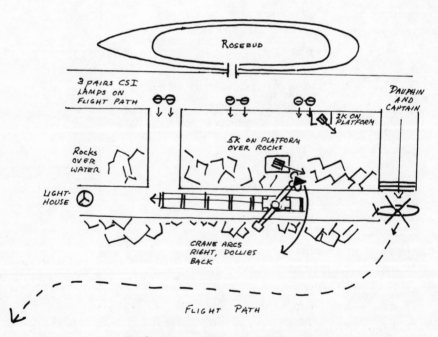

Helicopter Shot—Juan-les-Pins

346

DAILY CONTINUITY REPORT

Production: ROSEBUD

Cameras & Set ups: ? Panaflex
Crane - Pan & Track
75mm 30/20/15/35/18ft.
.2.8 Forced 1 stop

Date: June 8.1974

Set: Ext.Lighthouse, Breakwater and Rosebud

Time Shot: 30"

Screentime:

Weather:

SCENE NO. 39 Night	
SLATE NO. 47	

ACTION & DIALOGUE:

CAMERA SHOOTING FROM BREAKWATER..STARTS ON LIGHTHOUSE..KIRKBANE
JUMPS DOWN ONTO THE ROCKS..RUNS FORWARD TO MEET HACAM..KALEB AND
CHEIKH WHO RUN UP OVER ROCKS CARRYING BAGS OF EQUIPMENT..TORCHES ETC
CAMERA PANS LEFT WITH THEM TO ROSEBUD AND TRACKS IN..FRANK IS STANDING
AT TOP OF GANGWAY SMOKING CIGARETTE..KIRKBANE STAYS WITH FRANK..
CAMERA LOSES THEM AND PANS WITH HACAM..KALEB AND CHEIKH AS THEY GO
ON BOARD ..MOVE LEFT AND GO THRU GALLEY DOOR...

```
         Take 1.  NG cut.  End clappers.
         "    2.  NG camera
         "    3.  P.
         "    4.  P.
```

Note: Under "Cameras & Set-ups" she has indicated that the Panaflex, mounted on a crane, panned and trucked to follow action. A 75mm lens was used at F2.8 and development was pushed one stop (to compensate for low light levels). "30/20/15/35/18ft" refers to the different distances at which the camera was successively focused during the take.

OTING PRODUCTIONS S.A.

"ROSEBUD"

MOVEMENT ORDER 2.

JUAN LES PINS TO CORSICA

Due to the fact that we are making our move to Corsica during a busy period we have to move over several days. We accept the fact that this complicates the packing for everyone and ask for your co-operation. Please let the Production Office know if on reading this document you have any comments:- (no rude ones!)

SATURDAY 8 JUNE	NICE/BASTIA FERRY	
	Call at port:	8.00 a.m.
	Departure:	11.00 a.m.
	Arrival:	6.00 a.m.
	FIAT I	Driver (Yves Amoureux)
	FIAT II	Without driver
SUNDAY 9 JUNE	NICE/CALVI FERRY	
	Call at port:	7.00 a.m.
	Departure:	9.00 a.m.
	Arrival:	2.30 p.m.
	SOUND VAN (To take Cutting Room equipment)	Driver (Peter Downey) Passenger (Michel Naud)

On arrival in Calvi go to Hotel Napoleon Bonaparte at I'LLE ROUSSE and leave there cutting room equipment. (The projector to be taken on to Bastia for rushes there).
On arrival in Ille Rousse contact Mr. F▇▇▇▇▇ who will be waiting for you, then proceed as others to Bastia.

CATERING I.	Driver (Georges Blanchon) Passenger (Martine Blanchon)
CATERING II.	Driver (Francis Lorenzetti)
CATERING III.	Driver (Henriette Marello) Passenger (Louis Claude Marello)

On arrival proceed to Bastia (approx. 3 hour drive) to Hotel Marana, Transat Hotel Club, Furiani, Nr. Bastia. Tel. 31 70 81.

MONDAY 10 JUNE	Set up crane at Port Gallice to get shooting crane out of port to trailer.

TUESDAY 11 JUNE	NICE/AJACCIO FERRY	(In charge at port: Pierre Roubaud)
	Call at port:	2.00 p.m.
	Departure:	10.00 p.m.
	Arrival:	7.00 a.m. (12 June)
	CONSTRUCTION VAN	Driver (Vince Foley) Passenger (Mick Murchan)
	30KW GENNY	Driver (Alan Grayley) Passenger (Nobby Cross)
	LANDROVER GENNY	Driver (Ron Taberer) Passenger (Ray Evans)
	LAND ROVER & TRAILER CRANE	Driver (Bill Draper) Passenger (Ted Clayton)
	MINIBUS 7 to take remainder of editing equipment.	Driver (Yves Amoureux) Passenger (Florence Favre le Bret)
		(Wardrobe to travel air personal baggage.)
	ESTAFFETTE (To rent) to take offices, hair, makeup equipment)	Driver (Christian Palligiano) Passenger (Ami Amir)
	PROP MINIBUS	Driver (Tony Teiger)

(THOUGH THERE ARE NO CUSTOMS FORMALITIES IT IS ADVISABLE FOR THOSE VEHICLES CONCERNED TO TRAVEL WITH THEIR CARNETS SO PLEASE COLLECT THESE FROM THE PRODUCTION OFFICE)

348

On arrival in Bastia proceed to Hotel Marana, Transat Hotel
Club, Furiani, Nr. Bastia (approx. 6 hours drive) — Tel.
31 70 81.

If you have any problems please ask Christian Palligiano who
will be with you

FLIGHT AF 1630.   NICE/BASTIA.

Please have your luggage ready in hotel lobbies by 10.30 a.m.

Departure from Hotels in Juan les Pins around 11.15 a.m. by
cars and buses - detailed list on Monday.

Registration of people and luggage at 12.00 at Nice Airport.
Lunch at Nice Airport - 12.30 - 1.30 p.m.
Flight departs: 2.35 p.m.

Arrives Bastia: 3.15 p.m.

On arrival buses and cars will be waiting - list to be issued
before departure.

Bernard Mazauric and ████ F███████ will meet flight.

PASSENGER LIST

ERIK PREMINGER	COLIN JAMISON & MRS JAMISON & BABY
GRAHAM COTTLE	MIKE JARVIS
BARBARA ALLEN	DENISE VUILLAUME
CHANTAL BOTTI	BUD ROSENTHAL
WOLFGANG GLATTES	MICHEL ROSENCRANTZ
BERNARD COHN	KEITH HAMSHERE
RICHARD JENKINS	LAURENT PETITGIRARD & piano
JEAN MARIE PELISSIE	PETER THORNTON
HUGUES NONN	RUSS WOLLNOUGH
ANGELA MARTELLI	RON PEARCE
DENYS COOP & MRS COOP	TED GERSHUNY
JIMMY DEVIS	BIRGIT WIMSLOW
DEWI HUMPHRIES	KEN KAUFMAN
COLIN DAVIDSON	TONY GITTELSON
DAVID WHITE	
PIERRE FEVES	
ROBIN GREGORY	
TERRY SHARRATT	
MARC FREDERIX	
PAUL RABIGER	
MISS RANGER	

ROBERT MITCHUM & MRS MITCHUM
SHILOA
AMIDOU
SAID BOUSSOUAR
MOURAD MANSOURI
LALLA WARD
ISABELLE HUPPERT
DEBBIE BERGER
BRIGITTE ARIEL
KIM CATTRALL

BASTIA HOTEL:	HOTEL MARANA
	TRANSAT HOTEL CLUB
	FURIANI
	NR. BASTIA Tel. 31 70 81
PRODUCTION OFFICE:	41 Boulevard Paoli 31 48 17
	Bastia 31 48 27

WEDNESDAY	NICE/BASTIA FERRY	(In charge at port - Pierre Roubaud)
12 JUNE		
	Call at port:	6.00 a.m.
	Departure:	8.00 a.m.
	Arrival:	2.30 p.m.
	CAMERA CAR	(Driver (John Lake)
		Passenger (David Cadwallader)
	CONSTRUCTION 1.	Driver (D. Batrichevitch)

These vehicles will be met at port in Bastia.

AFTER FIRST THREE	HOTEL NAPOLEON BONAPARTE	
DAYS IN BASTIA:	I'LLE ROUSSE	
	CORSICA	Tel. 60 09 50

	CAR	Driver (Harold Sachs) - to be arranged.
SUNDAY	NICE/CALVI	
16 JUNE	Transport of Simulator.	

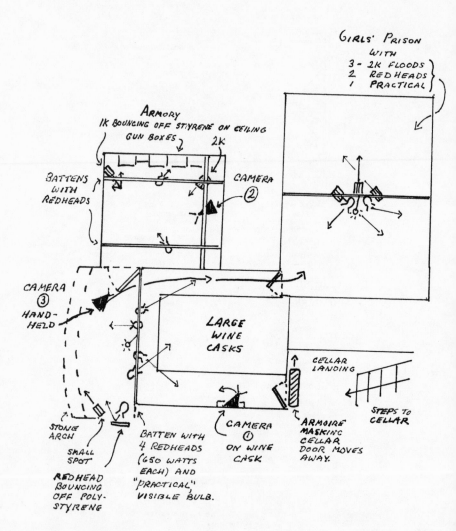

Camera position 1 pans Arabs from cellar door to armory door.

Camera position 2 picks up Arabs in armory and pans them out again.

Camera position 3 picks up Arabs leaving the armory and moves behind them, hand-held, into the prison.

Cave Plan

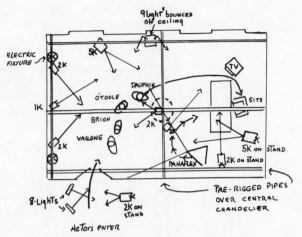

Night. Shades closed. Camera opens wide on Dauphin. Actors enter the wide shot. Camera moves with Dauphin to medium shot at desk.

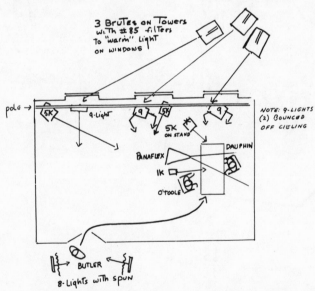

And then there was Fargeau's office by daylight. Shown is medium close shot on Fargeau at his desk, with lights rigged for wider angle of two men at desk and butler.

Fargeau Office

351

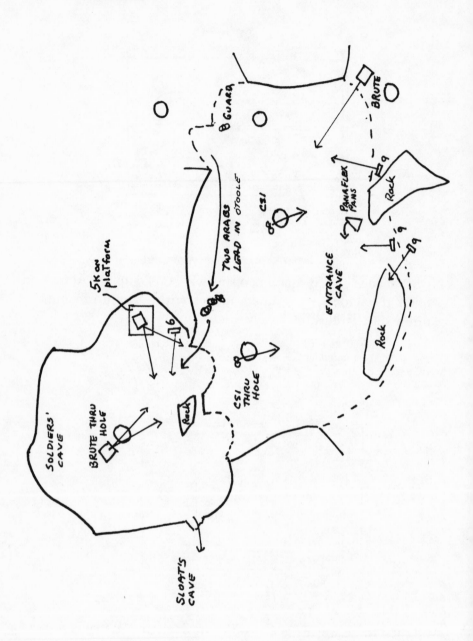

Desert Caves—as O'Toole is led in

Abbott, Maggie, 29
ABC, 300
Accounting, see Production, accounting
Actors, 76, 78, 182
  agents, see Agents
  arrival for shooting, 166–69
  casting of, see Casting
  credits, xx–xxii, 155, 156
  firing of, 176, 177, 179, 180–81,
    228–29, 230, 339
  insurance for, 171, 181, 288, 289
  publicity, see Publicity
  rehearsals, 177–80, 260–62
  see also names of individuals
Adam, Marie-Christine, 96
Advise and Consent, xv, 50
African Queen, 18, 58
Agents, 28, 29–34, 41, 46, 56, 61, 97,
    106, 118, 119–20, 138, 155, 156,
    158, 313
Agony and the Ecstasy, The, 322
Allen, Barbara, 125, 127, 131, 132, 133,
    134, 136–37, 144, 161, 171
Allen, Woody, 336
Alvina, Anicee, 96
American Cinema, The, 238
Amidou, 64, 222–23, 240, 241–42, 254,
    255, 256, 259, 266, 268, 284, 336
  directions from Preminger, 226–27
  editing of scenes with, 293, 294
Anastasia, 50, 98
Anatomy of a Murder, xv, 3, 4, 137,183
Andrews, Dana, 183
Angry Silence, The, 326
Apocalypse Now, 86, 340
Ariel, Brigitte, 179, 181, 211, 220, 226,
    233, 284, 285, 313
  directions from Preminger, 221, 223,
    236

love scene, 220–22, 234, 293, 294
Art department, 161, 163, 237, 257
  construction by, 254, 301, 312, 320
  salaries, 70–71
Art directors, 24, 46, 143–44, 254, 314
  prop location by, 143–45, 172
  replacement of, 257, 287
  salaries, 70
  site selection by, 47–48, 80–85, 88,
    116, 117, 139, 287
  staff of, see Art department
Asphalt Jungle, 241
Assistant directors, 27, 46, 53, 54–56,
    69, 78, 237, 296
  casting and, 101, 102, 103
  handling actors, 167, 168, 228
  on recces, 88–92, 106–107, 116–17,
    148
  scheduling by, 93–94
  during shooting, 248–50, 258,
    267–68, 270, 312
  staff chosen by, 148
Attenborough, Richard, 312, 317,
    325–29, 336, 337
Aubrey, James, 225
Avanti, 238
Avildsen, John, 69

Bankhead, Tallulah, 224
Barry Lyndon, 39, 311
Bass, Saul, 6, 8
Bates, Alan, 120, 278
Battle of Algiers, The, 275
Baum, Marty, 31
Baum, Raoul (pseudonym), 144, 163,
    229, 237, 249, 250, 258, 307
Becket, 278
Beller, Georges, 230, 232, 233–34, 235,
    238–39, 242, 288–89

353

INDEX

INDEX